Cheaponomics

Do you really think you are getting a good deal when given that free mobile phone for switching service providers, if a multinational retailer undercuts its competitors or by the fact that food is relatively cheaper today in many countries than ever before?

Think again! As Michael Carolan clearly shows in this compelling book, cheapness is an illusion. The real cost of low prices is alarmingly high. It is shown, for example, that citizens are frequently subsidizing low prices through welfare support to poorly-paid workers in their own country, or relying on the exploitation of workers in poor countries for cheap goods. Environmental pollution may not be costed into goods and services, but is paid for indirectly by people living away from its source or by future generations. Even with private cars, when the total costs of this form of mobility are tallied it proves to be an astronomically expensive model of transportation. All of these costs need to be accounted for.

The author captures these issues with the concept of "cheaponomics." The key point is that costs and risks are socialized: we all pay for cheapness, but not at the point of purchase. Drawing on a wide range of examples and issues from over-consumption and waste to over-work, unemployment, inequality, and the depersonalizing of communities, it is convincingly shown that cheapness can no longer be seen as such a bargain. Instead we need to refocus for a better sense of well-being, social justice, and a balanced approach to prosperity.

Michael Carolan is Professor and Chair of Sociology at Colorado State University, USA. He is the author of several books, including *The Real Cost of Cheap Food*, *The Sociology of Food and Agriculture*, *Reclaiming Food Security*, and *Society and the Environment: Pragmatic Solutions to Ecological Issues*.

"*Cheaponomics* is a revelation! It uncovers the devastating truth behind the modern economy of 'bargains'. It turns out to be like a game of global Whack-a-Mole – when prices are pushed down in one place, the real costs pop up somewhere else, often in our own backyards. Michael Carolan finishes by describing a new game that would make 99 percent of us better off."

Clive Hamilton, Professor of Public Ethics at Charles Sturt University, Canberra, Australia and author of Growth Fetish, Affluenza *and* Requiem for a Species

"Michael Carolan has unearthed a fatal flaw in the economic status quo. That's quite a feat on its own. But more amazing is the way Carolan has sidestepped doom and gloom in *Cheaponomics* by providing logical examples, touches of humor, and plenty of solutions for societies that desperately need them."

Rob Dietz, former executive director of CASSE (the Center for the Advancement of the Steady State Economy) and co-author of Enough Is Enough: Building a Sustainable Economy in a World of Finite Resources

"While our consumer society has long been celebrated as an unrivaled mode of social organization, its gradual waning has now begun to focus attention on the fact that prevalent lifestyles are built on a mountain of ecological, financial, and societal debt. *Cheaponomics* expertly accounts for the costs that we have incurred and highlights alternative systems of exchange that promise to be immensely more satisfying in a world of increasingly constrained resources."

Maurie J. Cohen, Associate Professor of Sustainability Studies at the New Jersey Institute of Technology, USA and co-founder of the Sustainable Consumption Research and Action Initiative

"Michael Carolan presents a successful challenge to the conventional way we measure well-being. In sprightly prose and well-chosen data, Carolan shows that the costs of a race to the bottom in labor, environmental and social standards produces low retail prices that are opiates: addictive, destructive and unsustainable. More than a great teaching tool, *Cheaponomics* suggests an alternative – economic life whose goal, if we willed it, could be human fulfilment."

Robert J.S. Ross, Research Professor of Sociology and The Mosakowski Institute for Public Enterprise at Clark University, USA and author of Slaves to Fashion: Poverty and Abuse in the New Sweatshops

"Michael Carolan writes a great story, with numerous examples, on how we are addicted to cheap stuff with their massive societal costs like environmental pollution and negative consequences to our wellbeing. He concludes with practical recommendations for improvement. *Cheaponomics* is a must-read for all of us."

Philip Vergragt, Professor Emeritus of Technology Assessment, Delft University of Technology, The Netherlands, and a Fellow at Tellus Institute, USA

Cheaponomics

The High Cost of Low Prices

Michael Carolan

First published 2014
by Routledge
2 Park Square, Milton Park, Abingdon, Oxon OX14 4RN

and by Routledge
711 Third Avenue, New York, NY 10017

Routledge is an imprint of the Taylor & Francis Group, an informa business

© 2014 Michael Carolan

The right of Michael Carolan to be identified as author of this work has been asserted by him in accordance with sections 77 and 78 of the Copyright, Designs and Patents Act 1988.

All rights reserved. No part of this book may be reprinted or reproduced or utilized in any form or by any electronic, mechanical, or other means, now known or hereafter invented, including photocopying and recording, or in any information storage or retrieval system, without permission in writing from the publishers.

Trademark notice: Product or corporate names may be trademarks or registered trademarks, and are used only for identification and explanation without intent to infringe.

British Library Cataloguing-in-Publication Data
A catalogue record for this book is available from the British Library

Library of Congress Cataloging in Publication Data
Carolan, Michael S.
Cheaponomics : the high cost of low prices / Michael Carolan.
pages cm
Includes bibliographical references and index.
1. Prices. 2. Value. I. Title.
HG229.C334 2014
338.5'2–dc23
2013033345

ISBN: 978-0-415-73514-8 (hbk)
ISBN: 978-0-415-73515-5 (pbk)
ISBN: 978-1-315-81937-2 (ebk)

Typeset in bembo
by Taylor & Francis Books

Printed and bound in the United States of America by Publishers Graphics, LLC on sustainably sourced paper.

Contents

List of illustrations	vi
Acknowledgments	vii
1 Free enterprise, socialism, and cheaponomics	1

PART I
Cheap stuff — 19

2 You bought that computer but someone else paid for it	21
3 Free plastic bags (and other costly ephemeral commodities)	43
4 The high cost of cheap foods	64

PART II
Cheap economies and communities — 89

5 The real cost of automobiles and car-munities	91
6 Retail concentration and rock-bottom prices … but at what cost?	111
7 Working less for more	129

PART III
Transitioning toward affordability — 145

8 Comforting the productivist zombie	147
9 Real prosperity is priceless	168
10 Ten recommendations for the good, affordable, and affording	195
Index	211

Illustrations

Figures

4.1	Relationship between daily average per capita consumption of oils, fats, and sugars and average percentage of disposable household income spent on food	66
4.2	Breakdown of the amount of energy consumed by the US food system	67
4.3	Median average salary by ethnicity and gender	80
5.1	Relationship between Happy Planet Index and percent of total trips by walking, biking, or public transit for select high-income nations	107
6.1	Sales of top 10 companies for three sectors of the global food system	121
6.2	Food system concentration in the US and New Zealand	123
9.1	Relationship between life expectancy and GDP	171
9.2	Relationship between economic freedom score and happy life years	171
9.3	Relationship between health and social problems and inequality among selection of high-income countries	179
9.4	Relationship between spending on foreign aid and inequality among selection of high-income countries	179

Tables

3.1	Plastic packaging resins	55
9.1	Where the one percent fit in the hierarchy of income	175

Acknowledgments

Where does one draw the line when writing an acknowledgment section? I've always struggled with this question in previous books. With this project, however, the line is particularly unclear as my thanks goes out to literally thousands. There are my students, who contributed greatly by way of hours of brilliant classroom discussion. Then there are all those who gave up their time to come and hear me speak at various public lectures: so many wise questions and provocative observations which helped enormously in keeping my arguments grounded and clear. And how could I possibly list all of my colleagues: fellow critics of cheaponomics, many of whom I have never personally met, whose fingerprints are all over this book. A couple of these individuals were in fact kind enough to provide me with advanced copies of their yet-published materials: Kyle Knight (University of Alabama), John Rennie Short (University of Maryland), and Paul Tranter (University of New South Wales). To all: a heartfelt "Thanks." I am also indebted to Tim Hardwick. Were it not for Tim this book might have never seen the light of day. And, finally, the three irreplaceable constants in my life: Nora, Elena, and Joey. "Thank you" just doesn't convey my full appreciation. No words can.

Portions of this project were aided by the support of the National Research Foundation of Korea (Project No. 2013S1A3A2055243).

Chapter 1

Free enterprise, socialism, and cheaponomics

We desperately want things to be cheap. But at the same time we do not. As my six-year-old daughter recently remarked after some plastic toys broke not long after being brought back from the store, "Those cheap toys sure are cheap!" Sure, some terms, when used in slang, have their meanings turned upside down – like "bad," which can mean in some instances, loosely, "good." But cheap's double meaning has always been there (or at least for a long time according to the *Oxford English Dictionary*). Cheap as conventionally understood is something to be avoided and simultaneously strived for. Maybe, deep down, we really do know better. Perhaps our subconscious is whispering "anything that appears too good to be true probably is" (or "there is no such thing as a free – or even cheap – lunch"). And so we use the same word to describe what we know in our heart to be two sides of the same coin. But that has not stopped us from demanding cheaper and cheaper stuff – as long as it doesn't look, feel, or taste cheap.

I have been lecturing on the cost of cheap for a while now, particularly since my book *The Real Cost of Cheap Food* came out. It is not that I am against an economic system producing goods that we can afford. Indeed, that is precisely why I was compelled to write this book, because we cannot afford what the economic status quo is feeding us. As I will repeatedly show, cheap is terribly expensive.

I have been known to drop into big-box stores to conduct "research," occasionally even buying particularly cheap wares to use as props for my lectures on the subject. Not long ago I visited Walmart – my Machu Picchu of sorts as I never leave the site disappointed. On this particular occasion I came across a microwave for less than US$10. Can you believe it: I regularly spend more buying a large bag of broccoli from a local grower at my neighborhood farmers' market! We are talking about a device manufactured thousands of miles away in China, from plastics that while likely processed domestically were produced using petroleum from the Middle East. The steel to make the microwave oven's cavity could have also come from China, as they lead all nations in steel production. The magnetron (the heart of the device): also likely manufactured in China, though no doubt some of the materials that went into making it were imported. I also bet coal supplied the vast majority of the electricity that ran and illuminated the factory where it was assembled and packaged (China also leads the world in coal production). And let us not forget about the material that went into manufacturing the cardboard it dwelt in while traveling across the Pacific and a handful of states before ending up at the Walmart in Fort Collins, Colorado (where I live). These materials could have also come from China, or maybe not. How could that US$10 have paid for all those costs? Simple: it could not have. Had I taken the microwave home, I might have bought it but I would not have *paid* for it. A particularly egregious aspect of today's economy is that the individuals who most profit from it and who benefit from its cheap wares are not fully paying for their good fortune, leaving billions, and that is before factoring in future generations (trillions?), to foot the bill.

It is tempting to call these costs hidden. But are they? They may not have the immediacy of one's house being on fire but they undoubtedly have a presence, in our taxes and polluted oceans, in our changing climate, and in the faces of those who pay for them daily through hunger, sickness, and conflict. A recently released report sponsored by the United Nations estimates that the 3,000 largest publicly traded corporations in the world cost us US$2.2 trillion – that's trillion with a "t" – in environmental damage in 2008 alone.[1] And that is "just" costs to the environment, saying nothing of the price we pay for decreased public health, unjust labor practices, and low wages. Lest we forget, when a firm in, say, North America or Europe fails to pay its employees a suitable wage those employees often are able to qualify for government assistance programs. And who do you think pays for that?

Consumers do not give those costs much thought – or at least not enough to keep them from seeking out the next bargain. I doubt anyone that bought the US$10 microwave from Walmart thought while going through checkout, "I really should pay more for this," not that paying more in itself guarantees anything other than more profits for the retail giant. As a social scientist I am also deeply interested in *why* this is. We might not be able to articulate in precise terms what the ecological footprint of the world's largest 3,000 publicly traded companies cost us but we know – *all* of us – that those costs are there.

~

I give lectures on the cost of cheap. Recently, in an attempt to be more provocative, I have taken to starting these talks with the following three-question quiz.

- Do you believe in letting the market regulate itself?

If so, you might be a socialist.

- Do you think the right interests are being served by today's economy?

If so, you might be a socialist.

- Do you measure market "success" by how cheaply an economy is able to produce stuff?

If so, you might be a socialist.

I have long been struck by how the term "socialist" has been used, particularly in the United States. As far as I can tell, it refers exclusively to someone who promotes redistributive policies that seek to spread the wealth. Under this scenario, the *benefits* generated by an economy are spread – are *socialized* – to various degrees across society. Yet benefits are not the only things that can be socialized. *Costs* can too. While quick to brand their intellectual adversaries as socialists, proponents of the economic status quo have yet to catch on to the fact that they are also deserving of the "socialist" title. They strive to make society pay for the costs of this economic system while concentrating its benefits within the hands of a few. They are socialists too, though the type they promote I would argue is far more insidious, unjust, and unsustainable than that advocated by their antagonists. This brings me to the book's title: *Cheaponomics* – shorthand for *cost-socializing socialism*.

While this book is critical of the dog-eat-dog style of free market capitalism enveloping the world – what is commonly referred to as neoliberalism – the position it takes is not inherently political. It offers a big tent argument, which is to say my appeals are to those on both the political Right and Left. Granted, some will find this claim initially dubious, as criticism of the economic status quo has a history of orienting from so-called progressive or liberal camps. Yet, in the end, I believe conservatives will be just as appalled at the state of cheap once its exorbitant costs are laid out. These are not only costs we are paying for as taxpayers and citizens but which we are asking future generations to also bear. And as those on the Right rile against bankrupting future generations when talking about things like national debt I can only assume they will feel an equal visceral reaction to all forms of future "debt." As I tell family members and friends that ally themselves with political conservatism and who claim to have never met a tax they liked: "When you socialize costs you necessitate higher taxes, either for present and/or future generations, because, in the end, *someone* has to pay for those costs." Conservatives take note: by bankrupting future generations, through higher taxes, reduced individual well-being, diminished environmental integrity, lifeless communities, and rising levels of inequality, cheaponomics is the antithesis of fiscal (or any form of) responsibility.

~

We adopted an economic strategy long ago that hinged on the production of ever-cheaper commodities. In an earlier book, *Reclaiming Food Security*, I detail how this practice first took root in nineteenth-century Great Britain in

4 Free enterprise, socialism, and cheaponomics

the context of food. The ruling class was confronted with the problem of how to feed the growing mass of workers streaming into cities from the countryside. Yet their motives were far from altruistic, having to do more with anxieties about social unrest. In short, the goal was not about feeding the poor well, but well enough to keep them from rioting in the streets. If calories were cheap, or so the reasoning went, employers would have a greater chance of getting away with paying their workers a pittance; a mindset that has not entirely been abandoned, as anyone that studies contemporary international food policy knows. I am not saying that prices of consumer goods today are artificially low to mask worker oppression. If anything, cheapness is less the mask and more the catalyst of depressed wages, environmental ruin, and taxpayer exploitation. Regardless of why and how it started, we have gotten locked into a system where one of its primary goals is to produce cheap stuff.

While supply-side economics has closely been aligned with the policies of President Ronald Reagan, which is why it is occasionally referred to as Reaganomics, economic policy since World War II has been preoccupied with the production of cheap goods – with, in other words, supply. This fixation upon retail price would be less problematic if we lived in a world where costs could be fully (and fairly) monetized while remaining affixed to the commodity or service from whence they came. Unfortunately, in a free market economy the incentives collectively encourage firms to externalize costs, as many as they can get away with. That which remains, what we call a commodity's retail price, comes nowhere close to representing a thing's total expense. But it is even worse than that, as firms under this model have an incentive to punch as many holes into the pricing system as possible, by, for example, offshoring, polluting, or employing undocumented laborers. It is what we call having a comparative advantage, even though it places certain populations – namely, those that have to pay for these socialized costs – at a tremendous disadvantage.

That is one approach to prosperity, what I call supply-side. The alternative, or at least one of them, which receives considerably less attention, is what I refer to as a demand-side approach to prosperity. There is one thing I have never been able to figure out: what are the benefits of cheap products if wages fall proportionately with – or even faster than – the price of goods? Sure, the price of, say, food has dropped considerably since 1970 in the United States, from taking up 14 percent of the average household's disposable income to 9 percent today. But the hourly minimum wage during that same period, after adjusting for inflation, has dropped nearly 50 percent. And those low wages trigger still additional costs. It has been calculated that California taxpayers are spending US$86 million annually providing healthcare and other public assistance (food stamps, subsidized housing, and the like) to the state's 44,000 Walmart employees. If competing retailers were to adopt Walmart's wage and benefit levels the bill to this state's taxpayers would increase US$410 million annually.[2] Low wages cost everyone. Cheaponomics is not about saving anything other than the present economic environment and the income inequalities it generates and is predicated upon. Cheap has become a substitute for equality of income. Cheaponomics creates a false sense of hope, which makes large income inequalities tolerable. As long as we think products will become continually cheaper the American dream remains within reach, even if our paystubs and the environment say otherwise.[3]

What are we to do? The matter is admittedly complex. A demand-side approach to prosperity does involve paying people higher wages, recognizing that if people were paid better they could afford more accurately priced goods. But there is more to it than that. The great twentieth-century economist John Maynard Keynes accurately predicted some 80 years ago that by the dawn of the twenty-first century we would be witness to remarkable productivity increases. His predictive abilities faltered, however, by suggesting we would choose to take advantage of those increases in productivity by choosing leisure over work. Let us also remember how this addition in leisure time for each worker would have meant more opportunity for employment. An economy with a 20-hour work week can employ twice the number of people as one with a 40-hour work week. In this alternative universe over-consumption is neither possible, as a shortened work week would not allow it, or desired, recognizing that with everyone in the same boat the social pressures to over-consume become dramatically weakened. Considering the alternative, only a madman could have predicted the path ultimately taken: longer work hours so we can buy products that do nothing to enhance our well-being but which deplete our natural resources while destroying the health of ourselves and our planet. As it turns out, we are all crazy; though I am hopeful our insanity is temporary.

~

Western thought dating back to Ancient Greece has been fascinated with knowledge. Epistemology – a branch of philosophy concerning the subject of knowledge – is not for the faint of heart. It is serious business. Books, careers, and university courses are devoted to this subject. And while we still do not seem to know if trees that fall in an uninhabited forest make a sound (or if I really am if I think), we continue to ponder weighty questions surrounding the nature and scope of human knowledge.

What, then, about ignorance? On this subject those books, careers, and courses are surprisingly silent. Fortunately, the sciences are starting to fill this void. For example, a team of cognitive neuroscientists at Emory University in Atlanta scanned the brains of 15 self-identified Democrats and 15 self-identified Republications while they read quotes attributed to President George Bush and the then Democratic presidential candidate John Kerry. Some quotes fell in line with the political ideology of Bush and Kerry, others did not. When confronted with contradictory information from "their" candidate the scans revealed not only that neural pathways linked to reasoning shut down but reward circuits kicked into overdrive to positively reinforce the faulty reason being produced.[4] This research, and endless others like it, point to something we can all personally attest to: that we selectively filter information by clinging onto data that support our beliefs while ignoring that which tells us we are dead wrong.

We need to be careful, however, not to take from this research the idea that our fates are sealed. While neural mechanisms might play a role in filtering information those biological structures did not originally determine whether the subjects were Bush or Kerry supporters. The same principles are at work with cheaponomics. Difference is scary. No one likes change. That is why we have come up with alternative fuels rather than *alternatives to* fuel; why we have focused on developing electric cars rather than on coming up with an entirely different method of human mobility; and why our attention has focused almost entirely on the last of the Three Rs of Environmentalism – Recycle – even though its ecological benefits pale in comparison to the first two (Reduce and Reuse). I suppose one could even point to certain evolutionary advantages that go along with change avoidance – after all, change is risky.

All of this talk about cognitive filtering and neural pathways, however, has one glaring omission. What about power? This is where the social sciences can add considerably to the conversation. As opposed to just an absence of knowledge, ignorance involves supporting social structures and practices as complex as those involved in knowledge production and maintenance. As Robert Proctor notes while describing the politics of cancer research in *Cancer Wars*, we must:

> study the social construction of ignorance. The persistence of controversy is often not a natural consequence of imperfect knowledge but a political consequence of conflicting interests and structural apathies. Controversy can be engineered: ignorance and uncertainty can be manufactured, maintained, and disseminated.[5]

Ignorance can be manufactured in the sense of knowledge that has been lost. As Nancy Tuna points out:

> obstetricians in the United States, for example, no longer know how to turn a breech, not because such knowledge, in this case a knowing-how, is seen as false, but because medical practices, which are in large part fueled by business and malpractice concerns, have shifted knowledge practices in cases of breech births to Caesareans.

In her words, knowledge of how to turn a breech in the professional medical community has "actively disappeared."[6]

To talk about ignorance in the context of cheaponomics is to talk about a verb. There is some active disappearing going on, as I detail in the chapters that follow. Rather than temporary insanity, then, I think we can plead ignorance. But that does not reduce our level of blame. The benefit of being ignorant – over insane – is that you can actually change that state. Though to do this will require a collective rolling up of our sleeves.

~

What lies ahead? The book performs a social autopsy. In the social sciences such examinations are meant to be performed prior to "death" in the hope of curing the social body from a particular ill, which in this case is cheaponomics. The procedure spans three parts. Part I focuses on cheap *stuff*, from electronics (Chapter 2) to plastics (Chapter 3) and food (Chapter 4). These chapters serve to biopsy (continuing with the medical analogy) components of the diseased body. But sociology is about seeing the general in the particular. So in interrogating particular things we find pathologies endemic to society. While we feign concern about the cost of everything, it turns out we are actually making things that are tremendously expensive. Why is this? What are its broader effects? Later chapters seek to understand the source and outcomes of these pathologies in the hope of identifying workable sustainable alternatives. Part II looks at how we have organized society, at great expense, before the altar of cheap, in term of our car-munity environments (Chapter 5), big-box economies (Chapter 6), and notions of labor, leisure, and the civic life (Chapter 7). Finally, Part III (Chapters 8, 9, and 10) tackles the question of what society would look like if cost really mattered; where, instead of prioritizing cheapness and cost socialization, the focus was on making things that were affordable and that afforded everyone the ability to achieve ends of their own choosing.

Before briefly overviewing each chapter a quick word about why I choose to use the term "cost socialism" over the more economically (politically?) correct "cost externality." Perhaps it is the sociologist in me but I do not care for how the latter seems to imply that those costs *could* be internalized: after all, any costs that can be external can also be internal, right? Not all costs socialized, however, can be – nor, I would contend, would we want them to be – internalized and therefore included in the retail price of goods and services. For example, do we really want to pay more for something that costs those manufacturing it their health and well-being? Doesn't it make more sense – and cents – to produce goods in a more humane and just manner to begin with? (This is not a rhetorical question: it does make more sense – and cents – as argued in later chapters.) It is also my experience, after spending hundreds of hours in the classroom and on the lecture podium talking about the subject, that to call a cost "externalized" hides, through mystifying technocratic language, the fact that certain segments are paying for those costs *now*. And what, precisely, are these costs external *to*? No wonder folks seem less interested in them when tagged with this adjunctive. Isn't that a natural reaction to things said to be pushed to the "outside". Isn't that, for example, why we build homes:

to protect ourselves from the elements by externalizing them with the intent of creating a safe place to live, eat, and sleep?

"So when a cost is externalized that means we no longer have to worry about it, right?" That is an honest to goodness question, word for word, which I was recently asked by someone while talking about my newest book project. *That's* the problem I have with the term cost externality. And it's your problem too, because you pay for it.

Chapter 2: you bought that computer but someone else paid for it

Were it not for cheaponomics the Digital Age, as we know it today, would have looked decidedly different. How else could something predicated on the sale of a billion units annually, with each embodying literally tons of waste (and often powered by coal), be praised for marshaling the overthrow of matter without some serious cost redistribution occurring? This chapter attempts to detail these costs – to public and worker health, taxpayers, the environment, and future generations – so others can continue to have cheap (and easily replaced) electronic gadgets. The chapter looks at the costs incurred through the mining of the necessary materials, such as lead, cadmium, and mercury, before discussing those associated with the manufacturing process, ultimately concluding with the pricy problem of electronic waste – or e-waste. Between 40 and 70 million metric tons of e-waste are generated worldwide annually, very little of which is actually recycled. And of course it is anyone's guess at the amount of e-waste that will be generated once the three billion residents of India and China reach a level of e-affluence comparable to what is found in the West.

Chapter 3: free plastic bags (and other costly ephemeral commodities)

They are made using billions of gallons of oil annually. Their toll on natural resources is matched by the collective destruction they bring to wildlife, killing roughly one million sea creatures every year, such as birds, whales, seals, and sea turtles. Retailers in the United States spend approximately US$4 billion a year on these things. We use them once, which equates to about half a trillion units consumed annually, but they last forever. And – here's the kicker – they are free. I am talking about plastic bags. Cheaponomics is to a throwaway society as hydrogen and oxygen are to water. I enter into the subject of the ephemeral commodity – a commodity whose principal identity is that of waste – by starting with an examination of the "free" plastic bag, a case of cheaponomics taken to its illogical extreme. From there, while also exposing the costly practices of planned obsolesce and cost–benefit analysis, attention turns more generally to the rise of the disposable society.

Chapter 4: the high cost of cheap foods

Occasionally when giving public lectures on food I come bearing props. Two of my favorites are a six-pack of Pop-Tarts and two red bell peppers. Why: because they cost me the same to purchase – roughly US$4.00. This is truly a remarkable feat. There are more than 50 different ingredients in the Chocolate Fudge Pop-Tart. There is even a "Pop-Tart World" that recently opened in Times Square, New York, joining the Hershey Store and M&M World at this internationally renowned location. Each pastry is a robust 200 calories, making the entire US$4.00 box worth a gut-busting 1,200 calories. As for the two red bell peppers: one ingredient (itself!); no "Red Bell Pepper World" (in fact not much of any ad campaign); and roughly 50 calories a piece (assuming they are large) or 100 calories in total. It is a sad commentary on the state of cheap to learn that while average-income Americans need to spend roughly 15 percent of their food budgets on fruit and vegetables to meet government guidelines that figure would jump to 70 percent among low-income households – if, that is, those households actually did eat the recommended amount of fruit and vegetables (most do not because they cannot afford to). One obvious place these costs are being realized is in healthcare. In the 1970s households spent roughly 14 percent of their disposable income on food and 7 percent on healthcare. Today, the average household spends roughly 15 percent on healthcare and 9 percent on food. But healthcare is just one of the many expenses associated with cheap food. There are also costs to the environment and to individual and community well-being, recognizing specifically the links between cheap food and food deserts and malnutrition. That's right; rather than being a solution to hunger cheap food policies are directly responsible for the malnutrition of millions. Let us also not forget about the army of laborers who also pay, with their health and the well-being of their families, so we can eat as we do. Cheap food is far from affordable. In fact, it's extremely expensive.

Chapter 5: the real cost of automobiles and car-munities

Think the cost of that new car is captured in its window sticker? Think again. Road accidents are annually responsible for 1.3 million deaths and up to 50 million injuries globally. These figures are expected to account for 5 percent of the total global disease burden by 2030 at a cost of roughly US$2.5 trillion. Road accidents cost developing countries approximately US$100 billion annually – that is twice the amount of aid monies that these economies receive. Noise from road traffic has been linked to sleep disturbance, hypertension, and hyperactivity in children. The AAA (formally known as the American Automobile Association) places the average annual cost to own and operate a car in the United States at US$8,946. And let us not forget: the average household in the United States owns 2.29 vehicles. Then there is "free" parking. Who pays for that? We all do, as taxpayers, regardless of whether you use it or not. Or what about the current lump-sum pricing practice for auto insurance that is so common in places like the United States? It is widely recognized that, just as an all-you-can-eat restaurant encourages more eating, all-you-can-drive insurance pricing encourages more driving, which also means more accidents, congestion, and greenhouse gas emissions. It is also terribly inequitable, in that miles driven is positively correlated with income. Low-mileage (and low-income) drivers therefore subsidize insurance costs for high-mileage (high-income) drivers. Then there are the problems of air pollution, CO_2 emissions, and climate change linked to the automobile, costs that are anything but insignificant. For example, a study from the July 2013 issue of *Environmental Research Letters* estimates that worldwide air pollution kills more than two million every year (many of the pollutants highlighted attributable to the automobile).[7] Yet perhaps the most egregious expense of all is the automobile's costs to civic disengagement and community integration. The car is therefore not just a drain on our wallets but, as we shall see, on human well-being, social cohesion, and, even, to democracy itself.

Chapter 6: retail concentration and rock-bottom prices ... but at what cost?

The goal of this chapter is to roll back the veil masking the costs of so-called megastores (and Walmart in particular given its market enormity). It has been estimated that public coffers in the United States lose more than US$1 billion annually through what is known as vendor discounts, of which over US$100 million goes to Walmart. A vendor discount is essentially a service fee designed to compensate store owners for recording sales tax collections and remitting them to revenue agencies. When first adopted, shopkeepers laboriously kept records by hand. Today, of course, this is all handled electronically and is automatic. Then there are the studies – like the one mentioned earlier – that describe how taxpayers effectively subsidize the low wages and poor benefit levels that are increasingly becoming the norm among hypermarket employees. Thanks to Walmart, and others that are following their "lead," over 100,000 employees in the United States qualify for public assistance that otherwise would not if they were just paid better. Add to that the costs of these superstores to local communities. A study released in 2012 focusing on retailers in Salt Lake City is par for the course, at least among those looking at economic impact. Independent and locally owned shops and restaurants returned 52 percent and 78.7 percent, respectively, of their revenue back into the local economy. National chain stores, conversely, recirculated on average 13.6 percent of all revenue back into local markets while national restaurant chains recirculated at an average of 30.4 percent.[8] The chapter concludes by discussing how these firms, which rival high-income countries in terms of revenue generated, are altering the very foundations of our society; a change that comes at the expense of a broader understanding of what constitutes an economic system, which was originally recognized by the Ancient Greeks but has since fallen by the wayside. Included in this broader understanding is a vast array of exchange relationships including kinship, neighborhood, and community; a space where *real* productivity was thought to have occurred but now all such relations are being sacrificed in the name of cheap.

Chapter 7: working less for more

I use the subject of vacations and leisure as an entry point into a broader conversation about how we are organizing ourselves and the notions of prosperity that spring from those relationships. Recall the point made earlier about how economist John Maynard Keynes incorrectly predicted that productivity increases would translate into shorter work weeks and more leisure for the average American worker. Instead, we followed a different path, involving more work, stress, and status-seeking behaviors. Not only that, vacations have become just as taxing as work. Why is that? Perhaps part of an answer lies in how we currently equate "vacation" with "going away"? Maybe if we enhanced the attractiveness of communities we would feel differently. This would clearly have ecological benefits, as the real cost of vacations, after factoring in for air travel and everything else one does when touring a distant land, far exceeds the immediate out-of-pocket expense paid to a company like Expedia.com. But it would also help dampen the need we feel to over-work, as we would no longer have this large expense looming on the horizon. Working less, it turns out, is not only good for our mental health and overall well-being. It would help infuse communities with people who have struck a balance between being gainfully employed and gainfully leisured. If we have learned anything from the last 50 years it is that community cannot be bought; there is no substitute for it in the marketplace. We have to work for it. And we cannot do that if we spend all our time working, so we can, among other things, vacation as far away from our communities as our credit cards allow. In sum, we need to reflect upon whether cheaponomics actually makes *anyone* feel better off. Clearly it does not for those having to pay for their unfair share of the costs, a point made repeatedly in earlier chapters. But can we assume that those receiving their unfair share of the benefits profit from these arrangements, in terms of enhanced well-being? The evidence suggests they do not. So if few – if any – qualitatively benefit from cheaponomics, why continue down this path?!

Yet, as I said earlier, the subject of leisure is but an entry point into a broader conversation. We do need more leisure but not the resource-intensive (aka "commercial") type that has become so prevalent in high-income countries. To do that – to have the time to actually do leisurely leisure – we need to also think about work, or more accurately we need to have a conversation about the amount of (paid) work we do. Now is not the place to describe this position in detail, as it cannot be explained thoroughly in just a couple of sentences. What I will be unpacking in this chapter is the erroneous notion that we need to work more to have more (and be happy). We can actually do a lot more if we worked less. And we can do it all with lower incomes too.

You will have to wait until Chapter 7, however, to discover how we square that circle.

Chapter 8: comforting the productivist zombie

Ever notice how solutions to all the world's ills, or at least most of them, are framed in productivist terms? Problem: climate change. Solution: renewable energy. Problem: food insecurity. Solution: a second green revolution. Problem: peak oil. Solution: electric cars. We need not worry about producing less, according to this mindset; just producing differently. That will fix everything. Wouldn't that be nice? It certainly is an easy way forward. After all, if all we have to change is how we produce stuff then we really do not have to change much at all. Tweaking production maintains the status quo, for the most part, as it allows us to continue doing what we have been doing for decades. Changing *how* the grid is electrified, for example, requires zero alterations to consumer behavior. At most, we might have to get used to occasionally plugging in our cars. Otherwise, consume away! But what good do these "solutions" do if they perpetuate – and perhaps even ramp up – energy-intensive, cheap ways of living? So what, for example, if some of our energy comes from renewable sources? If it is all going to power transportation across and between sprawling cities, the lighting, heating, and cooling of homes that continue to grow in size and be filled with cheap stuff, and, more generally, fuel a system that has gotten really good at socializing most of its costs, are we really creating any saving over the long term? Or are we, by focusing so intently on producing our way toward a just and sustainable society, merely speeding up the very system we ought to be changing? Before answering that question answer this one. By finding alternatives to non-renewable resources are we weaning ourselves from their use or, albeit inadvertently, intensifying our consumption of them (an outcome that goes by such names as the Jevons paradox and the rebound effect)? It is a matter of simple supply and demand. As the alternatives generate more supply they reduce the market price of the commodity in question and therefore encourage its demand. The promises of productivism, as a sole solution for delivering us from cheaponomics, do not hold up to empirical scrutiny. Yet this ideology continues to live. This chapter seeks to behead this undead creature so it can, finally, have eternal rest, with the help of such macabre devices as collaborative consumption, taxes and regulations, and good old-fashioned talk (mixed in with some collective action).

To be perfectly clear, this chapter is not about having *more* or *less*: electricity, comfort, lighting, freedom, etc. Cheaponomics lives off of these false choices, as they keep us sufficiently distracted by thinking that the alternatives are even worse. As opposed to the mind-numbing effects that arise from embracing this false dichotomy, an affordable society finds its freedom in its rejection. As spelled out in this chapter, affordable alternatives center on doing consumption, government, markets, liberty, and the like *differently*.

Chapter 9: real prosperity is priceless

Cheaponomics assumes the worst of people. We should let a free, unencumbered market decide the fate of the world because anything else would be tainted with the petty, selfish jealousy that clouds otherwise rational human judgment. That is why proponents of the economic status quo cringe when their form of socialism is challenged, because the other form, in their minds, "rewards laziness" and "disincentivizes work." The data, however, tell a different story. People are no more inherently lazy than they are inherently selfish. The egoistic rational actor seems to only exist in the pages of economic textbooks and in the minds of economists. Worse still, when left to their own accord the animal spirits of free market capitalism end up consuming themselves – a point made all too clear in the wake of the recent global financial collapse (though other examples are all around us, most notably climate change). This chapter contemplates what a more balanced approach to prosperity would look like. Topics discussed include inequality, how rights presuppose responsibilities, the limits of individual (consumer) action, the relationship between growth and happiness and well-being, and participatory democracy. Excessive forms of benefit-socializing socialism are problematic but so too are the types of cost-socializing practices detailed throughout the book. Rather than aiming for cheap, I suggest devising a system predicated on outcomes that are afford-able. The term's original meaning originates from the Old English word *geforthian*: to carry out. Affordability, following this usage, speaks to an object's or system's enabling ability. Just like the sun affords plants the energy to grow, we ought to want an economic and social system that affords people and nations the capabilities to develop and enhance their overall well-being. Sadly, cheaponomics has just the opposite effect: it disables.

Fortunately, however, it has not affected us to the point where we cannot turn things around.

Chapter 10: ten recommendations for the good, affordable, and affording

To conclude, I offer some suggestions – ten to be exact – to help get the conversation going on how we can make society more enabling for *everyone*. Doing away with cheaponomics is no guarantee, in itself, that real prosperity will be attained. At least by doing away with it an affording prosperity has a fighting chance.

~

It is not often that I agree with Milton Friedman – the feisty, diminutive, brilliant professor that oversaw the Chicago school of economics' rise in influential political circles. But on this point I think we would see eye to eye: that the recent Great Recession (of 2008), which the world economy continues to struggle to recover from, has been catastrophic and in being so it offers a unique opportunity. For Friedman (and this is where we part company), it offers an exciting market opportunity. For me, the opportunity I see is in a noticeably different direction. You will have to read the rest of the book to find out just what that vision looks like but it certainly is not in the direction of an even more entrenched status quo. Friedman observed that "only a crisis – actual or perceived – produces real change. When that crisis occurs, the actions that are taken depend on the ideas that are lying around."[9] For Friedman and his legion of disciples, their strategy was "to develop alternatives to existing policies, to keep them alive and available until the politically impossible becomes political inevitable."[10] Consider this book as a food stockpile of sorts, of alternative ideas to nourish collective action.

Let us be clear on just what the catastrophe is. Part of it is a real example of disaster capitalism, in the sense that there are a lot of pieces that still need picking up, in the form of homes worth less than their mortgage (aka underwater mortgages), millions of unemployed and uninsured, and a middle class whose purchasing power is disappearing with every passing month. But it is also a catastrophe *for* Friedmanites and their free-market ideas. As I discuss in later chapters, the so-called engine of economic growth, as a job creating, well-being generating force, which has been spewing smoke, leaking oil, and killing pedestrians (and riders) for years, has never performed more poorly than in recent years.

The Dow Jones Industrial Average closed at 15,464.30 today (July 14, 2013), an end of the day milestone never before reached. Every day brings with it the potential for a new record high. The "good old days" were never *this* good, as least as far as the stock market is concerned. The Dow has recovered more than all of its losses after hitting rock bottom in March of 2009 – the third-strongest bull market for the Dow since World War II. And yet: the job market has recovered only 5.5 million of the 8.7 million jobs lost because of the financial crisis – the worst labor-market recovery since World War II – and the inflation-adjusted average income is presently 8 percent *lower* than in 2007.[11] There are a number for reasons for this, as explained in later chapters. Two big ones include the fact that firms have found ways to do more without adding individuals to their payroll, which is to say they are choosing capital-intensity (or more accurately *energy*-intensity) over

6 Tuana, N. (2004) "Coming to understand: Orgasm and the epistemology of ignorance," *Hypatia*, 19(1), pp. 194–232, p. 196.
7 Silva, Raquel, Jason West, Yuqiang Zhang, Susan C. Anenberg, Jean-François Lamarque, Drew T. Shindell, William J. Collins, Stig Dalsoren, Greg Faluvegi, and Gerd Folberth (2013) "Global premature mortality due to anthropogenic outdoor air pollution and the contribution of past climate change," *Environmental Research Letters*, 8(3), http://iopscience.iop.org/1748-9326/8/3/034005/article, last accessed July 15, 2013.
8 Civic Economics (2012) "A national comparative survey with the American Booksellers Association," Indie Impact Study Series, American Booksellers Association, Salt Lake City, UT, www.lvfiba.org/Las_Vegas_Client_120717.pdf, last accessed September 16, 2012.
9 Friedman, Milton (2002 [1962]) *Capitalism and Freedom: Fortieth Anniversary Edition* (Chicago, IL: Chicago University Press), p. xiv.
10 Ibid., p. xiv.
11 Gongloff, Mark (2013) "Dow hits record high: Here's why it doesn't matter," *Huffington Post*, March 5, www.huffingtonpost.com/2013/03/05/dow-record-high_n_2783096.html?view=screen, last accessed April 9, 2013.
12 Noah, Timothy (2013) "The one percent gobbled up the recovery, too," *New Republic*, February 12, www.newrepublic.com/article/112397/one-percent-gobbles-economic-recovery#, last accessed April 10, 2013.

Part I

Cheap stuff

Chapter 2

You bought that computer but someone else paid for it

Conducting 100 Google searches, $0.00; watching two ten-minute videos on YouTube, $0.00; viewing webpages heavily populated with images, figures, and tables for one hour, $0.00: total CO_2 footprint of these "free" acts ... 1,660 grams. That is the cost I imposed upon the atmosphere by engaging in online research for the previous sentence: 1,660 grams of CO_2 equivalents. From behind my desk using a purely digital medium (allegedly), those actions emitted as much CO_2 as had I instead chose to drive my car a little over two-and-a-half miles to consult with the reference librarian at my neighborhood library. I alone may have retrieved this information but I alone am not paying these costs. You are too. So: thank you.

Perhaps you would like to know what you and your children (and your children's children ...) paid for. What those 1,660 grams of carbon dioxide "bought" was some rather surprising information about the true cost of internet activity. Harvard physicist Alex Wissner-Gross calculates that the average Google search accounts for seven grams of CO_2 emissions, whereas an image-intensive webpage or one streaming a video emits 0.2 grams of CO_2 for each second viewed.[1] Thanks to the energy-intensive server farms that "house" the information superhighway, free e-data is far from free. On the bright side: at least I did not create an avatar to track down this information. It has been calculated that inhabitants of Second Life each consume 1,752 kWh per year – almost as much as a real person (the average inhabitant of Earth consumes 2,436 kWh per year)![2]

In 1994 the boldly titled essay "Magna Carta for the Knowledge Age," written by notable futurists including Alvin Toffler, was published. It got some things right, such as when it referred to computers and the internet as "more ecosystem than machine." But it stumbled terribly by viewing this ecosystem as being inhabited purely with information and by predicting the eventual revolution of "the overthrow of matter."[3] The wizard behind the digital veil giving this ecosystem the air of, well, air – after all, we now refer to much of it as "the cloud" – remains solidly material, composed of things like coal, carbon dioxide, taxpayers, cancer, water, corrosive chemical concoctions (aka piranha baths), and open-pit mines. The Digital Age may have the appearance of floating on a cloud but it has legs and they are every bit as solid as the namesakes of the Bronze and Iron Ages.

Looking online – and, in light of my earlier findings, at the cost of a couple dozen grams of CO_2 – I found the company Kocaso selling its ultra-slim laptops for US$79. We all know the price cycle of technology: when new, it is expensive (I remember my dad spending a couple hundred dollars for a VHS recorder in the early 1980s); once established, the price drops precipitously (before disappearing from the store's shelves, VHS recorders were sold at Walmart for less than $10 in 2006). If you ask an economist about this, they will likely say something about economies of scale – the cost advantages obtained through expansion. These economies are both "internal" and "external," in that they are the result of price savings not only from manufacturing more units but also from "efficiencies" obtained in related sectors, such as when raw materials are made cheaper due to a reorganization of extractive industries. And of course it doesn't take long until supply and demand become self-reinforcing, as cheaper products drive demand which in turn causes prices to drop even further. But *US$79* ... really?

This chapter is not about that US$79 computer. It is not about any particular electronic device. You see, that is where we start getting ourselves into trouble, by thinking about these items in isolation and their associated costs as one-off. When purchasing that US$79 computer it is easy to be lulled into believing that you have paid fully for – or, in economic parlance, internalized – its costs the moment you submit your credit card number. Yet unless you plan on never using it, and encasing it in a lead tomb so that its end-of-life phase is of no consequence, someone continues to pay for it. Someone, that is, other than you. Remember, we are talking about something that is more ecosystem than machine. The manufacturing and functionality of computers, tablets, and mobile phones are predicated on a complex external web. Not one of us is Harry Potter and this is not Hogwarts School of Witchcraft and Wizardry. We have to rely on good old-fashioned matter – and the breaking up of matter – when bringing these gadgets forth into the world and giving them life, not magic for witches and wizards.

So what precisely are all these costs? That is where things get tricky. We cannot really say, precisely. But neither *should* we say, precisely. I have never been particularly fond of the idea of monetizing the universe. I could no more, for example, put a price on the health of my family than the poet Robert Burns on love (or roses). We need to be honest with ourselves: some things just do not – and should not – have a price. But even if we could put a price tag on everything we need to realize that these costs are not fixed. Let us say, hypothetically, that the earlier mentioned US$79 computer, after all charges are accounted for, costs society and future generations in excess of US $1,000. Does this mean that I am arguing that computers should not be widely available, as most people in the world could not afford the US$1,000+

expense? Absolutely not. That US$1,000+ price tag is inflated because we currently allow so many costs to go unaccounted for. Cost *maximization* is presently the norm, as long as the most egregious can be externalized. Cheaponomics tends to produce things that are the *most* expensive for society. Minimizing costs socialized would undoubtedly bring *total costs* down, leading to things that are ultimately less expensive for us all. Taking this step would also incentivize the making of things that are repairable and reusable, so we would not be purchasing a new mobile phone and computer every 18 and 36 months, respectively (which is how frequently the average American replaces these devices). So as retail prices go up with the internalization of costs we need to be mindful of how these added consumer expenses would be offset by reduced purchase frequency. That is to say, *if* we would even choose to still buy these goods. A discussion on the freedom of access and onerous weight of ownership, however, will have to wait for later chapters.

My three-ton laptop

The term "virtual" is used a lot when talking about resources that go into making things – virtual water, energy, CO_2 equivalents, etc. – but there is nothing virtual about them. They are real, though you would not know it by looking at my laptop. Dell advertises that it weights a fairly trim 3.97 pounds. Its virtual weight: as best as I can calculate, over 6,000 pounds.

Here are the numbers I have come up with:

- approximately 1,000 pounds of rock and ore waste to extract minerals from open-pit mines;[4]
- 529 pounds of fossil fuels, 49 pounds of chemicals, and 3,307 pounds of water during the manufacturing phase (this is equivalent to the waste generated when producing a mid-size vehicle);[5]
- 772 pounds of CO_2 equivalents for its entire life cycle (with an assumed four-year use-life).[6]

That comes out to 5,657 pounds. But that is just the computer itself. I use this device – a lot. I tracked my Googling for the last week. I average more than 100 searches during the weekday; slightly less, but not much, on weekends. Taking the earlier mentioned estimate that each Google search accounts for seven grams of CO_2 emissions, that comes out to 700 grams a day and 255,500 grams (563 pounds) annually – just for using an internet search engine! To put that into some perspective, I would have to drive my car roughly 360 miles to emit the equivalent. Then there are all the videos I (or more accurately my kids) stream on Netflix. That is taxing an energy-intensive server somewhere in the world (energy likely being generated from a coal-powered plant) and therefore contributing further to my laptop's CO_2 footprint. And that is just my computer. More than one billion PCs and tablets are

24 Cheap stuff

now sold annually, most of which will be replaced in just a few years due to their becoming "obsolete."[7] At a couple tons a piece, that is a lot of not-so-virtual waste.

President Obama was re-elected in 2012 running on the often-touted slogan, "We are all in this together." The economics underlying the Digital Age operate under a similar credo, at least when it comes to the issue of who pays for costs. How else could something predicated on the sale of a billion units annually, with each embodying literally tons of waste, be praised for marshaling the overthrow of matter without some serious cost redistribution occurring? Returning to my laptop: 3.97 pounds in front of me; 6,000+ pounds scattered elsewhere. In other words, I am responsible for 0.0005 percent of its total weight. The remaining 99.9995 percent is someone else's problem. *That* is cost-socializing socialism. Like it or not, we are all in this together. Though, as we will soon see, some are losing more in this egregious game of cost redistribution than others.

Virtual blood, cancer, miscarriages, suicides ...

Some virtual costs can be converted to numerical form: virtual water, CO_2 equivalents, tons of rock and ore waste. Others cannot, or at least should not be, like virtual cancer, conflict, and death. Virtual blood flows through our electronic devices.

Ever hear of coltan? My guess is no, even though you would likely say it is essential to your way of life after learning of its properties. It has played a key role in miniaturization, allowing capacitors to handle high voltages at high temperatures in small spaces. Your ultra-thin mobile phone, the ubiquitous iPad, portable GPS devices: all progeny of coltan. The industrial application of this ore spans the electronic spectrum, from pacemakers to missile guidance systems, cellular phones, gaming consoles, and laptops and tablets. It is no wonder that it has been classified as a "strategic mineral" by the US Pentagon.[8]

Coltan is a combination of two rare ores, columbium (also known as niobium) and tantalum. Demand for these ores collectively results in the rape, torture, and murder of hundreds of thousands of innocent Congolese people per year. While remarkably resource rich and in possession of a high-volume river system with the potential to supply much of the continent's electricity needs, Congo has been stricken by conflict, most recently due to militias (many from neighboring countries) battling for control of the country's coltan mines. While currently accounting for a small percentage of global coltan production – presently 80 percent of this ore comes from mines in Australia – roughly 80 percent of the world's known reserves are thought to be in Africa, with 80 percent of those located in the eastern region of Congo.[9]

A number of these mines are under the control of rebels and militia groups, meaning many coltan miners are under rifle rule – a great many of whom are children and prisoners.[10] Even coltan from legal mines has blood on it, as owners are often illegally taxed by rebel militias or members of the Congolese army to bankroll fighting that has resulted in the killing of as many as 45,000 civilians a month since 2000.[11] As Peddar Panga, a former soldier of the Democratic Republic of Congo (who came to the United States in 2005 to pursue a nursing degree), recently explained to a group of students in Austin, Texas, "There is blood on your cell phone, death on your laptop. Rape is in your car."[12] The last point is a reference to the rampant violence against Congolese women in areas of conflict, crimes that have led to increased rates of HIV and AIDS in regions already devastated by poverty, food insecurity, and ethnic tensions. In the Shabunda territory, for example, roughly 3,000 rapes were recorded between 2006 and 2009.[13] Undoubtedly a conservative figure in a country where gendered (read: female) violence remains the norm and where rape is commonly used as a weapon of warfare and a tool of ethnic "cleansing" through forced pregnancy and as a means of propagating HIV/AIDS among rivals.

So: does my two-plus ton laptop also have blood on it? Electronic firms claim we will never know for sure, explaining that the global coltan commodity chain cannot be properly policed as the ore changes hands at least a half a dozen times before reaching manufacturers whose brands we are familiar with. Some NGOs, however, claim this to be a lie and have successfully traced the supply chains of coltan.[14] As for the prospect that blood coltan will one day receive the same global notoriety as blood diamonds: well, we can hope. A mining official, interviewed for an article in a Pakistani newspaper, was doubtful:

> There is a cold and calculated cruelty about the massacre (of people) and (the clearing) of forests for coltan, but blood diamond sounds glamorous, and blood coltan doesn't mean anything. I cannot imagine Leonardo DiCaprio making that movie. Maybe George Clooney? Maybe not.[15]

If not a movie about conflict coltan perhaps George Clooney would sign on to play a "clean room" worker for a nameless computer chip manufacturer in Silicon Valley; a place with among the highest concentration of Superfund sites in the country. (Superfund was established by US Congress to pay for containment, cleanup, and/or remediation of abandoned toxic waste sites.) The processes involved in the making of semiconductors and chips are continually evolving, as are the chemicals that do the work of etching, cleaning, and dissolving. The pace of this change is so great that for many chemicals we have no idea of their public health and environmental effects, as no comprehensive health and safety analyses have been conducted. A couple hundred different ingredients can go into the making of a single semiconductor; a list that can differ widely depending on the type of semiconductor being manufactured. And in most cases the specifics of each "recipe" are locked up under the guise of an industry trade secret, making this all one giant guessing game.

In sum, even if we wanted to regulate this industry we could not – under existing laws – because that would require a knowledge of what was being regulated.

The clean room is an OSHA (Occupation Safety and Health Administration) inspector's dream space, if the safety and health of computer chips – versus workers – were their primary concern. Air is filtered to ensure it is free of any particulate matter. "What about air fumes?" you might ask. They are of no bother as they pose no threat to the chips' well-being. The air, which is constantly recirculated and therefore free of dust, often remains thick with noxious chemical vapors. Over the course of any workday workers can inhale or come into contact with dozens of known or suspected carcinogens. Workers in this space do wear protective clothing, which includes the head-to-toe "bunny suit." Yet, again, what at first blush look to be steps taken to safeguard humans are really about keeping chips free from contamination. The bunny suits are more for keeping hair and flecks of skin from the worker *in* than about keeping toxins *out*. And the chemicals: there is a reason the various acids and solvents used to imprint and etch silicon wafers are called "piranha baths." They will eat about anything, including the protective gloves of workers.[16] Yet it is not the gloves we ought to be worried about.

A number of high-profile cases have been filed against IBM by former workers over the last 20 years. These lawsuits center on the high rates of cancer among one-time employees and the equally alarming rates of birth defects among their children. Bob Herbert wrote a series of *New York Times* Op-Ed pieces in 2003 detailing these statistical anomalies. He notes, in reference to the children:

> There is a long list of young people and children who have suffered tragic birth defects – spina bifida, missing or deformed limbs, a missing kidney, a missing vagina, blindness – whose parents (in some cases both parents) worked for IBM and are now suing.[17]

Herbert also highlights the work of Dr. Richard Clapp, an epidemiologist from Boston University, whose work shows not only elevated rates of breast cancer, non-Hodgkins lymphoma, and brain cancer among IBM employees but that these cancers are occurring in IBM employees at ages younger than the US average.[18] Dr. Clapp was led to this conclusion after reviewing records previously known only to IBM management. As it turns out, IBM should have known something was up, given the fact that since 1969 they kept death records for nearly all their US employees.

Richard Clapp was also in the news a few years back when the journal *Clinics in Occupational and Environmental Medicine* revoked an invitation to publish a paper he wrote based on the aforementioned data. According to a spokesperson for the publisher of the journal, "It was determined that it was original research and the format of it wasn't appropriate for *Clinics*, which is a review journal." The guest editor of the issue in question and many of its contributing authors, however, say that this is not the real reason for the paper's removal, contending instead that the invitation was revoked because of pressure placed on the journal by IBM. A review of *Clinics* issues for the two years preceding the proposed special issue justifies such suspicions, as no fewer than six original research studies were published during this time period.[19] The paper in question analyzes mortality records for 32,000 IBM employees over 32 years. The findings it presents are stark. Workers in the sample were two to six times more likely to develop certain cancers than the national average. Legal maneuvers by IBM also kept Clapp from publishing his findings in any other journal. After more than two years in limbo, a New York court issued an injunction prohibiting IBM from interfering with Dr. Clapp's efforts to publish his corporate mortality study.[20] It has since been published in the peer-reviewed journal *Environmental Health*.[21]

Yet, as is all-too-often the case, cost socialization does not stop at national borders. In fact, many of the costs attributed to electronics are shipped overseas, placing them at the feet of populations who are already paying dearly for the "prosperity" peddled by cheaponomics.

Like most other firms, electronic companies are aggressively seeking out cheap labor and lax regulatory environments in lower income countries. Take, for example, the high-profile case involving the use of N-hexane among Apple workers in China. N-hexane is a fast-evaporating solvent, which makes it easier for workers to clean the screens of their products. N-hexane is also a neurotoxin – a poison that acts on the nervous system – that has been linked to loss of control of the hands, skin cancer, and leukemia.[22] Another common exposure reported among Chinese laborers in the electronics industry is to the solvent glycol ether. Overexposure has been linked to inhalation injuries, birth defects, miscarriages, and testicular damage.[23] Then there are the stories coming out of South Korea involving their Samsung manufacturing plants, which tell of leukemia, lymphoma, brain cancer, and other diseases striking relatively young workers at unusually high rates.[24]

As for some of these socialized costs, allow me to do some back-of-the-envelope calculations using breast cancer to make my point. Based on current incidence rates, 12.4 percent of women born in the United States today will develop breast cancer at some point in their lives.[25] According to Richard Clapp's research, female workers in "clean rooms" have a rate of breast cancer that is double what would be expected in the general population. Worldwide, the total number of these workers is estimated at over one million, roughly one-quarter of whom perform jobs that routinely put them into direct contact with the toxic chemicals.[26] Let us say half of these are women. If they have twice the incident rate of breast cancer as the general female population (in the United States) then well over 10,000 women are acquiring this disease annually so we can satisfy our addiction for cheap gadgets. And that is just breast cancer, saying nothing of testicular cancer, leukemia, lymphoma, brain cancer, miscarriages, neurological disorders, birth defects …

There is also ample evidence pointing to how the new Digital Age relies upon the very old practice of labor abuse. This is exemplified by the wave of suicides that took place in 2011 and 2012 at Foxconn factories in China, where iPads and iPhones (among other gadgets) are manufactured. The cause of these acts: inhumane working conditions. It had gotten so bad that Foxconn management required new staff to sign pledges that they would not attempt to kill themselves. If they did, their families could only seek the legal minimum in damages.[27] Undeterred by these threats, close to 150 Chinese workers threatened to commit suicide in January 2012 by leaping from their respective factory roofs in protest of how they have been treated.[28]

Since then, Foxconn and Apple have been engaged in a vigorous public relations campaign touting recent improvements in the working conditions of their factories. Closer inspection, however, makes one more than a little skeptical on just how deep the makeover goes. A report issued in September 2012 by the group Students and Scholars Against Corporate Misbehavior (SACOM) cites the continuation of a number of labor rights abuses.[29] The following is a sample of what their investigative research uncovered.

- Excessive overtime: monthly overtime hours at between 80 and 100 hours in some of the production lines at Foxconn – a total that is two to three times that allowed by Chinese law.
- Unpaid overtime: on some production lines workers were forced to reach production targets before being allowed to stop even if that meant working overtime without pay.
- Denial of ergonomic break: Foxconn and Apple promised to offer two daily ergonomic breaks for workers but most interviewed received no such respite from work.
- Meager wages: wages earned are still insufficient to meet basic needs, especially among workers who have dependents.
- Arbitrary relocation of workforce: workers are brought in from other provinces to meet production goals. Many workers claim to not have any choice in the matter and often do not know how long they will be away from their families.
- Occupational health and safety: workers express concern for their health due to inadequate training involving practices that bring them into direct contact with chemicals. Workers were also worried about the general long-term health impacts of working around particular chemicals and odors.
- A culture of distrust toward workers: workers are required to obtain an "off-duty permit" for things like a bathroom break.

Next time you are queued up in front of an Apple store waiting to get your hands on their newest iPhone, look around. There is very likely a similar scene unfolding in the Economic Processing Zone in Zhengzhou, China. Yet whereas your compatriots are bursting with excitement for what awaits beyond the locked Apple doors, the line in front of the Foxconn plant is far more subdued. And why wouldn't it be: that mass of bodies is helping pay for the cost of your soon-to-be-purchased gadget. You could say, in some cases at least, they are queuing up to literally internalize certain externalized costs, in the form of cancers, birth defects, suicides, and shame – all for you and the companies that profit from your purchase.

Floating on a cloud ... of fossil fuel emissions

"The cloud" is an apt term, but not for the reasons you think. The name cloud in the context of the IT (information technology) sector does not have any single definition. The term is frequently applied to refer to a wide range of internet-based platforms and services – from Facebook to Flickr, LinkedIn, and Google Maps – that store and deliver data from an online source to the gadget in front of you. The metaphor of a cloud certainly builds on the futurist's utopia of having finally overthrown matter. Cloud computing consumes nothing more than 1s and 0s. Right?

I recently had a student proudly announce in class that he lives "digitally off the grid" – those were his words. Turns out he has some photovoltaic cells that charge a couple of batteries which he then plugs his electronic devices into at night before going to bed. He admitted to being a heavy data user, though this fact failed to register with him as having any ecological significance. In addition to daily sending out "dozens of texts" and an equal amount of emails he confessed to streaming at a minimum two movies from Netflix every evening while listening to hours of Pandora (internet radio) during the day. But because he did all of this off of a solar-, rather than a coal-, charged iPad and iPhone he thought he had zeroed out his energy footprint. Not that he is alone in thinking this way. When polled not a single student, out of more than 100, in my Global Environmental Issues class came anywhere close to realizing just how energy-intensive it is to Google, tweet, and stream.

Yet I do find the term apt, if the right metaphor were evoked. Cloud computing *clouds* our ability to see beyond the liquid crystal display (LCD) in front of us. If "the cloud" were a country it would have the fifth largest electricity demand in the world, at more than 700 billion kWh.[30] Yet this demand is practically invisible. Perhaps we are living in Hogwarts School of Witchcraft and Wizardry after all, as it takes some special wizardry to make an entire country's energy footprint disappear from plain sight. And the *type* of energy being consumed to sustain this invisible country: if that is "clean" then black is the new green and coal the new solar. To give a perverse example: the anti-virus software firm McAfee calculates that the electricity required to transmit the trillions of spam emails sent annually is equivalent to the amount required to power more than two million homes in the United States and produces the same greenhouse gas emissions as over three million cars.[31] Facebook's first two data centers in Oregon and North Carolina, while using a highly energy efficient design and technology, were both located in areas where more than 60 percent of the electricity came from coal. So while the US Environmental Protection Agency (EPA) continues to work with the IT sector to expand its EnergyStar rating system to apply to data centers the fact that these server farms continue to obtain a significant amount of their energy from coal largely cancels out any efficiency gains made in server technology.

Something else that further cancels out these efficiency gains: the comatose server, which has reached epidemic proportions.

At the request of the *New York Times*, the consulting firm McKinsey & Company analyzed energy use by data centers used by pharmaceutical companies, military contractors, banks, and government agencies and found them to be using, on average, only 6 to 12 percent of the electricity powering their servers to perform computations. The remaining energy – roughly 90 percent of it! – went to idling servers. An example of cheaponomics pure and simple as the practice represents "cheap" insurance – as IT firms strike sweet deals with electric companies to obtain underpriced electricity – against the rare event of a massive surge in activity that could crash operations.[32] The energy wasted on these "farms" is as much as 30 times greater than the amount used to process and transmit data.[33] Then there are the banks of batteries and diesel power generators standing by just in case there is a power disruption on the grid. Amazon, for example, has been fined hundreds of thousands of dollars by Virginia's Department of Environmental Quality for installing and running diesel generators without obtaining the necessary environmental permits required by the state. As for the permits issued in the IT haven that spreads out across 14 counties in Virginia (due to cheap electricity and various tax breaks and subsidies): those diesel generators alone could supply enough electricity to match one nuclear power plant.[34] Two percent of world CO_2 emissions is what the IT sector is said to be responsible for – a carbon dioxide footprint, it is worth mentioning, that is as large as global air traffic.[35]

There is no reason to believe that this footprint will lighten anytime soon, even as firms like Facebook, Apple, and Google pledge to derive more of the energy that powers their server farms from renewables like solar and wind. Demand for additional centers is growing exponentially. Between June 2006 and June 2011, the number of internet users jumped from 1.043 billion (16 percent of the world's population) to 2.11 billion (30 percent of the world's population). The number of so-called "smart" phones is projected to rise from 500 million in 2011 to two billion by 2015. As for the total number of websites in existence, that figure increased from 18,000 in August 1995 to roughly a quarter of a billion by 2009.[36]

As for what is fueling this growth: primarily coal. A single 500MW coal-fired power plant emits three million tons of CO_2 and costs us more than US $500 *billion* a year when all the economic, health, and environmental impacts associated with each stage in the life cycle (extraction, transportation, processing, and combustion) are totaled.[37] Breaking this figure down a bit: US $74.6 billion are "paid" by Appalachian communities — where and by whom much of the coal is extracted — in terms of increased healthcare costs, injury, and death; costs linked to emissions total more than US$187 billion; and the mercury set loose into the environment, due to its negative effects upon human health, come with a price tag of almost US$30 billion. And let us not forget about climate change. Each 500MW coal-fired plant, in terms of climate change costs, passes onto the public (and future publics) an annual bill that can total more than US$200 billion annually.[38] Again, this is just *one* coal-fired power plant.

There are well over 500,000 data centers worldwide.[39] Some are so large that they can be seen from space and consume the same amount of energy as roughly 180,000 homes.[40] With renewables, these clouds could have a silver (or more accurately "green") lining, if we can wean ourselves from cheap coal. GreenQloud, a cloud computing service that markets itself as offering cloud servers and online storage that run on 100 percent renewable energy, has its operations on a former NATO Air Force base in Iceland.[41] (Nearly all of the electricity in this country is renewable thanks to geothermal and hydropower energy sources.) In October 2011, Facebook unveiled plans for its third data center. The site will be 60 miles from the Arctic circle in Lulea, Sweden. The center will be powered by a nearby dam that generates twice as much power as Hoover Dam and will be cooled eight months of the year using outside air. Yet, like other server farms, its financers have taken out a cheap (for them, not you) insurance policy to protect their investment from power disruptions: diesel power. Fourteen backup diesel generators will be at the site, which, one must assume, will be constantly running to supply real-time backup electricity.[42]

If you think phones have a lighter ecological footprint given their smaller stature, looks can be deceiving. By the end of 2012, the number of mobile subscriptions exceeded the world population for the first time. As of January 2012, India had 904 million mobile connections and looks to soon overtake China, the world's largest mobile phone market with 988 million subscribers. Two hundred million of India's mobile connections are for rural subscribers. Over 70 percent of India's more than 400,000 mobile towers stand in rural and semi-urban areas where grid-connected electricity is either not available or intermittent. Consequently, many of these towers rely on diesel generators to power their network operations. The amount of diesel consumed by these generators is roughly three billion liters annually, an amount that stands second only to that consumed by India's railways. Collectively, these lung-clogging power plants, which literally reflect nineteenth-century technology, are responsible for more than ten million tons of CO_2 emissions annually. As India's rural mobile subscription rates continue to increase — right now the adoption rate is about 25 percent — this figure will undoubtedly increase.[43]

A different "farm" subsidy

Here is a farm subsidy you will never find listed in any US Farm Bill: US$70 billion a year. That is how much, by one estimate, state and local governments – and thus taxpayers – give away to IT companies every year in order to attract their business.[44] Washington state, for example, subsidizes a Microsoft server farm in the municipality of Quincy to the tune of US$34 million a year. Why? For jobs, of course. But there is a catch. The center employs fewer than 70 people, who service things like its air conditioning systems and provide security. The "skilled" (cheap) programmers overseeing the site's daily operations can be located on the other side of the globe. The subsidies and incentives work out to roughly US$486,000 per job.[45] Elsewhere, Yahoo received US$268 million in state and local tax benefits and discounted energy to build a data center in Lockport, New York, to create employment for 125 citizens – or US$2.144 million per job. Verizon received US$614 worth of various incentives to locate its server farm in Somerset, New York. That US $614 million helped create about 200 jobs – a return in taxpayer investment of US$3.07 million for each new employee.[46] In 2010, the North Carolina Legislature debated for less than a minute before agreeing to provide Apple with US$46 million in tax breaks to construct a server farm in Maiden, which itself sweetened the deal by agreeing to slash Apple's property taxes in half and local taxes on its assets by 85 percent. The payoff: 50 jobs.[47] One more example: in August, 2012, Apple announced plans to build a US$1 billion server farm in Reno, Nevada – a deal only made possible thanks to US$88 million in state and local tax breaks. The company estimates that the new facilities will employ a little over 200 people earning an average of US$25 an hour; all for a job that costs taxpayers US$400,000 per employee.[48]

Other socialized costs take the form of underpriced energy. For utility providers, server farms represent the goose that lays golden eggs. Consequently, the former aggressively work to lure the latter onto their grid with promises of abundant cheap energy. Take, for example, a city ordinance recently debated in the town of Council Bluffs, Iowa. This law, if passed, would cap electricity fees for energy-intensive server farms at US$400,000 for the first four years; US$450,000 for years five through ten; and US$500,000 for years 11 and thereafter.[49] In other words, beyond a certain point these farms would essentially be consuming *free* energy, which would be coming primarily from large coal-fired power plants.

Free for Google, Twitter, Yahoo, and the like; damn costly for the rest of us.[50]

The cost of e-waste

Cultural theorist Walter Benjamin utilized a particular "natural history" method whereby he looked to the obsolete commodities that populated late-nineteenth-century arcades in Paris as he sought to understand the world from whence they came.⁵¹ These "fossilized" remnants included "the briefcase with interior lighting, the meter-long pocket knife, or the patented umbrella handle with built-in watch and revolver."⁵² For Benjamin, such "waste" not only illuminates past cultural states of fashion but also speaks to us about very real economic and material forces that led to their emergence and eventual decay. What will future generations, by employing this method, learn about us, after digging down and finding an entire stratum composed of wires, CPUs (central processing units), silicon chips, and broken LCD screens all interlaid with smashed pieces of plastic of various shapes and colors? Will this waste be used to define our epoch – E-wasteocene – by future geologists and archeologists? Following Benjamin, it certainly says something about the epoch's predominant economic and material forces which I have summed up in a single term: cheaponomics.

Just how much waste are we talking about? Based on recent trends, roughly 400 million computers are expected to be sold worldwide in 2013.⁵³ By 2015, the number of computers in use will top two billion.⁵⁴ If we are to believe industry estimates, which place the average life expectancy of a computer at between three and four years and global recycling rates for computers at less than 10 percent, then most of those two billion computers will be landfilled by 2020.⁵⁵ And that is just computers. There are more than four billion cell phone users worldwide; a number that is growing annually. The materiality of these devices might last forever – as they are largely non-biodegradable – but for the average cell phone owner "forever" is ephemeral, as ownership barely extends beyond a year.⁵⁶

Commodities, by their very definition, are supposed to be consumed. If that is the case then electronic commodities are peculiar as many are apparently made just to be thrown away. A 2011 report from a Ghana-based organization found that of the almost one-quarter of a million tons of electronic waste imported into the country annually, 30 percent was brand new but deemed "obsolete."⁵⁷ Annie Leonard in *The Story of Stuff* tells about a visit she had to an e-waste recycling facility in Roseville, California. Watching a series of printers get smashed before being pilfered of any recyclable material she noted that they all still had those plastic tags on them that must be pulled before they can function. They were all new. She then learned from her guide that about half of all the e-waste processed at the plant was like this: never used. As the guide went on to explain: "The companies don't want this stuff coming back to them through their warranty programs and then have to be responsible for it. It's easier for them to just destroy it."⁵⁸

The rates at which we can expect e-waste to increase are sobering. According to the United Nations Environment Program, by 2020, e-waste from computers will increase, from 2007 levels, by 500 percent in India and by 400 percent in China. They further predict e-waste from cell phones, over the same time period, to increase 700 percent in China and 1,800 percent in India.⁵⁹ So while the majority of e-waste today ends up exported overseas to less affluent nations – it is estimated that shipping e-waste to China, for example, is ten times cheaper than handling it in the United States – those countries will soon have their own electronic waste problems to deal with.[60]

Mercury is one of the more pernicious components of e-waste. Roughly 22 percent of the world's annual use of mercury goes into the making of such electronic devices as thermostats, sensors, mobile phones, batteries, and flat panel monitors.[61] As electronics in poorer nations are typically "recycled" out in the open mercury can easily come into contact with water producing the highly hazardous methylmercury. (A quick – though not free – YouTube search of "e-waste" will reveal numerous videos of individuals hunched over cooking stoves attempting to melt down, and thus melt out, precious metals.) Methylmercury is particularly dangerous to children and fetuses because it can have long-lasting cognitive effects. It is also a bioaccumulative environmental toxicant, meaning that, once ingested, it is readily and completely absorbed by the gastrointestinal tract. This is particularly concerning when it enters organisms like fish, as it then becomes more concentrated as it travels up the food chain through predatory consumption.

Cadmium, a heavy metal used in computer batteries, circuit boards, semiconductor chips, and CRTs also carries with it tremendous costs to society and the environment. Acute exposure to cadmium fumes can produce flu-like symptoms, referred to occasionally as "the cadmium blues." More severe exposure can cause tracheo-bronchitis (inflammation of the mucous membrane of the trachea and bronchi), pneumonitis (inflammation of lung tissue), and pulmonary edema (abnormal buildup of fluid in the air sacs of the lungs). Inhaling cadmium-laden dust can lead to respiratory tract and kidney problems which can quickly turn fatal. Ingestion of cadmium can cause immediate poisoning and damage to the liver and the kidneys.[62] And then there is lead: the fifth most widely used metal in the electronic industry after iron, aluminum, copper, and zinc. (Lead is found in things like solder, lead-acid batteries, and cable sheathing.) Overexposure to this heavy metal can produce vomiting, diarrhea, convulsions, coma, and even death. Lead is particularly dangerous for children as it can have profound neurological and behavioral effects.[63]

Recent studies have found extremely high levels of toxic pollutants in the air and soil around the Chinese city of Guiyu, home to the largest e-waste site on earth, and in the bodies of its residents.[64] Eighty percent of the residents of this city of over 200,000 people work in the recycling and dismantling of e-waste.[65] One pollutant causing grave public health concerns in this city of waste is Polybrominated Diphenyl Ethers (or PBDEs). PBDEs are compounds used as flame retardants, commonly used throughout the electronic industry. While we are only beginning to understand the effects of exposure to this compound the preliminary data are not promising. According to the US Environmental Protection Agency (EPA), overexposure to PBDEs can cause liver, thyroid, and neurodevelopmental toxicity.[66] More concerning still, a 2010 study found that children with higher concentrations of PBDEs in their umbilical cord blood at birth scored lower on tests of mental and physical development between the ages of one and six. Among those with the highest prenatal exposure, verbal and full IQ scores were reduced between 5.5 to 8.0 points.[67] PBDE blood sera levels among e-waste recyclers in Guiyu exceeded those reported by the government by a factor of between 50 and 200.[68]

BackTalk, a project of Massachusetts Institute of Technology's (MIT's) Senseable City Lab, set out to better understand what becomes of millions of tons of e-waste produced in the United States annually. A little of this waste actually gets reused, such as through a project involving the Peace Corps, which sends obsolete computers to lower-income countries. BackTalk donated laptops to this program loaded with tracking software and a functioning webcam. The devices were labeled with stickers announcing that they would be recording their whereabouts and sending this information back to researchers at MIT. And then off they went, to such faraway places as schools in Nepal and libraries in Africa. Once booted up at their new homes the devices proceeded to send out location updates and snapshots of their surroundings – and often of their users – every 20 minutes, telling a mesmerizing visual story to those receiving this data in the process.[69]

With e-waste, the three Rs of environmentalism hierarchy – reduce, reuse, and recycle – is turned on its head. There is no talk of reducing our consumption of these devices, even though we ought to know by now that access and ownership are not the same things. In fact, Kevin Kelley, founder of the influential magazine *Wired*, has gone as far as to argue that "access is better than ownership" (more about this in later chapters).[70] And while, as illustrated in the previous paragraph, some of these devices find a second life through reuse programs the vast majority are either landfilled or recycled, though, sadly, in practice these two ends remain practically identical. Even after the metals have been extracted the majority of e-waste, in terms of its overall weight, is not worth recycling, as it is cheaper to just start from scratch. So off to the landfill it goes – or the nearest ditch, as is the case in many lower-income countries.

When the subject of e-waste comes up in my class I always find time to show the video, *Ghana: Digital Dumping Ground*.[71] Produced by Frontline, this exposé follows computers that were passed along to a reputable e-waste facility in California. After the undercover camera crew is promised their waste will be recycled "safely" and "locally" the crew leaves the drop off facility. On the way out, however, they are careful to take note of the identification numbers on the shipping container in which their computers were placed. Using public records they then trace where the container was sent. Its final destination: the port of Hong Kong.

Planning the obsolescence of planned obsolescence

Planned obsolescence is a catch-all term to describe an assortment of ways used to increase purchase frequency (this concept is discussed in still greater detail in Chapter 3). This technique has taken many forms, some more sinister than others. There was the proposal, which thankfully was never implemented, within General Electric to intentionally shorten the life of their light bulbs in the hopes of increasing sales by as much as 60 percent.[72] A more common technique involves designing devices that cannot be repaired. Given the economy's penchant for socializing costs it is far more cost-effective – aka cheaper – to make a device using pre-molded plastics that do not allow for easy disassembly. Better, from an efficiency and profitability standpoint, to make commodities that are disposable than repairable, particularly given how firms presently bear no responsibility for their products beyond the life of their warranties. Why make products that can be repaired when it is "cheaper" not to?

Alfred Sloan, long-time President and CEO of General Motors, is widely "credited" for popularizing planned obsolescence and establishing an industry standard in the process. The automobile industry by the 1940s faced tremendous uncertainty. They had accomplished what just a couple of decades earlier seemed unimaginable: near market saturation. What was Detroit to do once everyone who could afford to buy a car had one parked in their garage? The answer: get people to replace their car with a new one every couple of years. (This was before the idea of multiple-car households took hold.) But how? A well-maintained car could function perfectly well for decades. (This was also back when cars were considerably easier to repair.) Planned obsolescence in this case involves making the automobile sitting in one's garage obsolete by way of its appearance – that's why models are radically redesigned at least once every ten years. Add to this a propaganda campaign that would make Stalin blush, to make owners feel that their present model leaves them unfulfilled while simultaneously expanding the perceived "needs" that their car must fulfill (for a rearview camera, satellite radio, and televisions in every headrest) and voilà: planned obsolescence.

If only General Motors manufactured computers.

In October 1965 Gordon Moore published observations that would eventually become known simply as "Moore's law" – that the number of transistors on integrated circuits (and thus chip performance) doubles approximately every two years. Moore's law is essentially a law of obsolescence. And forget every two years. Thanks to Moore's law a computer ceases to be state of the art the moment it rolls out of the factory – what is known in the IT sector as being "death dated" as it can be predicted practically to the month when electronic devices are rendered "obsolete."[73]

Raymond Kurzweil, a well-known futurist and technological optimist, noting how "computers are about one hundred million times more powerful for the same unit cost than they were a half century ago," exclaimed that "if the automobile industry had made as much progress in the past fifty years, a car today would cost a hundredth of a cent and go faster than the speed of light."[74] Moore made similar remarks, claiming if Detroit had made advances at the same rate as Silicon Valley that cars today would get 150,000 miles to the gallon.⁷⁵ What's wrong with these statements? They conflate cheap with affordability. After calculating in *all* the costs, including those of "cloud" computing and any associated with the billions of tons of hazardous e-waste generated annually, I am not convinced Silicon Valley really has anything over Detroit other than perhaps having had greater success at socializing costs – though, as discussed in Chapter 5, the automobile owes much to cheaponomics.

Yet Moore's law is, well, a *law*, so that means obsolescence is inevitable, which also means the mountains of e-waste we generate annually are inevitable too – right? This leap in logic, from obsolescence to waste, is understandable as we presently live in a throwaway society. The two, however, do not have to be linked. Designing devices that could be upgraded could go a long way in reducing e-waste. As Harvey Molotch points out, design determines as much as 90 percent of an artifact's economic and ecological costs, from the raw materials used to gases emitted, people hurt, and amount sent to the landfill.⁷⁶

We could also do a much better job recycling whatever cannot be upgraded. But things have to first be *made* to be recycled. Earlier I mentioned that it is currently ten times cheaper to ship e-waste to China than to handle it in the United States. Is that because the e-waste recycling technology in China is ten times more efficient than that found in North America? Of course not. It might be cheaper for recycling firms, electronic manufacturers, and consumers to have this waste shipped to China but that is only because Chinese laborers (and their families) are paying – in the currency of cancer, birth defects, and a spoiled environment – for ten times more than what their counterparts in the United States would put up with. If recycling firms, electronic manufacturers, and consumers had to pay for all those costs I am confident our electronic gadgets would be better designed to be repaired, upgraded, and recycled.

We cannot entirely fault corporations. There is currently little incentive for them to design and build machines with this never-ending-point in mind. At present, the time horizon most electronic firms have extends no further than the warranty. And, not surprisingly, their design reflects these parameters. It is not realistic to expect firms to always act altruistically, especially when such altruism could place them at a distinct market disadvantage and thus into bankruptcy leaving a market captured entirely by the most selfish firms. Yet we cannot put all of our eggs in the basket of regulation either, as I discuss in Chapters 8, 9, and 10.⁷⁷ This brings me back to a point made earlier about needing to think about these devices in the context of access rather than ownership. Right now you have to own, in most cases, in order to have access to the so-called Information Age. That has proven to be entirely unsustainable as it leads to the over-consumption of scarce resources and the spoiling of public and environmental health. But it also creates terrible asymmetries in terms of access as not everyone can afford these gadgets, even though they are incredibly "cheap."

So how do we divorce access from ownership? You will have to wait for the answer as that gets us into deeper structural changes than what I am ready to discuss at this early stage. I will tell you this much, however: the outlook is quite hopeful. The recommendations, while necessarily systemic in their scope, are well within our reach as they are all things already being done somewhere in the world. Topics to be discussed include collaborative consumption, the substitution of "cheap" capital (and energy) for affordable (and affording) labor, and greater governance (not to be confused with "more government"). Yet you will have to hold out until Chapters 8, 9, and 10 to get the particulars.

Notes

1 BBC News (2009) "'Carbon cost' of Google revealed," *BBC News*, January 12, http://news.bbc.co.uk/2/hi/7823387.stm, last accessed October 1, 2012; Gombiner, Joel (2011) "Carbon footprinting the internet," *Consilience: The Journal of Sustainable Development*, 5(1), pp. 119–24.
2 *Guardian* (2006) "Avatars don't have bodies, but do leave footprints – carbon ones," *Guardian*, December 5, www.theguardian.co.uk/technology/blog/2006/dec/05/avatars dontha, last accessed October 1, 2012.
3 Dyson, Esther, George Gilder, George Keyworth, and Alvin Toffler (1994) "Cyberspace and the American dream: A Magna Carta for the Knowledge Age," *Future Insight*, August, www.pff.org/issues-pubs/futureinsights/fi1.2magnacarta.html, last accessed October 1, 2012.
4 Grossman, Elizabeth (2006) *High Tech Trash: Digital Devices, Hidden Toxics, and Human Health* (Washington, DC: Island Press), pp. 27–33.
5 William, Eric (2004) "Energy intensity of computer manufacturing: Hybrid assessment combining process and economic input – output methods," *Environment, Science and Technology*, 38, pp. 6166–74.
6 Stutz, Markus (2010) "Carbon footprint of a typical business laptop from Dell," Dell Company, May, http://i.dell.com/sites/content/corporate/corp-comm/en/Documents /dell-laptop-carbon-footprint-whitepaper.pdf, last accessed October 6, 2012.
7 Arthur, Charles (2011) "Post-PC? What Apple's iPad sales and PC trends tell us about computing future," *Guardian*, July 21, www.guardian.co.uk/technology/blog/2011/ jul/21/post-pc-apple-products-show, last accessed October 6, 2012.
8 Molango, Matteo (2008) "From 'blood diamond' to 'blood coltan': Should international corporations pay the price for the rape of the DR Congo?" http://works. bepress.com/maheta_molango/1, last accessed October 8, 2012.
9 IPIS (2002) "Supporting the war economy in the DRC: European companies and the coltan trade," IPIS report, International Peace Information Service, Antwerp, Belgium, January, www.grandslacs.net/doc/2343.pdf, last accessed October 8, 2012.
10 Molango (2008).
11 Najm, Fatima (2010) "Blood coltan: Is your cell phone soaked in Congolese blood?" *The Express Tribune*, October 13, http://tribune.com.pk/story/67995/blood-coltan-is-your-cell-phone-soaked-in-congolese-blood, last accessed October 8, 2012.
12 Ayala, Elaine (2012) "Conflict coltan cited Congo genocide talk by SAC student," *My San Antonio*, February 21, www.mysanantonio.com/news/local_news/article/ Conflict-coltan-cited-in-DRC-genocide-3344769.php, last accessed October 8, 2012.
13 Allen, Karen (2009) "Human cost of mining in DR Congo," *BBC News*, September 2, last accessed October 8, 2012.
14 Najm (2010).

15 Najm (2010).
16 Stranahan, Susan (2002) "The clean room's dirty secret," *Mother Jones*, March/April, www.motherjones.com/politics/2002/03/clean-rooms-dirty-secret, last accessed October 9, 2012.
17 Herbert, Bob (2003) "IBM families ask, why?" *New York Times*, Op-Ed, September 15, www.nytimes.com/2003/09/15/opinion/ibm-families-ask-why.html, last accessed November 11, 2013.
18 Herbert, Bob (2003) "Sick and suspicious," *New York Times*, Op-Ed, September 9, www.nytimes.com/2003/09/04/opinion/04HERB.html?th=&pagewanted=print&position=, last accessed October 9, 2012; CBS News (2007) "Did IBM know of a cancer link?" *CBS News*, December 5, www.cbsnews.com/2100-500164_162-587573.html, last accessed October 9, 2012.
19 Blilar, John, Andre Cicolella, Dipl Eng, Robert Harrison, Joseph Ladou, Barry Levy, Timothy Rohm, Daniel Teitelbaum, Yung-Der Wang, Andrew Watterson, and Fumikazu (2007) "IBM, Elsevier Science, and academic freedom," *International Journal of Occupational Environmental Health*, 13, pp. 312–17.
20 Ibid.
21 Clapp, Richard (2006) "Mortality among US employees of a large computer manufacturing company: 1969–2001," *Environmental Health*, 5, www.ehjournal.net/content/5/1/30, last accessed October 9, 2012.
22 EpiAnalysis (2012) "Occupational health in the electronic age: Disease in the new sweatshop," *EipAnalysis*, January 23, http://epianalysis.wordpress.com/2012/01/23/esweat/, last accessed November 11, 2013.
23 EpiAnalysis (2012); Herbert, Robert (2003) "Early warnings," *New York Times*, Op-Ed, September 3, www.nytimes.com/2003/09/12/opinion/early-warnings.html, last accessed October 10, 2012.
24 Grossman, Elizabeth (2011) "Toxics in the clean rooms: Are Samsung workers at risk?" *e360 Yale*, June 9, http://e360.yale.edu/feature/toxics_in_the_clean_rooms_are_samsung_workers_at_risk/2414/, last accessed October 10, 2012.
25 Howlader, N., A. Noone, M. Krapcho, N. Neyman, R. Aminou, S.F. Altekruse, C.L. Kosary, J. Ruhl, Z. Tatalovich, H. Cho, A. Mariotto, M.P. Eisner, D.R. Lewis, H.S. Chen, E.J. Feuer, and K.A. Cronin (eds) (2013) *SEER Cancer Statistics Review, 1975–2009* (Vintage 2009 Populations), National Cancer Institute, Bethesda, MD, http://seer.cancer.gov/csr/1975_2009_pops09/, last accessed October 10, 2012.
26 Stanaham, Susan (2002) "The clean room's dirty secret," *Mother Jones*, March/April, www.motherjones.com/politics/2002/03/clean-rooms-dirty-secret, last accessed November 11, 2013.
27 *Daily Mail* (2011) "You are NOT allowed to commit suicide," *Daily Mail UK*, May 1, www.dailymail.co.uk/news/article-1382396/Workers-Chinese-Apple-factories-forced-sign-pledges-commit-suicide.html, last accessed October 11, 2012.
28 Moore, Malcolm (2012) "Mass suicide protest at Apple manufacturer Foxconn factory," *Telegraph*, January 11, www.telegraph.co.uk/news/worldnews/asia/china/9006988/Mass-suicide-protest-at-Apple-manufacturer-Foxconn-factory.html, last accessed October 11, 2012.
29 SACOM (2012) *New iPhone, Old Abuses: Have Working Conditions at Foxconn in China Improved?* Students and Scholars Against Corporate Misbehavior, Hong Kong, September 20, www.scribd.com/doc/106445655/New-iPhone-Old-Abuses, last accessed October 11, 2012.
30 Cook, Gary (2012) *How Clean is Your Cloud?* Greenpeace International, April, Amsterdam, The Netherlands, www.greenpeace.org/international/en/publications/Campaign-reports/Climate-Reports/How-Clean-is-Your-Cloud/, last accessed October 23, 2012.

31 Farrar, Lara (2009) "Greening the internet: How much CO2 does this article produce?", *CNN.com*, July 13, http://edition.cnn.com/2009/TECH/science/07/10/green.internet.CO2/, last accessed October 28, 2012.
32 Glanz, James (2012) "Power, pollution and the internet," *New York Times*, September 22, www.nytimes.com/2012/09/23/technology/data-centers-waste-vast-amounts-of-energy-belying-industry-image.html?nl=todaysheadlines&emc=tha2_20120923&_r=1&, last accessed October 24, 2012.
33 Ibid.
34 Ibid.
35 Dworschak, Manfred (2008) "Server farmers as polluting as air traffic," *Businessweek*, March 31, www.businessweek.com/stories/2008-03-31/server-farms-as-polluting-as-air-trafficbusinessweek-business-news-stock-market-and-financial-advice, last accessed October 24, 2012.
36 Bianchini, Ron (2012) "Are data centers the new global landfill?" *Wired*, October 22, www.wired.com/insights/2012/10/data-centers-new-global-landfill/, last accessed October 24, 2012.
37 Epstein, Paul, Jonathan Buonocore, Kevin Eckerle, Michael Hendryx, Benjamin M. Stout, Richard Heinberg, Richard Clapp, Beverly May, Nancy L. Reinhart, Melissa M. Ahern, Samir K. Doshi, and Leslie Glustrom (2011) "Full cost account for the list cycle of coal," *Annals of the New York Academy of Sciences*, 1219, pp. 73–98.
38 Ibid.
39 Bianchini (2012).
40 Cook (2012).
41 Ibid.
42 Waugh, Rob (2011) "That's really cool: Facebook puts your photos into the deep freeze as it unveils massive new five acre data center near Artic circle," *Daily Mail* October 28, www.dailymail.co.uk/sciencetech/article-2054168/Facebook-unveils-massive-data-center-Lulea-Sweden.html, last accessed October 25, 2012.
43 Cook (2012).
44 Sherter, Alain (2011) "How Microsoft, Google and other tech giants exploit strapped US states," *CBS News*, March 4, www.cbsnews.com/8301-505123_162-43551522/how-microsoft-google-and-other-tech-giants-exploit-strapped-us-states/, last accessed October 25, 2012.
45 Ibid.
46 Ibid.
47 Harkinson, Josh (2012) "Apple's US$88 million tax break doesn't compute for Nevada," *Mother Jones*, August 8, www.motherjones.com/politics/2012/08/apple-nevada-88-million-tax-break, last accessed October 25, 2012.
48 Ibid.
49 City of Council Bluffs (2012) "City council minutes," February 14, www.councilbluffs-ia.gov/Files/AgendaCenter/Agendas/40/Minutes/PC%20Minutes%202-14-12.pdf, last accessed October 25, 2012.
50 Eller, Onnelle (2012) "Is state spending to entice data farms worth it?" *Des Moines Register*, March 3, www.desmoinesregister.com/article/20120304/BUSINESS04/303020064/Is-state-spending-entice-data-farms-worth-, last accessed October 25, 2012.
51 Benjamin, Walter (1999) *The Arcades Project* (Cambridge, MA: Harvard University Press).
52 Ibid., p. 203.
53 Gartner (2010) "Gartner says worldwide PC shipments to grow 20 percent in 2010," *Gartner.com*, March 4, www.gartner.com/it/page.jsp?id=1313513, last accessed November 1, 2012.
54 Grossman (2006), p. 31.

55 Electronics Take Back Coalition (2010) *Facts and Figures on E-Waste and Recycling, Electronics Take Back Coalition,* San Francisco, CA, June 4, www.electronicstakeback.com/wp-content/uploads/Facts_and_Figures, last accessed November 1, 2012.
56 Ibid.
57 Green Advocacy Ghana (2011) "Ghana e-waste country assessment," SBC E-waste Africa Project, http://ewasteguide.info/files/Amoyaw-Osei2011_GreenAd-Empa.pdf, last accessed November 2, 2012.
58 Ibid., p. 204.
59 UNEP (2009) *Recycling: From E-waste to Resources, United Nations Environment Program,* July, www.unep.org/PDF/PressReleases/E-Waste_publication_screen_FINALVERSION-sml.pdf, last accessed November 2, 2012.
60 Kutz, Jennifer (2006) "You've got waste: The exponentially escalating problem of hazardous E-waste," *Villanova Environmental Law Journal,* 17, pp. 307–29.
61 Templeton, Nicola (2012) "The dark side of recycling and reusing electronics: Is Washington's e-cycle program adequate?" *Seattle Journal for Social Justice,* 7(2), Article 21, http://digitalcommons.law.seattleu.edu/sjsj/vol7/iss2/21, last accessed November 2, 2012.
62 United States Department of Labor (n.d.) "Cadmium," www.osha.gov/SLTC/cadmium/index.html, last accessed November 2, 2012.
63 Sanborn, Margaret, Alan Abelsohn, Monica Campbell, and Erica Weir (2002) "Identifying and managing adverse environmental health effects," *CMAJ,* 166(10), pp. 1287–92.
64 Chien-Min Chung, "Guiyu, largest e-waste site on earth," www.china-pix.com/multi media/guiyu/, last accessed November 2, 2012.
65 Ni, Hong-Gang and Eddy Zeng (2009) "Law enforcement and global collaboration are the keys to containing e-waste tsunami in China," *Environmental Science and Technology,* 43, pp. 3991–4.
66 EPA (2008) *Toxicological Profile for Decabromodiphenyl ether (BDE-209) Integrated Risk Information System,* Environmental Protection Agency, June, www.epa.gov/iris/toxreviews/0035tr.pdf, last accessed November 2, 2012; EPA (2008) *Toxicological Profile for Pentabromodiphenyl ether (BDE-99) Integrated Risk Information System,* Environmental Protection Agency, June, www.epa.gov/IRIS/toxreviews/1008tr.pdf, last accessed November 2, 2012.
67 Herbstman, Julie, Andreas Sjödin, Matthew Kurzon, Sally A. Lederman, Richard S. Jones, Virginia Rauh, Larry L. Needham, Deliang Tang, Megan Niedzwiecki, Richard Y. Wang, and Frederica Perera (2010) "Prenatal exposure to PBDEs and neurodevelopment," *Environmental Health Perspectives,* 118(5), pp. 712–19.
68 Betts, K. (2007) "PBDEs in electronics-recycling workers in China," *Environmental Science and Technology,* 41, p. 5576.
69 Foster, Joanna (2011) "A global pinball game: Tracking e-waste," *New York Times,* July 25, http://green.blogs.nytimes.com/2011/07/25/a-global-pinball-game-tracking-e-waste/, last accessed November 4, 2012.
70 Kelly, K. (n.d.) "Access is better than ownership," *Exponential Times,* www.exponentialtimes.net/videos/access-better-ownership-0, last accessed July 3, 2012.
71 Frontline (2009) *Ghana: Digital Dumping Ground,* Frontline, Public Broadcast Station, June 23, www.pbs.org/frontlineworld/stories/ghana804/video/video_index.html, last accessed November 4, 2012.
72 Slade, Giles (2006) *Made to Break: Technology and Obsolescence in America* (Cambridge, MA: Cambridge University Press), p. 5.
73 Ibid., p. 196.
74 Kurzweil, Ray (n.d.) "The age of spiritual machines: When computers exceed human intelligence," *New York Times,* www.nytimes.com/books/first/k/kurzweil-machines.html, last accessed November 5, 2012.

75 Giles (2006), pp. 197–8.
76 Molotch, Harvey (2003) *Where Stuff Comes From: How Toasters, Toilets, Cars, Computers, and Many Other Things Come to Be As They Are* (New York: Routledge), p. 238.
77 See also Carolan, Michael (2013) *Society and the Environment: Pragmatic Solutions to Ecological Issues* (Boulder: Westview Press), see chapter 13.

Chapter 3

Free plastic bags (and other costly ephemeral commodities)

It doesn't add up. Worldwide, we use somewhere between 500 billion and one trillion plastic bags a year – that's between 16,000 and 32,000 bags a second.[1] Disposable bags are produced using non-renewable fossil fuels that have taken 70 million years to make. "How much fossil fuel?" you ask. It takes roughly 4.3 billion gallons (or 137,000,000 barrels) of oil to produce one trillion plastic bags.[2] At US$100 a barrel, that comes out to be approximately US$13.7 billion worth of crude. The bags are responsible for the deaths of roughly one million sea creatures every year, from birds to whales, seals, and sea turtles.[3] A recent attempt to assign value to certain marine species finds willingness-to-pay values ranging from US$40 per household for recovering Puget Sound Chinook salmon to US$73 per household for recovering the North Pacific right whale.[4] Extrapolating from this study, a conservative willingness-to-pay value for the million marine animals lost annually thanks to plastic bag waste, for all 115 million households in the United States, is in the order of hundreds of millions of dollars. What would you pay for something that every year consumes billions of dollars of oil and which costs the environment, in terms of non-human lives and biodiversity lost, hundreds of millions of dollars annually? If we are talking about the disposal plastic bag the answer can be plainly stated: nothing.

The free plastic bag seems the economic equivalent to the paradox of Achilles and the Tortoise in philosophy, where the concept of motion is denied. In both instances, what seems impossible on paper is refuted before our eyes. The free plastic bag should not exist. But it does – trillions of them, in fact. What appears a paradox, however, is really just egregious accounting, as the bags are not really free. All the aforementioned costs are being paid, just not by those using this product with a functional use-life that can be measured in minutes but which is made from raw materials almost 100 million years in the making.

Critics of plastic bags occasionally speak of how these products are gobbling up precious landfill space. If only they were. A more serious problem lies with all those bags that end up elsewhere, clogging everything from the gastrointestinal tracks of wildlife to sewer drains. It is estimated that 19 percent of all storm drain litter in Los Angeles county is accounted for by plastic bags. This trash has cost Californian taxpayers almost US$2 billion over the last 20 years, as regulations require that the drains remain clear of trash which otherwise could be swept out to sea.[5] It is remarkable how a product specifically intended to be thrown away after one use can be designed so poorly for the waste phase of its life cycle. Less than one percent of the plastic bags consumed annually are recycled (or more accurately "down-cycled" into another product), which should not come as much of a surprise as they are not designed for this end. This helps explain why recycling one ton of plastic bags costs US $4,000, resulting in a raw material worth US$32.[6]

The Great Pacific Garbage Patch: "It's a giant trash island, as big as Texas!" I frequently hear this about the massive floating field of waste trapped by the North Pacific Gyre. (The North Pacific Gyre, located in the northern Pacific Ocean, is one of five major oceanic gyres, which are large systems of rotating ocean currents caused by the Coriolis Effect.) This is where a lot of the renegade plastic goes after having escaped the municipal waste stream. Unfortunately, it is not actually an island of waste. If it were, cleaning it up would be considerably easier – like plucking a piece of lawn furniture from a swimming pool after it mistakenly blows in. Now imagine that the patio chair is hundreds of tiny (microscopic, in many cases) Lego pieces and the pool is actually a jetted hot tub. A "galaxy" is a more accurate descriptor of the Great Pacific Garbage Patch; a dystopian universe populated by trillions of objects ranging in size from a tennis ball to the far more populous miniaturized bits of plastic.

Part of the reason the Great Pacific Garbage Patch is mistaken for an island is due to a common misunderstanding about plastic. When people hear that plastic hangs around for hundreds of years they assume that means *in its present form*. After all, plastic is not biodegradable. But plastic does break down. That is part of the problem. As opposed to being consumed by microorganisms and transformed into compounds found in nature, plastic is broken down into ever smaller pieces as sunlight photodegrades the bonds in its polymers. Plastic never goes away. The pieces just break down and thus multiply in number, making it easier for plastic to find a pathway into organisms and the food chain. And that is precisely what is happening. Plastic pieces now outweigh surface zooplankton in the Great Pacific Garbage Patch by a factor of 6 to 1.[7] Further compounding matters is the fact that plastics take even longer to break down in seawater than on land, as cool seawater and ultraviolet-ray-blocking seaweed act as preservatives. Thus, except for what is picked up manually during sea-cleaning expeditions, every piece of plastic to find its way into the ocean over the last half century is still there.[8]

According to United Nations estimates, roughly 80 percent of the debris in the Great Pacific Garbage Patch originates from land. Another 10 percent (or about 705,000 tons) comes from free-floating fishing nets.[9] The remaining waste has been traced to recreational boaters, offshore oil rigs, and large cargo ships, which annually drop approximately 10,000 shipping containers into the sea holding anything from rubber ducks to computer monitors, resin pellets, and Lego.[10]

As 63 percent of the world population lives more than 100 kilometers from a coast – and 99.999 percent at a distance greater than 100 kilometers from the Great Pacific Garbage Patch – the sea represents the ultimate "away" as far as trash disposal is concerned.[11] But for millions of species of wildlife it is anything but away. It is home. For example, of the half a million albatross chicks born each year on Midway Atoll (a 2.4-square-mile atoll in the North Pacific Ocean), about 200,000 die of starvation, as adults mistake plastic trash for food and end up feeding it to their chicks.[12] Opening their carcasses reveals a body cavity literally brimming with plastic. A recent study found that 97.5 percent of all the albatross chicks on this tiny island had plastic in their stomachs.[13]

It is no wonder why plastic bag taxes and outright bans have been implemented in certain countries and some cities. Yet while plastic waste is a monolithic problem the sociologist in me wants to know how and why we have gotten ourselves into this situation. The next time you are in a superstore look around. *Everything* around you will likely be carried out the front door in a plastic bag; recognizing too that before any of it could come in through the back it had to first be encased in a plastic tomb (a third of all plastic produced is used for packaging).[14] And, more likely than not, the thing being enveloped by layers of petrochemicals is itself plastic. Unless we come to grips with how this came to be, banning or taxing disposable plastic items is not going to solve anything.

Gone today here tomorrow

We have become such pigs.

John Stuart Mill, the great nineteenth-century utilitarian philosopher and economist, famously wrote that "it is better to be a human being dissatisfied than a pig satisfied; better to be Socrates dissatisfied than a fool satisfied."[15] I find it odd that proponents of cheaponomics would seek to justify their dog-eat-dog style of economics with an approach that views them as satisfied pigs. (Well before Mill, Adam Smith argued that the hand of the free market is both utility maximizing and just and therefore ought to be left alone.) What would you call someone who supports a system that not only gave rise to but actively encourages the so-called disposable society: Socrates or a fool? Pigpen economics – where the notion of limits does not exist – fails to add up in the real world.

Growing up in rural Iowa I spent a lot of time around pigs. As a child, I remember marveling at how they were supplied with an unending supply of food and water and how ready they were to defile their environment only to have this waste shuttled *away*. I image the worldview from a pigpen to look a lot like that of a century ago, when disposability and obsolescence emerged as solutions to the economic ills at a time and when resources and aways were seemingly infinite. While the concept of planned obsolescence was introduced in the previous chapter when discussing electronics it is necessary to return to and interrogate it further. If we hope to one day move toward an economy that produces commodities that we can afford and which affords us all the ability to enhance our overall well-being we will need to first address the drivers of disposability.

Prosperity through waste. That was – and is – essentially the rationale underlying planned obsolescence, provided, of course, that the costs of all that waste are socialized. A book published in 1928 longingly points to the economic advantages that disposability opens up: "If what had filled the consumer market yesterday could only be made obsolete today, that whole market would be again available tomorrow."[16] Four years later Bernard London, a Manhattan real estate broker, took this position to the extreme, calling upon the government to "assign a lease of life ... to all products of manufacture," after which:

> these things would be legally "dead" and would be controlled by the duly appointed government agency and destroyed if there is a widespread unemployment. New products would constantly be pouring forth from the factories and marketplaces, to take the place of the obsolete, and the wheels of industry would be kept going.[17]

That same year (in 1932) the book *Consumer Engineering* came out. In it, the authors proudly tout disposability as the "new technique of prosperity."[18] At one point the authors ask, "Does there seem to be a sad waste in the process?"[19] Their response: "Not at all. Wearing things out does not produce prosperity but buying things does."[20] While acknowledging that all this waste consumes resources, their pigpen worldview makes this recognition fleeting: "We still have tree-covered slopes to deforest and subterranean lakes of oil to tap with our gushers."[21]

Initially, there was something uniquely American about planned obsolescence. Its earliest proponents, such as Christine Frederick in her book *Selling Mrs. Consumer* from 1929, used the concept as an attack upon "European cultural domination" and "the Old Antique-Worshipping Standards" which believed in "treasuring the old" and "disdaining the new."[22] Europeans were mocked for their purchase of artifacts that were made from "very substantial, everlasting materials" which "you would never need to buy again if you can help it."[23] Americans at this time were attempting to carve out their own unique identity, distinct from their European counterparts.[24] And, understandably, as there was far less old that could be treasured (the country was, and still is, young relative to European standards), a collective identity sought to be nurtured around the new.

There is also a geographical component to all this that deserves mention. Long after all the "aways" disappeared in Europe they remained plentiful in North America. Thinking about resources and waste sinks reflected, at least in part, this away-multitude. The US Census Bureau defines a "frontier county" as any county that has "six or fewer people per square mile." According to the US National Center for Frontier Communities, 56 percent of the land area in the United States, *to this day*, has a frontier designation.[25] I once had a conversation about the frontier concept with a friend from the Netherlands. After grasping the concept, which took a while, he could only give a chuckle signifying disbelief. As he explained, somewhat jokingly, it would be hard to locate a single spot in their country that would place an individual outside earshot of another.

Yet, ultimately, planned obsolescence is an inevitable outcome in a system that seeks to maximize costs socialized, which explains its eventual exportation to most other parts of the world – even the Netherlands. Disposability represents the limestone bedrock in cheaponomics' race to the bottom. When an economic system adopts the goal of producing products as cheaply as possible, disposability is the inevitable outcome, as cheap products – by nature of being "cheap" – never last long.

As discussed in the previous chapter, planned obsolescence can take many forms. In some cases the form is downright sinister, like in the early twentieth century when a European light bulb cartel (known as Phoebus) colluded to engineer light bulbs that lasted less long.[26] In other cases, purchase frequency is increased by largely aesthetic changes, such as when cars are made to look obsolete with the help of a redesigned exterior and interior. More often still, planned obsolescence occurs whenever products are made cheaply, which is to say, with cost socialization in mind. Planned obsolescence, in other words, represents business-as-usual under cheaponomics.

I have talked with many designers and engineers involved in the making of anything from vacuum cleaners to cars, kitchen appliances, and children's toys. Not one – and I have had this conversation with over 100 individuals – admitted to willfully designing anything to last less long. What they all acknowledged is an unrelenting pressure to be mindful of cost. As I was told recently by a designer of mechanical toothbrushes: "Ultimately, it's about cost; quality is certainly important, as long as it doesn't impinge on the bottom line." A retired designer of kitchen appliances explained it to me this way: "We can design products that last forever but where's the incentive if that product is going to end up costing the consumer one hundred times more than a base model?" These comments point to an economic reality that punishes product longevity and cost internalization over disposability and cost externalization. Yes; long-lasting products tend to have a higher retail price. But rather than stopping the conversation there we need to ask the follow-up question: relative to what and over how long of a time frame? The yardstick is skewed as the products they are being compared to have artificially low retail prices thanks to practices of cost socialization. Lest we forget, "cheap" should not be mistaken to mean "less expensive." When all costs are totaled, we should not be surprised to find the higher priced non-disposable item, especially when used repeatedly over a long lifetime, to be less expensive than the so-called cheaper alternative.

As for enhancing well-being, there is no evidence that planned obsolescence does this. If anything, it makes people feel worse off. It is more than a bit disingenuous to link planned obsolescence with prosperity when people like Brooks Stevens, the American designer who popularized planned obsolescence in the 1950s, wrote of the need to make "the American consumer unhappy with the product that he has enjoyed the use of for a period," after which they will feel the need to "pass it on to the second hand or second used market, and obtain the newest product with the newest possible look."[27] How can a practice that actively seeks to make people unendingly unsatisfied and unhappy be equated with prosperity?

Moreover, the idea that all "obsolete" products will somehow enjoy a second life as used goods belies evidence all around us, such as overflowing landfills and the Great Pacific Garbage Patch. (And even for those that do enjoy a second life, they rarely enjoy a long one because they are not designed for it.) Another way the system works against used goods is through the supporting networks that encourage those "unhappy" consumers to replace old with new. Unlike, say, the relatively robust pre-owned automobile market that exists in many countries most second-hand goods do not enjoy networks and financial structures to support resale. Finally, a consumption model where the wealthy are encouraged to continually replace old with new while those of less means are urged to purchase second-hand will only stigmatize used products and inevitably lead to status-driven consumption; a recipe that will lead to a societal wide keeping-up-with-the-Joneses mindset that makes society collectively worse off.

From scarcity to plasticity

Approximately 75,000 elephants were being killed annually by the late 1800s to produce the 800 tons of ivory required to satisfy world demand.[28] All this ivory went to make objects ranging from billiard balls to flat spatulas, combs, and piano keys. Even the ivory dust produced during the manufacturing process was saved and sold to florists, "who claimed," according to a book from 1886 written on the subject, "that its results upon roses and other choice flowers are astonishing."[29] Almost 20 years earlier, in 1867, an article in *The Friend: A Religious and Literary Journal* notes that because "an enormous number of elephants are destroyed in the course of every year … it is by no means improbable, that long before our human story is over the elephant will be numbered with extinct species."[30]

Saviors come in different sizes and shapes. Some are said to sport long beards and possess the ability to turn water into wine. Others are inanimate, made from materials that are initially malleable but which can be hardened into almost any form. Forget about conscious raising, education, or regulation, it was to be plastics that delivered the pachyderm from the brink of extinction. As John Hyatt, the inventor of celluloid, argued in a late-nineteenth-century pamphlet:

> as petroleum came to the relief of the whale [so] ... has celluloid given the elephant ... a respite in their native haunts; and it will no longer be necessary to ransack the earth in pursuit of substances which are constantly growing scarcer.[31]

The road to hell is paved with good intentions. Like the car, which won praise from street cleaners, public health officials, and politicians a century ago for delivering urban dwellers from a major environmental ill at the time – namely, the horse manure that had begun to blanket urban streets – plastics would someday be responsible for far more public health and environmental ills than those they initially delivered us from. Indeed, far from saving the earth from being ransacked, as Hyatt had assured, plastics took us one giant leap closer toward that end.

It all started with a $10,000 reward.

The popularity of billiards was growing. No longer for exclusively the leisure class, the expansion of pool halls across the United States and Europe began democratizing the sport. Yet only eight balls could be carved from the tusks of a large Asian elephant.[32] So, paradoxically, its expanding popularity was hastening the sport's demise as ivory become increasingly dear. In 1858, Michael Phelan, considered by many to be the Father of American Billiards, offered the kingly sum of US$10,000 to anyone who could discover a suitable substitute for ivory. Phelan, knowing that the future of the sport he loved hinged on such a discovery, pleaded that "if any inventive genius would discover a substitute for ivory, possessing those qualities which make it valuable to the billiard player, he would make a handsome fortune for himself, and earn our sincerest gratitude."[33]

A 20-something inventor by the name of John Wesley Hyatt read about the reward and started experimenting behind his house. Eventually he stumbled upon what he later called celluloid (meaning "like cellulose"), as it was created using the cellulose in cotton. Hyatt never collected the reward, perhaps because his billiard balls did not perform the same as the ivory balls he was hoping to replace. When they collided on a billiard table, the story goes, they produced such a loud crack that it sounded much like a gun going off; a noise that could have proved deadly in American pool halls during the late 1800s, especially those out West.[34] While not the first and certainly not the last material of what would later be called "plastic," celluloid opened a door that has proven impossible to close. As Jeffrey Meikle explains in *American Plastics*: "By replacing materials that were hard to find or expensive to process, celluloid democratized a host of goods for an expanding consumption-oriented middle class."[35] Celluloid brought costs down and suggested, for a time at least, that one really could keep up with the Joneses. Things have not been the same since.

Something very curious also happened with costs as we moved toward a model of consumption driven heavily by low "cost" plastics and other synthetics. With plastics, costs are more dispersed and easier to socialize, which helps drive down their retail price and therefore increase demand. This in turn further intensifies levels of cost socialization, making these products, in the end, far more costly than the materials they are replacing. Let me be clear, the natural products used previously – like ivory – were obviously not harvested in a sustainable manner. There was undoubtedly cost socializing occurring with ivory, most clearly to elephants themselves, the ecosystems they "serve," and to future generations who almost lived in a world where these beings were never again to roam. Even so, the price of goods made of ivory was rising relative to the increasing scarcity of this mammal teetering on the brink of extinction; though this, admittedly, was part of the problem, as it made ivory into what is known as a positional good. Items made from ivory thus began to be sought out precisely due to their scarcity, as ownership signified status. The thing about plastics is that the same costs are being externalized and then some. Plastics might have saved elephants in the short term. Yet if we continue to muck up our atmosphere and ruin ecosystems around the world in our quest to exploit whatever fossil fuel reserves remain, which is in part driven by our appetite for cheap plastics, elephants will not be the only species to go extinct.

The remainder of the chapter focuses on this " … and then some." These costs are dispersed in a variety of different ways, making them difficult to track. One dispersal technique, under the guise of being an "objective" policy-making tool, is the cost–benefit analysis. Learning about this tool will help us better understand how proponents of cheaponomics can sleep at night.

The costs of cost–benefit analysis

"There are three kinds of lies: lies, damned lies, and statistics." Mark Twain, who popularized this aphorism, lived before formal cost–benefit analyses became a cornerstone of the policy-making process. Were he alive today, he might be talking about four kinds of lies.

Though the first formal applications by government occurred in the United States in the 1930s, involving water projects, it was not until the 1980s, with the rise of Reaganism and Thatcherism – two "-isms" tied closely to cheaponomics – that cost–benefit analysis took center stage in shaping policy outcomes. At its face, cost–benefit analysis makes a lot of sense. Indeed, this approach to valuing the world has seduced many into falling blindly in love with it. And I emphasize *blindly*, for cost–benefit analyses cannot be trusted to faithfully deliver upon their promise, which is to produce outcomes of maximum benefit and minimal cost. Upon more critical reflection, we find that the approach in fact delivers just the opposite, which is to say it often produces outcomes of maximum cost, though many of these are shielded from view thanks to its ability to socialize them.

But I am getting ahead of myself. More on these socializing techniques in a bit. It is important first to understand the aims of the cost–benefit analysis.

The problem with decisions, so the argument goes, is that subjective value judgments always manage to creep in, pointing them in directions not always in line with so-called rational thought. Stripping emotion, cultural values, and politics from the regulatory process would not only result in more objective decision-making but produce outcomes that avoid thorny ethical questions. Why? Reducing the world to a single commensurable value, which allows all "costs" and "benefits" to be added up, produces decisions that are *non*-ethical. For example, it is not a matter of whether the value of four ought to be greater than that of two – that's just the way it is. Enter cost–benefit analysis. By monetizing the world, cost–benefit analyses claim to shield us from the dark recesses of humanity where things like love, aesthetics, compassion, and empathy lurk.

Hmmm; I always thought those traits were good as they are what make us human.

Back in the 1990s W. Kip Viscusi conducted a series of studies where the costs and benefits of cigarette smoking in the United States were added together.[36] His conclusion was that states actually saved money when their residents smoked because they died early. Therefore his policy recommendation was that "cigarette smoking should be subsidized rather than taxed."[37] In another study, economists Paul Carlin and Robert Sandy thought it would be interesting to determine what it was worth to mothers to save the lives of their children from car accidents through the use of car seats.[38] (The very fact that they thought a monetary value could be assigned to this underscores the lunacy of this approach.) They did this by estimating the amount of time required to strap their children into their seats correctly and then assigned a value to the time based on the mothers' actual or imputed (for those without a formal salary) hourly wage. Mothers cutting corners and thus not buckling their children in correctly, the researchers assumed, were saving time and because, as we all know (or do we?), time is money, those mothers were implicitly placing a value on the safety of their little ones' lives. So what was the average child's life worth to its mother? $500,000. I have yet to meet a mother – or father – who would be willing to part with their child for *any* dollar amount. Either they were all lying or this approach makes wrongheaded (not to mention offensive) assertions about how we value things. You could say that the cost–benefit analysis tells us the price of everything and value of nothing.

52 Cheap stuff

Do you live in a low-income country? If so, you are worth less than me; at least, that is the conclusion of dozens of cost–benefit analyses.

One analysis calculates that the well-being of citizens in less affluent nations is 1/2,000 of the value of an American citizen.[39] A widely circulated and infamous memo from the early 1990s, leaked from the World Bank, was premised on precisely this reasoning. Penned by Lawrence Summers, then chief economist for the World Bank (who was later appointed US Treasury secretary during the Clinton administration and subsequently served as president of Harvard University), it argued that the lower marginal cost of waste disposal in a poor country compared with the higher marginal cost of waste disposal in a waste-producing affluent country justifies the latter polluting the former. It concludes by reasoning that the poorest countries of Africa are vastly *under-polluted* as they are underutilizing what affluent countries desperately need, namely, waste sinks. As the lives of the people in these nations are worth less than the higher-income earners in countries like the United States the report argues that it is "economically efficient" to disproportionately expose the former to environmental risks.

When we reduce human life to statistical terms we deny people the dignity to be thought of as humans. Similarly, by putting a price tag on ecosystems and non-human life, we miss out on the opportunity to value things on their own terms. Instead, the predominate practice is to assign lower values to populations of lower socioeconomic status as well as to particular racial minorities, as certain ethnic groups are disproportionately overrepresented among lower-income strata. Because they have lower incomes and thus less buying power, welfare economics – a branch of economics that deals heavily in the currency of cost–benefit analysis – sees these people as having less value, literally, than those with higher incomes. Therein lies justification for environmental racism.[40] But that is OK, according to proponents, as this action "would not be the result of a government decision to take racial characteristics into account; in fact it would not be a product of any group level discrimination on the government's part."[41] The fact, however, remains: discrimination justified with statistics is still discrimination.

Then there is the tricky question of what to do about future generations. This is where the issue of discounting comes into the picture. Discounting offers a way to evaluate investments that generate future income. It is based on the premise that $100 received today is worth more than $100 received next year. Why? Because that $100 could be placed, at the very least, into a low-risk savings account and earn some interest. Suppose you invested that $100 today in something that earned five percent interest over the next year. That $100, at five percent interest, would become $105 next year. That $100, in other words, has a present value that is greater than $100 next year. As others point out, using conventional cost–benefit analysis methodology, one death this year, at a five percent discount rate, counts for *more* than a billion deaths in 400 years.[42] Suddenly, the foot-dragging and egregious cost-socializing that we have been witnessing in regards to everything from e-waste to cloud computing, plastic bags, and climate change starts making sense. Thanks to discounting, it is entirely possible to settle on a policy option that may knowingly result in human extinction hundreds of years from now but because it also lowers the well-being of some today it is deemed unacceptable. Thanks to this practice, the costs of many proposed regulations are said to be too high – even those that might one day save us from calamity – as a result of future benefits being heavily discounted. Douglas Kysar, a Professor of Law at Yale University, colorfully refers to this as "tyranny of the present."[43]

So when we talk about the some 80,000 chemicals that are now traded in the global market, many of which go into the making of plastics, it is no wonder why governments like the US government are resistant to their regulation. At a five percent discount rate, a popular rate among welfare economists, one cancer death 40 years from now has a present value equivalent to one-seventh of a cancer death today.[44] With discounting, short-term benefits can quite easily be made to outweigh long-term costs, by often showing little more than that a compound will bring some economic benefits today; a task effortlessly accomplished as it is usually the regulated firms who are asked to supply governmental agencies with information about compliance "costs."[45] Plastics in particular benefit from costs–benefits analyses, given their magnitude and scope. In the United States alone, the plastics industry accounts for more than $374 billion dollars in annual shipments and directly employs nearly 900,000 people.[46] That is a whole lot of happy consumers buying "cheap" disposable items, a whole lot of jobs, and a whole lot of content shareholders. By discounting all of the benefits gained by better regulating this industry, even those that will result in lives saved, cost–benefit analyses stack the deck in favor of the status quo: cheap plastics.

The recycling loophole

"I know plastic is bad but I recycle." I've lost count of how many times I have heard this rather obstinate declaration (or a close variation of it). Perhaps you have even said it yourself. We know from life cycle analyses, for example, that aluminum requires 96 percent less energy to make from recycled cans than when processed using bauxite. Recycled plastic bottles save us about 76 percent of the energy that would otherwise be consumed if raw materials were used; newsprint, about 45 percent; and recycled glass, 21 percent. Across the board, recycled goods come out on top, as the energy and materials used to produce non-recycled products are an order of magnitude higher than what is used to recover the same material through recycling.[47] The devil, however, is in the details. And the devilish details in this case center on the fact that the above statistics involve actual "recycled goods." The Faustian-like bargain we have struck by fetishizing recycling lies in the simple fact that the vast majority of plastic that we set out for weekly pickup will *never* meet this end.

Just because a plastic container has a recycling symbol on the bottom of it does not mean it can be recycled. I like to bring a garbage bag of plastic containers into class and ask students to identify which, in Fort Collins, Colorado, are likely to end up baled and sold as a "reclaimed" product. Out of more than 100 students I rarely get more than one or two that come close to identifying correctly the fates of these various petroleum shells. Granted, theoretically they all *could* be recycled but the data show the better bet is in them ending up in the landfill.

Technically speaking, the recycling symbol (and accompanying number) only identifies the plastic resin used in the making of the article in question, never mind that the chasing arrows that prominently envelope the resin code is the internationally recognized symbol used to designate *recyclable* materials. The recycling rates of each resin code vary greatly from one recycling facility to another (see Table 3.1). And even when a facility is capable of recycling a particular resin a whole host of other variables enter into the picture that could cause it to still be landfilled. The following recycling rates represent averages for the United States as a whole. Number 1 plastic, also known as Polyethylene Terephthalate (PET or PETE), the resin most likely to be recycled, has a recycling rate of 13 percent. Number 2, High Density Polyethylene (HDPE), has a recycling rate of eight percent; number 3, Polyvinyl Chloride (PVC), less than one percent; number 4, Low Density Polyethylene (LDPE), six percent; number 5, Polypropylene (PP), less than one percent; and number 6, Polystyrene (PS), less than one percent. Finally, number 7, the enigmatic category called simply "other," has a US average recycling rate of 7.5 percent.[48]

Recycling facilities are also in the business – lest we forget they are businesses too – of making money. And they are paid by the quality of the bales they produce. Not surprisingly, the less contaminated bales are typically worth more. Recycling facilities therefore tend to focus on those plastics sure to capture a price premium: namely, clear narrow-neck (e.g., soda and water) bottles made with PET/PETE (aka number 1 plastic). As Luke Vernon of Eco-Products explains, recyclers "have come to trust [that these plastics are most likely to be contaminate-free] as nearly fact which also means their buyers of bales also trust it as fact."[49] And since it is relatively easy to spot bales composed of alternative-shaped plastic objects many facilities ignore those containers entirely so as not to risk obtaining a lower market price, even those made with PET/PETE. The risk for buyers is two-fold: odd-shaped containers have a higher likelihood of not only being made of an alternative resin, which cannot be easily recycled; they also run a higher risk of being contaminated. Ever wonder how that empty Tide laundry detergent container gets clean enough to have its resin reclaimed? The answer is simple: it doesn't.

Moreover, most plastic can only be recycled twice. This is why I prefer the term down-cycle, as most reprocessed plastic from single-use bottles and food containers end up as something like plastic lumber, carpet backing, or park

Table 3.1 Plastic packaging resins

Resin codes	Descriptions	Product applications	Products that could be made with recycled content
1	Polyethylene Terephthalate (PET/PETE)	Plastic bottles for soft drinks, water, juice, sports drinks, beer, mouthwash, ketchup, and salad dressing. Food jars for peanut butter, jelly, jam, and pickles. Microwavable food trays.	Fiber for carpet, fleece jackets, comforter fill, and tote bags. Containers for food, beverages (bottles), and non-food items.
2	High Density Polyethylene (HDPE)	Bottles for milk, water, juice, cosmetics, shampoo, dish and laundry detergents, and household cleaners. Bags for groceries and retail purchases. Cereal box liners.	Bottles for non-food items, such as shampoo, conditioner, liquid laundry detergent, household cleaners, motor oil and antifreeze. Plastic lumber for outdoor decking, fencing and picnic tables. Pipe, floor tiles, buckets, crates, flower pots, garden edging, film and sheet, and recycling bins.
3	Polyvinyl Chloride (PVC)	Rigid packaging applications include blister packs and clamshells. Rigid applications such as pipe, siding, window frames, fencing, decking and railing. Flexible applications include medical products such as blood bags and medical tubing, wire and cable insulation, carpet backing, and flooring.	Pipe, decking, fencing, paneling, gutters, carpet backing, floor tiles and mats, resilient flooring, mud flaps, cassette trays, electrical boxes, cables, traffic cones, garden hose, and mobile home skirting. Packaging, film and sheet, and loose-leaf binders.
4	Low Density Polyethylene (LDPE)	Bags for dry cleaning, newspapers, bread, frozen foods, fresh produce, and household garbage. Shrink wrap and stretch film. Coatings for paper milk cartons and hot and cold beverage cups. Container lids. Toys. Squeezable bottles (e.g., honey and mustard).	Shipping envelopes, garbage can liners, floor tile, paneling, furniture, film and sheet, compost bins, trash cans, landscape timber, and outdoor lumber.

Table 3.1 (continued)

Resin codes	Descriptions	Product applications	Products that could be made with recycled content
5	Polypropylene (PP)	Containers for yogurt, margarine, takeout meals, and deli foods. Medicine bottles. Bottles for ketchup and syrup.	Automobile applications, such as battery cases, signal lights, battery cables, brooms and brushes, ice scrapers, oil funnels, and bicycle racks. Garden rakes, storage bins, shipping pallets, sheeting, trays.
6	Polystyrene (PS)	Food service items, such as cups, plates, bowls, cutlery, hinged takeout containers (clamshells), meat and poultry trays, and rigid food containers (e.g., yogurt). Protective foam packaging for furniture, electronics and other delicate items. Compact disc cases and aspirin bottles.	Thermal insulation, thermometers, light switch plates, vents, desk trays, rulers, and license plate frames. Cameras or video cassette casings.
7	Other	Three- and five-gallon reusable water bottles, citrus juice and ketchup bottles. Oven-baking bags, barrier layers, and custom packaging.	Containers and plastic lumber.

Source: Adapted from the American Chemistry Council (http://plastics.americanchemistry.com/Plastic-Resin-Codes-PDF).

benches – all ultimately un-recyclable products. When this happens, recycling (aka down-cycling) does little to reduce the use of virgin materials as those precious, non-renewable resources are still needed to make the plastic packaging that populates our lives.

There are also legitimate concerns that recycling might unintentionally be increasing the amount of raw material consumed and plastic landfilled. This brings us back to the earlier statement used to kick off this section: "I know plastic is bad but I recycle." There is considerable evidence that the ecological guilt and blame associated with using (as a manufacturer), consuming (as a consumer), and allowing (as a regulator and politician) excessive plastic packaging is assuaged with recycling.[50] This in turn leads to an acceleration of its pervasiveness, which in the end drives up the amount of resources consumed and plastics discarded. Of the close to half a million tons of plastic generated today in the United States only about 3.5 million tons (or roughly seven percent) is recovered. And the rest? Landfilled.[51] Investigations have in fact revealed that the amount of plastic sent to landfill actually *increases* when recycling programs expand to accept additional resin codes.[52]

What about the new generation of "biodegradable" plastics now available? Think the future lies not in the reduction, reuse, and recycling of plastics but in polymers that biodegrade? Think again. Substances biodegrade much quicker under aerobic conditions, as oxygen helps break the molecules apart. The problem, however, is that landfills are for the most part anaerobic because they are compacted so tightly. Lacking air (and for the most part even microorganisms) organic material can languish in a state of suspended animation for decades in a landfill environment. An "archeological study" of landfills by researchers at the University of Arizona uncovered still-recognizable 25-year-old hot dogs, corncobs, and grapes, and 50-year-old newspapers that were still readable.[53] In addition to not being biodegradable in a landfill, so-called biodegradable plastics are frequently viewed by recyclers as a "destructive contaminant" that can compromise the strength of the products they make. That's right: biodegradable plastics, in many applications, are neither biodegradable nor recyclable.[54]

Another unintended consequence of plastic recycling's growing influence upon our ecological psyche is that the relative "cheapness" of plastic is putting glass manufacturers, and thus glass recyclers, out of business. Unlike plastic, however, glass truly can be recycled, over and over again. Plastic versus glass: a case of the cheaper product winning out over the relatively more affordable. We have plastic recycling partially to thank for this.

More cheap frackin plastic

What are plastics made from? The answer to this question all depends on where in the world they are being manufactured. While per capita plastic consumption worldwide continues to skyrocket it is hard to believe that in many parts of the world its principal inputs are getting "cheaper."

In the United States, the vast majority of plastic is made from natural gas. Yet it could be worse, right? At least their source material is not coal, as in China (which is not surprising as they hold the world's largest coal reserves). The problem is that "natural gas" in the United States increasingly means "shale natural gas," which is obtained through the controversial practice of fracking. Shale gas is expected to account for close to 50 percent of total US gas production by 2035, up from a mere 19 percent in 2009.[55] Shale gas has been described by analysts as a "game changer" as it has allowed the United States to regain its position as a low-cost producer of all things plastic.[56] These cheap disposable commodities are in turn being exported around the world, as evidenced in the fact that the US exports of polyvinyl chloride – also known as PVC plastic – tripled between 2006 and 2011.[57]

The price of ethane, a natural gas component that is converted to ethylene when exposed to heat and pressure – a process called cracking – has fallen dramatically in recent years in the United States. Ethylene is a key ingredient for the manufacture of polymers. In 2012 alone the cost of ethane dropped by 67 percent among Gulf Coast processors driven in part by massive investments by chemical manufactures in Texas.[58] Chevron Phillips Chemical executive vice president Mark Lashier projects that his industry could spend more than US$30 billion to build facilities to convert cheap natural gas into plastics. To make sure his company does not get left behind in this cheap plastics revolution Chevron Phillips Chemical recently announced it will be investing US$5 billion to build a new cracking plant and supporting infrastructure in Baytone, Texas.[59] Brazoria county, located on the Golf Coast just south of Houston, has granted the chemical industry over US$6 billion in tax abatements for these expansions.[60]

For those unfamiliar with this process of fracking it works like this: a shaft is drilled several thousand feet into a shale formation and then "laterals" are drilled that fan out from the main vertical well. The fracking process itself involves pumping large amounts of water, sand, and a secret chemical mixture into the well. (Stories abound of health professionals struggling to obtain knowledge of the chemicals' identities in cases of exposure and running up against a close-lipped and obstinate industry.)[61] The pressure from this mixture fractures the shale, which in turn releases the natural gas. Once the fracking process is completed, the well goes into production, though over their lifespan wells often undergo multiple "frackings."

Fracking has been banned in Bulgaria and France over environmental concerns and most specifically risks to the wine industry in the event that groundwater stores were to become polluted. The people of France sit atop the continent's largest estimated shale natural gas reserves.[62] In the United States, fracking has come under increasing scrutiny; though, as indicated previously, this has not slowed the pace at which shale gas is being produced. Many home owners in areas where the practice is common say it has tainted their drinking water, either with methane or with the wastewater produced by the process. And the research is beginning to back up those claims. A study published in the *Proceedings of the National Academy of Sciences* examined 60 drinking-water wells in northeastern Pennsylvania and nearby areas in New York state.[63] Dissolved methane concentrations in water from the 34 wells located more than one kilometer from fracking operations were tested to have, on average, about 1.1 milligrams of dissolved methane per liter. In water taken from 26 wells within one kilometer of at least one fracking site, methane concentrations averaged 19.2 milligrams. Isotopic analyses of the carbon in the methane show it to have the same signature as that being recovered from nearby shale operations, thus implicating the fracking process. Other gases were also detected, which too were unique to the active gas-drilling areas. Ethane, another component of natural gas, and additional hydrocarbons were detected in 81 percent of water wells near fracking operations but in only nine percent of water wells farther away. Propane and butane were also more likely to be detected in wells closest to drilling areas.

The National Institute of Occupational Safety and Health recently warned that workers face an elevated risk of contracting the lung disease silicosis from inhalation of silica dust at fracking sites.[64] Silicosis is one of a family of dust-induced occupational ailments that produce roughly US$50 million in medical costs annually in the United States.[65] The process of fracking also contributes to the formation of ozone smog and particulate soot. Air pollution from shale gas drill sites in Arkansas led to estimated public health costs in excess of US $10 million in 2008.[66] The deforestation of the Pennsylvania countryside to make room for wells could lead to increased delivery of nutrient pollution into the already-threatened Chesapeake Bay and further enlarge the size of its dead zone (a low-oxygen environment inhospitable to life). One estimate places the cost of reducing the same amount of pollution as potentially generated by fracking at between $1.5 million and $4 million annually.[67]

Then there are the costs of methane emissions attributable to fracking.[68] Fracked wells leak between 40 to 60 percent more methane than conventional natural gas wells.[69] Methane has heat-trapping superpowers, at least when compared to carbon dioxide (CO_2). A molecule of methane traps 20 to 25 times more heat in the atmosphere than its CO_2 equivalent. These superpowers, however, last only about a dozen years. Methane in the atmosphere lasts for about 12 years before being scrubbed out by chemical reactions. Carbon dioxide, conversely, can last anywhere from 30 to 95 years. Nevertheless, it is expected that within 20 years methane will contribute 44 percent of the United States' greenhouse gas load – a sizable portion of which will be due to fracking.[70]

I mentioned earlier that fracking requires sand; a key ingredient in the fracking process. Sand is everywhere so we can be thankful that there is at least one seemingly inexhaustible resource used in the process, right? Wrong. The "sandprint" of fracking, it turns out, is just as problematic – and costly – as any other aspect of this process. That is because not just any sand will do. The type of sand required must be of a particular type: nearly pure quartz, well rounded, extremely hard, and of uniform size. Sand from younger glacial deposits as well as most beach and riverbank sand is too impure and too angular to be effective in the process. There is a fracking sand boom occurring in places like Wisconsin and northeastern Iowa as the geological formations there have created near-perfect fracking sand. Those regions may not possess the natural gas resources but what they lack in shale they make up for in their sandstone formations. Ground zero for fracking sand mining is western Wisconsin. As of November 2012, there were more than 60 functioning (or soon to be functioning) sand mines, up from five in 2010, all in an area spanning roughly three counties.[71]

I was born and raised in northeastern Iowa. Earlier last year (2012) I heard stories of small planes flying low in the area. I thought at first they were law enforcement looking for marijuana operations (growing up I remember the cops occasionally doing this). It turns out they were, of all things, sand prospectors. My uncle recently attended a meeting for landowners with large reserves of fracking sand on their properties. You will be surprised to learn where that sand could eventually end up. During that meeting residents were told that their sand could be shipped as far away as Saudi Arabia (theirs, apparently, doesn't meet the requirements for fracking). The carbon footprint of one barge full of sand traveling 2,000 miles down the Mississippi River to the Port of New Orleans and from there an additional 8,000 miles to Dammam's King Abdulaziz Sea Port (the largest port of Saudi Arabia) more than offsets any CO_2 "savings" achieved by the cheap natural gas extracted. Only in a world veiled by cheaponomics does it make sense to ship sand 10,000 miles to a *desert*.

In light of what we know about fracking there is nothing inexpensive about shale natural gas. Gas obtained through fracking, although cheap, comes with a hefty price tag. Yet the costs of fracking are just the first punch of a powerful one-two combination. The next comes in the form of distorted economies that further disincentivize the designing and manufacturing of products that can be either recycled (not down-cycled) or, better still, repaired. As long as plastic remains "cheap" – and at the moment it is only getting cheaper! – what incentive do producers have to manufacture, and consumers to buy, more affordable products with a longer lifespan?

None, at the moment. But it doesn't have to be this way. A whole new world of possibilities lies before us. If only, for example, energy were more accurately priced (Chapter 9). If only planned obsolescence were to become obsolete, as the economy shifted toward privileging access over ownership (Chapter 8). If only governance became more collaborative (Chapter 9). And if only we were to embrace a truly democratic regulatory politics, which extended from a product's conceptual cradle to its end-of-life grave (Chapter 10). Then what a world it would be.

Notes

1 Freinkel, Susan (2011) *Plastic: A Toxic Love Story* (New York: Houghton Mifflin Harcourt), p. 144.
2 McEachern, Diane (2008) *Big Green Purse: Use your Spending Power to Create a Cleaner, Greener World* (New York: Penguin Group), p. 182.
3 Moore, Charles and Cassandra Phillips (2011) *Plastic Ocean: How a Sea Captain's Chance Discovery Launched a Determined Quest to Save the Oceans* (New York: Avery).
4 Wallmo, Kristy and Daniel Lew (2012) "Public willingness to pay for recovering and downlisting threatened and endangered marine species," *Conservation Biology*, 26(5), pp. 803–9.
5 Freinkel (2011), p. 149.
6 Clean Air Council (n.d.) "Waste and recycling facts," Clean Air Council, Philadelphia PA, www.cleanair.org/Waste/wasteFacts.html, last accessed November 20, 2012.
7 Coulter, Jessica (2010) "A sea change to change the sea: Stopping the spread of the Pacific Garbage Patch with small-scale environmental legislation," *William and Mary Law Review*, 51, pp. 1959–95, p. 1962.
8 Ibid., p. 1962.

9 United Nations (2009) "Ghost nets hurting marine environment," United Nations Environment Programme, May 6, www.unep.org/Documents.Multilingual/Default.asp?DocumentID=585&ArticleID=6147&l=en, last accessed November 24, 2012.
10 McLendon, Russell (2010) "What is the Great Pacific Ocean Garbage Patch," *Mother Nature Network*, February 24, www.mnn.com/earth-matters/translating-uncle-sam/stories/what-is-the-great-pacific-ocean-garbage-patch#, last accessed November 24, 2012.
11 FAO (n.d.) "Climate impact on agriculture, Food and Agriculture Organization," Environment, Climate Change, and Bioenergy Division, Rome, Italy, www.fao.org/nr/climpag/pub/EIre0046_en.asp, last accessed November 25, 2012.
12 Weiss, Kenneth (2006) "Plague of plastic chokes the seas," *Los Angeles Times*, August 2, www.latimes.com/news/la-me-ocean2aug02,0,4917201.story, last accessed November 25, 2012.
13 Monterey Bay Aquarium (n.d.) "Laysan albatross and plastics," Monterey Bay Aquarium, Monterey Bay, California, www.montereybayaquarium.org/cr/oceanissues/plastics_albatross/, last accessed November 25, 2012.
14 Freinkel (2011), p. 142.
15 Mill, John Stuart (2010) *On Liberty and Other Essays* (Lawrence, KS: Digireads Publishing), p. 79.
16 Mazur, Paul (1928) *American Prosperity: Its Causes and Consequences* (London: Jonathan Cape), p. 99.
17 London, Bernard (1932) *Ending the Depression through Planned Obsolescence* (New York: self-published). Available at Library of Congress.
18 Sheldon, Roy and Egmont Arens (1932) *Consumer Engineering: A New Technique for Prosperity* (New York: Harper and Brothers).
19 Ibid., p. 7.
20 Ibid., p. 7.
21 Ibid., p. 65.
22 Fredrick, Christine (1928) *Selling Mrs Consumer* (New York: Business Bourse), p. 172.
23 Ibid., p. 172.
24 Sheldon and Arens (1932), p. 7.
25 National Center for Frontier Communities (n.d.) "The meaning of frontier," National Center for Frontier Communities, Silver City, New Mexico, www.frontierus.org/defining.php, last accessed November 27, 2012.
26 *The Light Bulb Conspiracy* (2010), documentary, Norway, http://topdocumentaryfilms.com/light-bulb-conspiracy/, last accessed November 11, 2013.
27 Quoted in Broadkar, Prasad (2010) *Designing Things: A Critical Introduction to the Culture of Objects* (New York: Berg), p. 183.
28 Holder, Charles Frederick (1886) *The Ivory King: A Popular History of the Elephant and its Allies* (New York: Charles Scribner's Sons), p. vii, 220.
29 Ibid., p. 222.
30 Stokes, John (1867) "The supply of ivory," *The Friend: A Religious and Literary Journal*, XL(48), pp. 377–8, p. 377.
31 As quoted in Freinkel (2011), p. 17.
32 Kahn, Jennifer (2009) "Plastic. Fantastic?" *Mother Jones*, April 21, www.motherjones.com/environment/2009/05/plastic-fantastic, last accessed December 3, 2012.
33 Phelan, Michael (1858) *Game of Billiards* (New York: H.W. Collender), p. 34.
34 Freinkel (2011), pp. 15–16.
35 Meikle, Jeffrey (1997) *American Plastic: A Cultural History* (New Brunswick: Rutgers University Press), p. 14.
36 Viscusi, W. Kip (1995) "Cigarette taxation and the social consequences of smoking," in *Tax Policy and the Economy*, edited by James Poterba (Cambridge, MA: MIT Press), pp. 51–102.

37 Ibid., p. 75.
38 Carlin, Paul S. and Robert Sandy (1991) "Estimating the implicit value of a young child's life," *Southern Economic Journal*, 58(1), pp. 186–202.
39 Kopczuk, W., J. Slemrod, and S. Yitzhaki (2005) "The limitations of decentralized world redistribution: An optimal taxation approach," *European Economic Review*, 49(4), pp. 1051–79.
40 Carolan, Michael (2013) *Society and Environment: Pragmatic Solutions to Ecological Issues* (Boulder: Westview Press), p. 215.
41 Sunstein, C. (2004) "Valuing life: A plea for disaggregation," *Duke Law Journal*, 54, pp. 384–445, p. 391.
42 Cowen, T. and D. Parfit (1992) "Against the social discount rate," in *Philosophy, Politics, and Society*, edited by P. Laslett and J. Fishkin (New Haven: Yale University Press), pp. 144–61, p. 147.
43 Kysar, D. (2010) *Regulating from Nowhere: Environmental Law and the Search for Objectivity* (New Haven, CT: Yale University Press), p. 148.
44 Ackerman, Frank (2008) *Poisoned for Pennies: The Economics of Toxics and Precaution* (Washington, DC: Island Press), p. 25.
45 McGarity, Thomas and Ruth Ruttenberg (2001) "Counting the cost of health, safety, and environmental regulation," *Texas Law Review*, 80, pp. 1997–2058.
46 The Plastics Industry Trade Association (n.d.) *About Plastics*, Washington DC, www.plasticsindustry.org/aboutplastics/, last accessed December 19, 2012.
47 Morris, J. (2005) "Comparative LCAs for curbside recycling versus either landfilling or incineration with energy recovery," *International Journal of Life Cycle Assessment*, 10(4), pp. 273–84.
48 Bhatti, Jawad (2010) "Current state and potential for increasing plastics recycling in the US," Master of Science Thesis, Department of Earth and Environmental Engineering, Columbia University, New York, www.seas.columbia.edu/earth/wtert/sofos/bhatti_the sis.pdf, last accessed December 20, 2012.
49 Vernon, Luke (2011) "Why all plastic containers can't be recycled," *Eco Ramblings*, February, http://ecoramblings.com/why-all-plastic-containers-cant-be-recycled/, last accessed December 20, 2012.
50 See, for example, Koestner, Richard, Nathalie Houlfort, Stephanie Paquet, Christine Knight (2001) "On the risks of recycling because of guilt: An examination of the consequence of introjection," *Journal of Applied Social Psychology*, 31(12), pp. 2545–60; Kage, Olle, Patrik Soderholm, and Christer Berglund (2009) "Norms and economic motivation in household recycling: empirical evidence from Sweden," *Resources, Conservation and Recycling*, 53(3), pp. 155–65.
51 Bhatti, Jawad (2010).
52 Ecology Center (n.d.) "Plastics task force: Seven misconceptions about plastics and plastic recycling," Ecology Center, Berkeley, CA, www.ecologycenter.org/ptf/miscon ceptions.html, last accessed December 21, 2012.
53 Rathje, William and Cullen Murphy (2001) *Rubbish! The Archeology of Garbage* (Tucson: University of Arizona Press).
54 State of California Department of Justice (2011) "Attorney General Kamala D. Harris sues plastic water bottle companies over misleading claims of biodegradability," Office of the Attorney General, Kamala D. Harris, Sacramento, CA, http://oag.ca.gov/news/press-releases/attorney-general-kamala-d-harris-sues-plastic-water-bottle-companies-over, last accessed December 23, 2012.
55 Kaskey, Jack (2011) "Cheap sale gas means record US chemical industry," *Bloomberg*, August 10, www.bloomberg.com/news/2011-08-10/cheap-shale-gas-means-record-u-s-chemical-industry-expansion.html, last accessed December 26, 2012.
56 Ibid.

57 Ibid.
58 Kaskey, Jack (2012) "Cheap gas from fracking fuels profits at LyondellBasell," *Bloomberg*, October 16, www.bloomberg.com/news/2012-10-15/cheap-gas-from-fracking-fuels-profits-at-lyondellbasell-energy.html, last accessed December 26, 2012.
59 Mapton, Stuart (2012) "Cheap US shale gas spurs plastics boom," *Bizmology*, March 12, http://bizmology.hoovers.com/2012/03/12/cheap-us-shale-gas-spurs-plastics-boom/, last accessed December 26, 2012.
60 Kever, Jeannie (2012) "Cheap natural gas fuels plant expansions," *Houston Chronicle*, October 31, www.chron.com/business/energy/article/Cheap-natural-gas-fuels-plant-expansions-3998350.php, last accessed December 26, 2012.
61 See, for example, Phillips, Susan (2012) "Pennsylvania doctors worry over fracking 'gag rule'," *National Public Radio*, May 17, www.npr.org/2012/05/17/152268501/pennsylvania-doctors-worry-over-fracking-gag-rule, last accessed December 26, 2012.
62 Klimasinska, Katarzyna (2012) "European fracking bans opens market for US gas exports," *Bloomberg*, May 23, www.bloomberg.com/news/2012-05-23/european-fracking-bans-open-market-for-u-s-gas-exports-1-.html, last accessed December 26, 2012.
63 Osborn, S., A. Vengosh, N. Warner, and R. Jackson (2011) "Methane contamination of drinking water accompanying gas-well drilling and hydraulic fracturing," *Proceedings of the National Academy of Sciences USA*, 108(20), pp. 8172–6.
64 United States Department of Labor (n.d.) "Worker exposure to silica during hydraulic fracturing," Occupational Safety and Health Administration, Washington, DC, www.osha.gov/dts/hazardalerts/hydraulic_frac_hazard_alert.html, last accessed December 26, 2012.
65 Dutzik, Tony, Elizabeth Ridlington, and John Rumpler (2012) "The costs of fracking: The price tag of dirty drilling's environmental damage," Environment America Research and Policy Center, Boston, MA, p. 2, www.environmentamerica.org/sites/environment/files/reports/The%20Costs%20of%20Fracking%20vUS.pdf, last accessed December 26, 2012.
66 Ibid.
67 Ibid.
68 Howarth, Robert, Renee Santoro, and Anthony Ingraffea (2011) "Methane and the greenhouse-gas footprint of natural gas from shale formations," *Climate Change*, 106 (4), pp. 679–90.
69 Fischetti, Mark (2012) "Fracking would emit large quantities of greenhouse gases," *Scientific America*, January 20, www.scientificamerican.com/article.cfm?id=fracking-would-emit-methane, last accessed December 26, 2012.
70 Howarth, Robert, Renee Santoro, and Anthony Ingraffea (2012) "Venting and leaking of methane from shale gas development: Response to Cathles *et al.*," *Climate Change*, 113(2), pp. 537–49.
71 Banerjee, Neela (2012) "Mining sand for fracking causes friction in Wisconsin," *Los Angeles Times*, November 19, http://articles.latimes.com/2012/nov/19/nation/la-na-wisconsin-sand-20121119-1, last accessed January 11, 2013.

Chapter 4

The high cost of cheap foods

"My mom tells me that when we were growing up eating out was a big deal. We didn't do it often because it wiped out an entire day's paycheck. It's a different world today. I can take my family [of four] out to eat for less than what I make an hour." This quote comes from an exchange I had with a man – let's call him Billy – while conducting research into why people make the food choices they do.[1] Billy was explaining to me the "value" places like McDonald's offer consumers.

"So," I inquired, "how much do you spend when you take the family out to eat and what do you all get?"

> We recently all went to McDonald's to celebrate [my daughter's] grades. I got two double cheeseburgers, which I should add are only US$0.99 each, a large fry, and a large Coke and one free refill; my wife, a fish filet [sandwich], large fry, and large Sprite; [my daughter], a cheeseburger, small fry and small soda; and [my son], Chicken McNuggets and a small soda. I paid for it all with a US$20 bill. Can you believe that? That's cheap.

It sure is. For less than US$20 Billy was able to purchase 3,990 calories and 139 grams of fat – or essentially the daily recommended caloric and fat intake of *two* adults (according to figures determined by the US Food and Drug Administration). Let me put this into some perspective. On a recent trip to a locally-owned grocery store I priced a salad supplied by alternative agrifood chains. This salad alone, had I purchased the ingredients, would have cost more than the entire meal – all 3,990 calories of it – purchased by Billy. Three locally grown red bell peppers, US$2 each; one bag of certified organic mixed lettuce, US$6; two locally grown cucumbers, US$1 each; one locally grown carrot, US$1; four ounces of certified organic sliced almonds, US$3; four ounces of fair trade quinoa, US$1.50; and a bottle of organic salad dressing, US$6. That comes out to US$25.50, before tax. I would submit, however, that while the former meal is cheap – without question – the latter may well be more affordable. Allow me to explain …

The United States Department of Calories

The first thing that needs to be acknowledged is that I am talking about cheap *foods*. Not all food is cheap, thank goodness. As for that which is, its celebrity is dubious at best.

Let us look first at precisely which foods, retail price-wise, are becoming less expensive. Research conducted in France finds that, after controlling for total caloric intake, a 100-gram increase in fats and sweets is associated with a 6 to 40-cent decrease in daily diet costs, while a 100-gram increase in fruits and vegetables is associated with a 22 to 35-cent increase in food expense.[2] Similarly, a study examining food items for sale at major retail supermarket chains in Seattle, Washington, found nutrient density negatively associated with energy density and positively associated with cost.[3] And this price disparity is only growing. The same research found that from 2004 to 2008 the price difference between healthy and unhealthy foods grew, as calorically-dense foods became cheaper and nutrient-dense foods more expensive. Turns out, Seattle is no outlier. A look at changes in food prices *throughout the United States* between 1985 and 2000 (converted to real 2002 US$) reveals soft drinks and fats/oils have gotten 25 percent and 15 percent cheaper, respectively, whereas the price of fresh fruits and vegetables have increased roughly 40 percent.[4]

I have spent a great deal of time elsewhere elaborating on how we have gotten to this point, to where we are now able to "efficiently" produce copious amounts of cheap food.[5] Extending back to at least the late 1940s, beginning in earnest with the green revolution, there has been a concerted push to increase the caloric output of global agriculture.[6] So confident were the architects of this single-minded emphasis on output that it was believed, at least for a time, that no other interventions were necessary to feed the world and alleviate global poverty. The head of the international body overseeing green revolution research, Syed Shahid Husain, for example, argued that gains in productivity were all the poor required and that "added emphasis on poverty alleviation is not necessary."[7] Not that this should be particularly surprising. Just look at, for instance, how we tend to frame issues of food policy in high-income countries: the United States Department of *Agriculture*, the US *Farm* Bill, and the European Union's Common *Agricultural* Policy. It's all about production. It's all about *more* – calories, bushels per hectare, liters of milk per head ...

Yet it is not just about calories produced. Practically all of the cheap calories consumed today are also *processed*. Figure 4.1 details the relationship between, across more than 100 countries, daily average per capita consumption of oils, fats, and sugars and average percentage of disposable household income spent on food. Not surprisingly, as oils, fats, and sugars become cheaper we tend to consume more of them. Yet the more important take-home message from the figure lies in the striking emptiness of its upper-right quadrant. National food

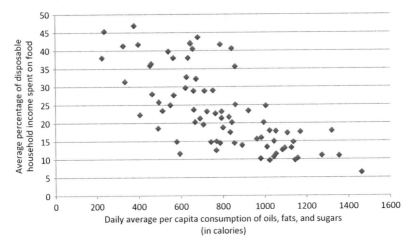

Figure 4.1 Relationship between daily average per capita consumption of oils, fats, and sugars (in calories) and average percentage of disposable household income spent on food ($15,000 or greater GDP per capita)
Source: Data obtained from the FAO and World Health Organization

systems that have managed to lower prices to levels where the average household is spending 15 percent or less of its disposable income on food are not excelling in making all food less expensive. Only certain types can be made *this* cheaply: namely, those we should not be eating in the first place – oils, fats, and sugars. In fact, cheaply is the only way they can be made.

I live in the United States, a country which has come to embody – all too literally – cheap food. Politicians and members of the conventional agriculture lobby frequently tout how we have the cheapest food in the world. Depending on where one gets the data from, the average household in the United States spends anywhere between 6 and 10 percent of its disposable income on food; a statistic that becomes all the more remarkable once it is revealed that close to half of all food consumed in the United States is consumed away from home.[8] This obsession with cheapness, however, has blinded us to a distinction that ought to be self-evident: not all calories are equal. And, unfortunately, the ones we have "succeeded" at producing so cheaply are precisely those we ought to be avoiding.

Cheap foods are actually incredibly expensive. I admit, at its face this point is a bit counterintuitive. But that is only because we've – we are all, to some degree, responsible for this (which also then means we can change things!) – become so good at socializing the costs of cheap food. Thanks to cheaponomics they appear, in terms of their retail price, to be affordable. They are not.

In business parlance, processed foods are said to have had "value" added to them. So, as consumers, we pay a little more for the added convenience: for example, pineapple that has been peeled and cored; soda packaged in various

The high cost of cheap foods 67

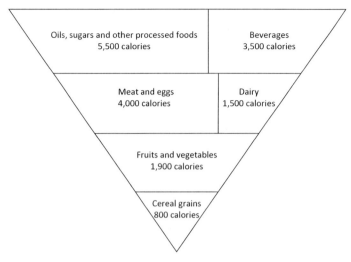

Figure 4.2 Breakdown of the amount of energy (17,000+ calories per day per capita) consumed by the US food system
Source: Based on Carolan (2013)

sized cans and bottles; and cookies, chips, and candy that are already made for us and packaged for trouble-free transportation. Yet, in adding value, food processors are also consuming, among other things, energy – a lot of it (see Figure 4.2). Value added is a euphemism for energy (and water, resources, pollution sinks, etc.) *subtracted*. "Value added" = "costs socialized." There's an equation you will not find in any economics or business textbook. What you *will* find is a whole lot of praise being heaped on the left-hand side of the equals sign. As for what is said about the right-hand side: chilling silence.

Corporate welfare by any other name would smell as cheap

Modern agricultural subsidies emerged in the United States in the early decades of the twentieth century and were initially implemented for purposes of income redistribution. Though we might like to romanticize farm life during this period, when agricultural prosperity is said to have been measured by whether or not every farmer had a chicken in their pot (to paraphrase a popular saying of the time), life was quite difficult for many producers. Farm incomes in the first half of the twentieth century were, on average, considerably lower and less stable than those of other sectors of the economy.[9] The rural voting electorate at this time was also considerably larger than today. The United States in 1930, for instance, had a population evenly split between cities and the countryside, meaning politicians could not afford to ignore the needs of this voting bloc, even the poorer segments of it. Much has changed in the intervening years. Rural residents in the United States now account for only 16 percent of the population, recognizing too that many of these inhabitants have no attachments to agriculture and might, as voters, have more in common with their more urban contemporaries. Average farm income is also up. In affluent countries, it is actually greater than the average non-farm household income.[10] This does not mean, however, that farmers are on the whole better off than their non-farming neighbors. Incomes among food producers are also far less equal today than in the 1930s. Back then, average farm incomes were low because farmers generally did not make a whole lot. Today, average income may be considerably higher, even after adjusting for inflation, but that is only because the mean is being elevated by a small percentage of highly profitable producers (who are often agribusiness firms rather than family farms). "Average," in this case, gives a distorted view of what the typical – or median, to use a statistical expression – farmer actually makes. Unlike three-quarters of a century ago, when subsidies acted as safety net to protect those most in need, the overwhelming majority of today's farm subsidies go to the largest and often most profitable farms/firms.

Between 1995 and 2009, the US government paid out US$211 billion in farm payments. Of this, 88 percent (US$186.5 billion) went to 20 percent of all farms, leaving US$24.5 billion to be distributed to the remaining 1,760,000 + smaller producers. The top recipient, from 1999 to 2009, was Riceland Foods, Inc. They received checks from US taxpayers totaling over US$554 million – that is more than what was paid to all the farmers in Alaska, Connecticut, Hawaii, Maine, Massachusetts, Nevada, New Hampshire, New Jersey, and Rhode Island. US farm subsidies also seem to take the idea of "the living dead" a little too seriously, as between 1999 and 2005 more than US$1 billion were paid to deceased landowners. That's right, to *corpses*. You can also be sure these acts of corporate (and cadaver) welfare are not confined to the United States. Equally generous handouts are being provided on the other side of the Atlantic. The Common Agricultural Policy of the European Union pays out roughly €50 billion annually in agricultural subsidies. And like in the United States, most of those end up in the bank accounts of what more resemble firms than farms. For example, the top recipient in recent years, the Dutch firm Campina, received €1.6 *billion* in taxpayers' money between 1997 and 2009.[11] That is an awful lot of taxpayer-funded support to hand to a single firm with annual profits approaching €483 million. We've come a long way from the days when government farm support went exclusively to farmers.

Processors too, those who make those cheap processed foods mentioned earlier, benefit considerably from agricultural subsidies. Take high fructose corn syrup (HFCS) manufacturers. HFCS represents close to half of the caloric sweeteners added to food in the United States. While average per capita consumption of all sweeteners in the United States increased from 123 pounds in 1966 to 151 pounds in 1999, per capita consumption of HFCS increased during that same period by 235 percent.[12] Between 1963 and 2005, thanks in significant part to subsidies (and import duties and fees on sugarcane imports to protect the domestic sugar industry but in doing so inflate the price of sugar), the price of HFCS remained 20 to 70 percent below that of sugar.[13] A further incentive to use HFCS is a government mandate that requires US food companies to use at least 85 percent domestically produced sugar in their products annually whenever sugar is used. Thanks to this cap on lower-priced sugar imports, US consumers are paying up to twice as much for sugar as compared to their European counterparts.[14]

So what sort of savings to food processors who use HFCS, precisely, can be attributed to agricultural subsidies? Thanks to an analysis by a pair of researchers at Tufts University, I have an answer to this question.[15] Had there been no subsidies for corn producers from 1997 to 2005, HFCS would have cost almost 12 percent more. These subsidies therefore saved HFCS producers US$2.19 billion during this period. As for soda manufacturers, as they are major purchasers of this input, it was calculated that had corn been priced at its full production cost they would have spent an additional US$873 million during that nine-year period. If we were to extend the window of analysis back to 1986, the savings to HFCS producers and soda companies grows to more than US$4 billion and US$1.7 billion, respectively.

Then there are the taxpayer-funded subsidies to get us to eat this cheap food. In the United States, advertising is a business expense and therefore can be used by corporations to reduce their federal tax liability. It has been estimated that the elimination of this tax break would reduce fast food advertising messages to children by 40 percent and by 33 percent for adolescents.[16] These merchants of cheap already have a megaphone, while others are confined to whispers. Why further reduce their tax liability and increase what are already highly inequitable messaging asymmetries? For every US dollar spent by the World Health Organization on preventing diseases caused by Western diets, more than US$500 is spent by the food industry promoting those diets. In the UK, the government spends £5 million annually on nutritional educational campaigns, while Coca-Cola alone spends £27 million on advertising to the very same population. Or what about the US$4.2 billion spent annually by the fast-food industry in the United States. Compare that to the entire annual budget of the Center for Nutrition Policy and Promotion (the USDA's subagency charged with improving the health and well-being of Americans): US $6.5 million.[17] It should therefore come as no surprise to discover that a diet based on observed food items advertised on television in the United States provides 2,560 percent and 2,080 percent of the recommended daily servings for sugars and fat, respectively. As for the recommended daily servings of vegetables and fruits offered by a US television advertisement-based diet: a paltry 40 percent and 27 percent, respectively.[18] As for the HFCS peddled through these billion-dollar glitzy ad campaigns: a recent study of 43 countries in the journal *Global Public Health* gives some sense of the costs to public health of this cheap additive beyond those attributed to sugar. Researchers found that adult type-2 diabetes to be 20 percent higher in countries that consume large quantities of HFCS even after controlling for sugarcane consumption. "The study adds," according to Michael Goran, of the University of Southern California Department of Preventive Medicine and co-author of the study, "to a growing body of scientific literature that indicates HFCS consumption may result in negative health consequences *distinct from and more deleterious than natural sugar*."[19]

Subsidies are also responsible for cheap meat, like the 99-cent double cheeseburgers mentioned at the beginning of the chapter. Between 1997 and 2005, animal agriculture saved approximately US$3.9 billion annually due to being able to purchase corn and soybeans at prices below the cost of production – that is a saving of almost US$35 billion over the nine-year period.[20] The swine industry, to zero in on one example, saved slightly less than US$1 billion annually between 1997 and 2005 thanks to underpriced (subsidized) feed. For Smithfield Farms, the largest hog producer in the United States, with more than 31 percent market share, that subsidized feed translated into a total saving (between 1997 and 2005) of US$2.54 billion and annual savings of US$284 million.[21] Research like this supports the view that the advantages confined animal feeding operations (CAFOs) have over smaller operations have less to do with actual efficiency gains and more to do with the large quantities of subsidized corn and soybeans that they feed their animals. Furthermore, it has been estimated that lax environmental regulations offset an additional 2.4 to 10.7 percent of a CAFOs' operating costs. When combined – discounted feed and a lack of environmental regulatory enforcement – the operating costs of large hog producers are reduced by between 17.4 and 25.7 percent. If these costs were folded back into our food system mid-sized diversified hog farmers would have a distinct market *advantage* over CAFOs.[22]

There is also considerable evidence that links agricultural subsidies with environmental degradation.[23] We know a couple things from this growing body of research. First, subsidies have been shown to have a technology "lock-in" effect that impedes the transition to alternative, less environmentally destructive policies. In other words, they tend to encourage investment in capital-intensive – aka energy-intensive (aka easily cost-socialized) – practices that are difficult to divest from once initial investments are made; practices linked closely with petrochemical use, habitat destruction, and land and water degradation. Agricultural subsidies are also negatively linked with biodiversity as they encourage mono-cropping, which in turn further adversely effects biodiversity by necessitating management practices that involve pesticide and herbicide use – toxins explicitly designed to reduce biodiversity by eradicating from farmers' fields species of insects (pests) and plants (weeds).

I return to some of the costs attributable to cheap food's reliance on petrochemicals later in this chapter. Before concluding this section I want to briefly address the main objective of the EU's Common Agricultural Policy (CAP), which, as stated on the European Commission's website, is "to ensure a fair standard of living for farmers and to provide a stable and safe supply at affordable prices for consumers." I think we can already take the European Commission to task over its understanding of a "fair standard of living" and "affordable," based on items discussed previously. Here is one more piece of evidence to add to that lot, looking specifically at the cost of price supports within the agricultural sector of the European Union. The stated aim of these subsidies is to guarantee a minimum level of income for farmers. Yet studies indicate that every €5 of additional subsidy leads to a €1 increase in farm income, while €4 leaks away (or you could say it is *socialized*) in the form of higher land and input prices. The costs of these supports add up further when combined with the fact that they also encourage fertilizer and pesticide use, demand for additional agricultural land, and the spread of monocultures.[24] It is laudable that the European Commission opts for the term "affordable" over, say, "cheap" as an expressed aim of the CAP. Too bad they do not practice what they preach.

Meanwhile, less than one-tenth of one percent of all agricultural subsidies in the United States – or less than one-hundredth of one percent of all agricultural subsidies *in the entire world* – go to supporting fruit and vegetable crops and more labor-intensive farming practices.

The unbearable lightness of obesity (and other health risks)

"We have gotten *too* good at producing cheap calories!" I occasionally start public lectures with this declaration. A blasphemous statement in the minds of many, until "cheap" is unpacked and King Cheaponomics is shown to be wearing no clothes. The truth of the matter is, the data supporting this opening salvo are overwhelming: calories *have* become too cheap and we *have* become too good at producing them. According to the Food and Agriculture Organization (FAO) of the United Nations (UN), the global food system produced 17 percent more calories per person at the dawn of the new millennium than it did 30 years earlier, even after factoring in a 70 percent population increase.[25] If evenly distributed, this factors out to everyone in the world having at least 2,720 kilocalories (kcal) per person per day. Hungry, therefore, is less about not producing enough and more about the inadequate distribution of what is currently available. That said, we do need to still be asking "Enough of what?", recognizing that while we produce sufficient calories to feed everyone in the world calories alone do not a secure food system make. If Morgan Spurlock's documentary *Supersize Me* (2004) taught us anything it is that humans cannot live on Big Macs, Shamrock Shakes, and Chicken McNuggets alone.

Reflect for a moment on this: worldwide, 12.5 percent (or almost 900 million people) of the population are presently hungry, while roughly 16 percent (or 50 million people) of US residents are defined as food insecure.[26]

If hunger and food insecurity were merely a function of not producing enough then how do you reconcile the fact that millions, living in a land of caloric abundance, lack access to nutritious and affordable food? The majority of the malnourished in the United States are actually food insecure not because they lack access to cheap calories but *because of it*. That ought to tell you something about this food, especially in terms of its costs to society.[27]

US caloric consumption increased from 2,234 calories per person per day in 1970 to 2,757 calories in 2003. Roughly 1,400 of those calories take the form of oils, fats, and sugars.[28] The United States is not alone in experiencing these trends. Around the world we are witnessing what I call an empty calorie nutrition transition.[29] Take the United States' neighbor to the south: Mexico. A significant influx in foreign direct investment (FDI) beginning in the early 1990s, most originating from transnational agrifood processors, has brought with it dramatic dietary changes. From 1997 to 2003 Mexico saw sales in the "snack" category increase annually by roughly 12 percent, while "baked goods" sales increased 55 percent.[30] More remarkable still are the reported increases in soft-drink consumption, which grew from 44 to 61 kcal per capita per day between 1992 and 2000.[31] As for the consumption of Coca-Cola, this increased from 275 eight-ounce servings per person per year in 1992 to a whopping 728 eight-ounce servings per person in 2012.[32] The average Mexican today drinks more Coke products than the average American (399), Britain (202), Chinese (32), and Indian (9) *combined*.[33] Meanwhile, from 1988 to 1999 the average Mexican diet went from having 23.5 percent to 30.3 percent of its calories coming from fat – that's a 28.9 percent increase. During the same period calories from carbohydrates declined from 59.7 percent to 57.5 percent of total calories consumed while consumption of refined carbohydrates increased.[34] These trends give some context to Mexico's second-place ranking behind the United States in a 2010 report listing the top 40 countries according to the proportion of their populations who are obese.[35] Mexico is certainly not unique among Latin American nations in this respect. Another example is Argentina. Eighteen percent of all household food expenditures in 1996 were on meals eaten outside the home. In 1970 that figure was a mere eight percent. This increase correlates strongly with a rise in FDI into the country, as much of it has been directed at the expansion of processed food chains.[36]

All this cheap food, however, has come at great cost to public health. There truly is no such thing as a cheap, let alone free, lunch (or meal of any sort). Starting with the United States, the global epicenter of cheap food policy:

- According to one estimate, the United States spent $190 billion on obesity-related healthcare expenses in 2005 – that's a whopping 21 percent of *all* medical spending.[37]
- Obesity has been found to be responsible for almost a third of the increase in inflation-adjusted health spending between 1987 and 2001.[38]

The high cost of cheap foods 73

- Total annual indirect costs (e.g., premature morality, disability) of obesity in the United States have been placed at over US$65 billion.[39]
- Estimates on the annual costs of absenteeism in the United States range from US$3.38 to US$6.38 billion.[40]
- Annual presenteeism costs attributable to obesity (impact of obesity on reduced productivity at work) in the United States have been calculated to be over US$9 billion.[41]
- Poor diet is a risk factor for four of the six leading causes of deaths in the United States: heart disease, cancer, stroke, and diabetes. When combined with obesity, these diseases have been estimated to cost US$556 billion per year.[42]

The story is much the same in Europe, where diets are increasingly emulating the North American national (cheap) cuisine.

- Total costs linked to obesity in the UK could increase by as much as 240 percent between 2007 and 2025. Obesity-related healthcare costs for the year 2007 were UK£10 billion. After factoring in for the wider costs to society and business the figure was closer to UK£50 billion.[43]
- Obesity-related illnesses costs Germany about UK£16 billion a year.[44]
- Obesity-attributed costs to absenteeism in France have been placed at US $155 million per year.[45]
- Total indirect costs associated with obesity cost Switzerland approximately US$450 million annually.[46]

The same holds for Australia:

- Overweight and obese adults cost the nation's economy, in terms of total direct and indirect costs, more than AU$56 billion annually.[47]

Canada:

- Total economic cost of overweight and obese individuals in Canada is approximately Cdn$300 billion a year: Cdn$127 billion in healthcare; Cdn$72 billion in loss of productivity due to total disability; Cdn$49 billion in loss of worker productivity due to higher rates of death; and Cdn$43 billion in loss of worker productivity due to disability of active workers.[48]

And finally China:

- Obesity-attributable costs of absenteeism are estimated at approximately US$50 billion annually.[49]
- Total direct and indirect costs attributed to obesity top US$53.6 billion annually – or more than four percent of the country's total GDP.[50]

I am not suggesting that all of these costs are attributable to cheap food. But a substantial portion of them undoubtedly are. Look at life expectancy at birth in the United States, which is holding steady ... for now. Yet a change is underway, at least in some parts of the country. The aggregate result of which might mean a *shorter* average lifespan for future generations. A study of county-level data shows that in hundreds of counties – most located in the South – life expectancy has actually fallen in recent years.[51] These counties also have some of the highest obesity rates in the nation, in addition to very high levels of (racial) inequality. The study implicates the nation's food system, as diet is shown to be a major risk factor in cutting short life expectancies. The authors of the study are also quick to highlight that while some US counties are performing particularly poorly all are negatively impacted by diet and other environmental factors. In the words of the study's authors, the "relative [life expectancy] performance for most communities continues to drop" across the United States.[52]

This is a delicate critique, however. Our beef ought to be with cheap food, not obesity per se. For example, there are some arguments, parroted frequently by well-intending individuals, which place significant climate change blame on the obese. A study of this ilk was recently published in the *International Journal of Obesity*. "Investigating the effects of a low-carbohydrate diet on body weight, body composition and resting metabolic rate of obese volunteers with type 2 diabetes," the authors estimated "that a 10 kg weight loss of all obese and overweight people would result in a decrease of 49.560 Mt of CO_2 per year, which would equal to 0.2 percent of the CO_2 emitted globally in 2007."[53] "A heavier body," according to Sarah Walpole, a UK-based researcher studying the links between health and climate change, "needs more food to be sustained."[54] Elsewhere, it has been pointed how the obese weigh on global gas mileage.[55] It has been calculated, for example, that for every 100 pounds in your car, assuming it gets an average of 31 miles a gallon, you can expect to add US$31.32 to your annual gas bill. In other words, the greater a car's "cargo" weight, the more gas it consumes, and the greater its greenhouse gas footprint.[56] The take-home message of this research: the Earth would be much better off if the obese lost weight.

Rather than blaming individuals I think real culpability lies in the system responsible for producing a glut of cheap calories – cheaponomics. There is an interesting link between obesity and climate change. But it is not the link you think. Conventional treatments of obesity parallel conventional prescriptions to combat climate change. In both cases, a disproportionate focus lies on individual consumption choices rather than on creating policies that would enforce corporate accountability or to mitigate their effects on those most harmed. Obesity and climate change are thus seen as "apolitical ecologies," which is to say that our explanations and solution each do not fully account for the asymmetries in power that produce and materially sustain them over time.[57] Both, in other words, are understood to be products of poor decision-making at the individual level. This move effectively absolves the system of any blame. And the status quo continues.

Here is another interesting link between obesity and climate change, though in this case the causal arrow points in the *opposite* direction – from climate change *to* rising obesity rates. There is good reason to believe that increases in food prices due to climate change will lead to higher obesity rates. All the talk about spikes in food prices in 2008 and again in 2010 failed to register the fact that the price of healthier foods (like fruits and vegetables) rose faster than processed foods.[58] As food prices continue to increase we can expect refined grains, sugars, and vegetable fats to replace healthier options as the latter will rise in retail price faster than the former. Why? We have cheaponomics to thank for that. The more energy-intensive – and, by extension, processed – a food is the easier it is to socialize its costs.

There is also a social justice issue here. The poor are more likely to be obese. As incomes drop energy-dense, nutrient-shallow foods become the best way to provide daily calories due to their lower retail price.[59] Those foods are also all-too-often the only ones available to low-income populations, a phenomenon known as a food desert. The evidence indicates that the poor would eat healthier if they could.[60] Their moral constitutions have not failed them. The food system has. Blaming them for their diets misses the mark. As for their culpability in contributing to climate change, let us not forget that by nature of living in poverty the poor also drive fewer miles (if they even own a car), own smaller homes (if they even own a house), and overall have less stuff. My point: their carbon footprint is a fraction of that of someone more affluent. The aforementioned obesity link to climate change is the rhetorical equivalent to a lot of hand waving. It distracts us from addressing the deeper systemic roots of things like climate change and obesity, which once exposed would better reveal cheap food's role in all of this.

Meat some other costs

Meat has gotten bad press as of late. As with obesity, we need to be careful to disentangle the food from the system whence it came. Animal agriculture can produce extremely affordable food, especially in places which are arable land poor and permanent pasture rich, such as in Sub-Saharan Africa where over 80 percent of the region is permanent pasture or rangelands. Unfortunately, most of the meat produced today is cheap. And that we cannot afford.

First, there is the matter of feed versus food. Growing up in rural northeastern Iowa, I have long been struck by one of the cow's most unique abilities, namely, its natural knack at converting something with zero nutritional value to humans (namely, cellulose), by way of various stomachs, into products our digestive tracts can better handle, like meat and milk. Yet "modern" cows also eat grains and legumes – things humans can eat directly. And they eat a lot of them.

Arjen Hoekstra, Professor of Water Management at the University of Twente and a leading water footprint (or in this case hoofprint) expert, calculates that the industrial beef cow consumes roughly 15,000 liters of water per kilogram of live weight gained.[61] The water-intensive nature of the industrial beef cow is a function of its diet in a CAFO environment. A conservative conversion ratio for a feed-intensive beef cow is 7 to 1. In other words, 7 kg of grain (23,150 calories/700 grams protein) are required for each kg (1,140 calories/226 grams protein) in live weight gain. Let us return briefly to Billy's 99-cent double cheeseburgers, mentioned at the beginning of this chapter. The real price of one hamburger has been placed, by one author, at over US$200.[62] The calculation assumes that the beef cow was fattened on pasture once covered by rainforest (an assumption that likely does not hold for Billy's burgers) and includes, among other things, ecological services that were provided by the now-lost ecosystem such as carbon sequestration and water cycling. Elsewhere, Raj Patel places the energy cost of the 550 million Big Macs sold in the United States every year at US$297 million (producing a greenhouse gas footprint of 2.66 billion pounds of CO_2 equivalent).[63] But why rely on these calculations by others. Let's do our own right now.

One 1,250-pound slaughter-weight cow produces roughly 100 pounds of hamburger meat (and 400 pounds of other meat cuts, including "alternative meats" like liver). Roughly 65 percent of the animal is carcasses.[64] (Let me write that again: 65 percent of each 1 kg live weight gain – for every 7 kg of grain consumed – is *inedible*.) McDonald's patties are an eighth of a pound, which means each cow produces roughly 800 regular burger patties or 400 double cheeseburgers. Assuming a 7 to 1 conversion ratio, each of Billy's double cheeseburgers thus has between an eighth and a tenth of a bushel of embodied corn within it. Corn is presently (February 2013) hovering around US$7 a bushel, though US$8/bushel corn is no longer out of the ordinary. That translates into roughly US$1 of corn within each burger, saying nothing of the embodied water, fuel, energy, greenhouse gases, fertilizers, herbicides, soil erosion, water pollution, and the like that went into its entire life cycle. And we still have yet to say anything about the costs of making the bun and cheese. That 99-cent price tag is not a deal. It is, quite literally, a *steal*.

But we have only just begun to scratch the surface …

There are also the costs of zoonotic diseases, which greatly threaten public health. Some of the more famous include the H5N1 virus – aka severe acute respiratory syndrome (SARS; more commonly known as bird flu) – which infected thousands and killed hundreds and the H1N1 virus – aka swine flu – which infected tens of millions and killed over 10,000.[65] While animal–human transfer of infectious agents has been occurring ever since animals were first domesticated, what we are seeing today is unprecedented in terms not only of the frequency of transfer but the virulency. The reason for this, according to the world's foremost expert on avian influenza, Robert Webster, is that "farming practices have changed." He goes on to explain that today:

we put millions of chickens into a chicken factory next door to a pig factory, and this virus has the opportunity to get into one of these chicken factories and make billions and billions of these mutations continuously. And so what we've changed is the way we raise animals and our interaction with those animals. And so the virus is changing in those animals and now finding its way back out of those animals into the wild birds.[66]

Compounding matters further is how we shuttle animals around the world. Modern animal transport systems have proven lush breeding grounds for disease. Animals from different herds or flocks are confined together for long periods of time in poorly ventilated environments, giving microorganisms and viruses every opportunity to move across the resident population. Then upon reaching the site where they are eventually slaughtered the animals are introduced to new herds or flocks, and *their* microorganisms and viruses. It is a veritable pathogen utopia and we are the financiers of this Paradise. What is amazing is not that some animals get sick but that they all do not.

Diane Carmen, writing in the *Denver Post*, notes that "if 19 million pounds of meat distributed to half of this country had been contaminated with a deadly strain of *E. coli* bacteria by terrorists, we'd go nuts. But when it's done by a Fortune 100 corporation, we continue to buy it and feed it to our kids."[67] The US Department of Justice estimates that foot-and-mouth disease, which is 20 times more infectious than smallpox, if used in an act of agroterrorism, would cost taxpayers as much as US$60 billion.[68] We already have had, thanks to cheap meat, the 2001 foot-and-mouth disease outbreak in the UK, which cost British taxpayers more than US$15 billion.[69] As for the costs of SARS to Asian countries: after taking into account loss of life (human and animal), healthcare costs, losses in productivity due to illness, and decreases in tourism and global consumer confidence toward Asian food imports, the WHO places the figure at somewhere between US$20 billion and US$60 billion, just in 2003.[70] Then there is the cost of microbial resistance to antibiotics in the United States, which is estimated to cost taxpayers US$4 billion annually.[71]

The costs associated with industrial animal agriculture go on and on. Below are a few more.

- Climate change: the livestock sector is currently responsible for at least 18 percent of human-induced greenhouse gas emissions.[72] These emissions are projected to grow by 39 percent by 2050.[73]
- Unhealthy diets: while levels of omega-6 fatty acids are roughly the same in the meat of corn-fed and grass-fed cattle, levels of omega-3 are higher in the fully-pastured cow. Consequently, the ratio of omega-6 to omega-3 in grass-fed beef is roughly 1.56:1, while in grain-fed beef it averages about 7.65:1. A healthy diet supplies these fats in the range of 1:1 to 4:1. Diets where meat is "cheap," however, have ratios in the range of 11:1 to 30:1,

which is hypothesized to be a significant risk factor in inflammatory disorders, colorectal cancer, and breast cancer among women.[74]

- Animal welfare: while you cannot put a price on animal pain and suffering, you can, perhaps paradoxically, put a price on their lives – that is, after all, exactly what a livestock market does. An estimated 80,000 pigs die annually in the United States just during *transport*, which equates to an US $8 million annual loss to the pork industry (a cost that does not include carcass disposal fees).[75] While cattle rarely die during hauling, transportation-associated injuries – which can include anything from broken bones to bruising and lacerations – lead to carcass devaluation. Bruising alone causes more than US$100 million in annual economic losses to US beef producers.[76] Stressed animals also lose weight, which is why "carcass shrinkage," as it is known in the livestock industry, is positively correlated with live transport distance.[77]

Take heart, carnivores. Meat is not inherently cheap. A good example of affordable meat can be found in the beef produced in northern Africa. The average cow in a typical northern African system consumes 25 liters of water per day over a two-year period to produce 125 kg of meat while living off crop residues, for which no additional water input is required. This equates to a direct water consumption of 146 liters per kilogram – far below the 100,000 liter statistic mentioned earlier to describe CAFO-beef. Yet even these figures overstate the animals' water requirements, as much of the water they consume is quickly recycled back into the soil as urine providing not only moisture but also ever-important nutrients for the soil. Certain animals, like pigs and chickens, can also consume organic food waste – indeed, they thrive on it. As you will discover later in this chapter, we have copious amounts of food waste. Animal agriculture might provide an avenue to re-capture some of that food – and all the embedded resources that go alone with it – and re-direct it back to feeding people versus landfills.

Costs to whom

Like everything discussed in this book, we cannot ask about "costs" without also inquiring about "cost to *whom*." People do not pay these costs evenly or fairly. There is an irreconcilable tension between efficiency and safety. The market is all about tradeoffs, as economists frequently remind me. And the relationship between efficiency and safety is no exception. Cheap food is about production efficiencies and economies of scale. Yet these "savings" also presuppose an organizational form that is inherently risky from the standpoint of worker and public health. Take industrial slaughter facilities. Mistakes are inevitable in an environment where line speeds continue to increase. So we have, for instance, an increasing occurrence of internal organs being cut open during the evisceration process exposing meat to fecal matter and dangerous bacteria. (One "solution" to this has been irradiation, which is the processing of exposing food to radiation which would kill all harmful bacteria. But isn't irradiated poop still poop?) When viewed collectively, animal agriculture industries rank among the most hazardous of all occupations. In CAFO environments, many worker injuries are attributed to accidents with machinery and animals, though chronic diseases due to environmental contaminants pose an increasing risk to worker health, especially as these facilities continue to expand in size.[78] Over 25 percent of CAFO workers, for example, suffer from respiratory diseases, ranging from bronchitis to mucous membrane irritation, asthma, and acute respiratory distress syndrome.[79]

Field laborers also pay a substantial cost for our cheap food. One study estimates that approximately 7.5 percent of all agricultural workers in Sri Lanka suffer from occupational pesticide poisoning every year.[80] In Costa Rica and Nicaragua, the rates of pesticide poisoning among field laborers are 4.5 and 6.3 percent, respectively.[81] A study investigating worker exposure to chemicals in the West African country of Benin found 81 percent of pineapple farmers and 43 percent of vegetable farmers reporting "considerable" negative health effects due to pesticide exposure (while only 1 percent reported "zero" negative effects).[82]

Grave income inequalities also embed our cheap food system. As detailed in Figure 4.3, we find that white men earn the highest wages in the United States, when looking at food production, processing, distribution, and retail/service sectors. The income disparities in the figure become even more striking once we factor in for the fact that racial minorities, most notably Latinos, pay for a disproportional share of the earlier-mentioned socialized costs that come with laboring in pesticide-laced fields and large-scale CAFOs.[83] Over 70 percent of workers in the United States who grade and sort harvested crops (a particularly low paying job) are Latino. Moreover, more than six out of every ten farm workers are undocumented immigrants. This population too is overwhelmingly Latino and, by nature of their "undocumented" status, incredibly easy to socialize costs on to as they lack many of the basic legal protections that come with citizenship.[84] And these income discrepancies are only increasing. For example, the weekly earnings for slaughter-plant workers in the United States in 1984 was US$700 (including overtime and adjusted for inflation, in 2009 US$). In 2010, those earnings had dropped to US$475.[85]

Rural communities and residents located near CAFOs also pay for a disproportionate share of these socialized costs. Neighbors of CAFOs have higher levels of respiratory and digestive disturbances in addition to having abnormally high rates of psychological disorders, such as anxiety, depression, and sleep disturbances.[86] Children living on or near large-scale hog farms have abnormally high rates of asthma; rates that increase proportionally with the size of the facility.[87] Middle schools in North Carolina that were within 4.8km (three miles) of one or more large hog-feeding facilities reported rates of asthma among the student population that were well above state averages.[88]

80 Cheap stuff

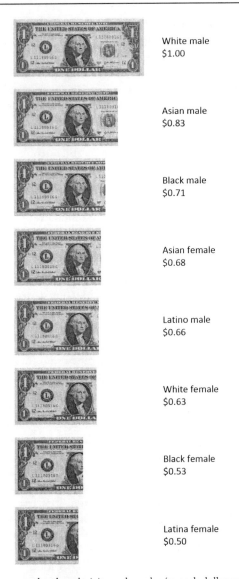

Figure 4.3 Median average salary by ethnicity and gender (to each dollar earned by white male) Source: Based on Liu and Apollon (2011; only those employed, working over 25 hours a week, and earning an income from employment were selected for analysis)

A study of six counties in Minnesota containing multiple large-scale livestock facilities recorded a number of negative impacts among residents living near these facilities, from widespread reporting of diminished quality of life to mid-sized farmers claiming their livelihoods were threatened due to limited access to markets and older producers expressing anxiety over the future of farming and rural life more generally.[89] There are also decades of studies documenting the relationship between industrial agriculture and its negative impact upon a variety of community quality-of-life indicators. The central thrust of this research notes that communities surrounded by large-scale, absentee, highly specialized farms tend to have a smaller middle class, lower mean family incomes, higher rates of poverty, higher rates of crime, poorer quality schools, and fewer churches, civic organizations, and retail establishments.[90]

Costs to when

We also need to ask questions about *when* some of these costs will become due? I am talking here about how our food system is costing the environment and thus future generations. One study, focusing solely on agricultural production in the United States, places the costs to natural resources, wildlife, biodiversity, and human health at between US$5.7 to US$16.9 billion annually. Again, while staggering, that figure ignores all the cost-socializing that happens after the farm as well as in the input sector.[91] Another calculates the socialized cost of UK agriculture – again, calculating only cost occurring *within* the farm gate – to be US$2.4 billion.[92] Those costs break down as follows: pesticides in water, US$200.6 million; nitrate, phosphate, soil, and *Cryptosporidium* in water, US$172.5 million; eutrophication of surface water, US$121.9 million; monitoring of water systems and advice, US$20.2 million; methane, nitrous oxide, and ammonia emissions to atmosphere, US$648.7 million; direct and indirect carbon dioxide emissions to atmosphere, US$158.2 million; off-site soil erosion and organic matter losses from soils, US$90.9 million; losses to biodiversity and landscape values, US$231.5 million; negative effects to human health from pesticides, US$1.8 million; negative effects to human health from microorganisms and BSE, US$666.4 million. As for the costs of pesticides, Cornell University ecologist David Pimentel places this figure at a staggering US$9.65 billion annually, which includes, among other things, public health impacts, honey bee and pollination losses, and groundwater contamination.[93] And this is the price tag of pesticides *just in the United States*.

One of the most neglected costs of cheap food and of pesticides more generally has been their impact upon pollinator services and the venerable honey bee in particular. Roughly 84 percent of the nearly 300 commercial crops are insect pollinated (90 percent of these services performed exclusively by honey bees).[94] Pimentel estimates the cost of pesticides due to pollinator poisonings and reduced pollination in the United States to be around US$283.6 million annually.[95] Another estimate, looking at the deciduous fruit industry of the Western Cape of South Africa, places the total annual value of insect pollination services and managed pollination at US$358.4 million and US$312.1 million, respectively.[96] Those services are slowly being eliminated thanks to current agricultural production practices, though you would never know it by looking at the retail price of many of our foods.

A core assumption of neoclassical economics is substitutability: that, eventually, human ingenuity will find suitable substitutes for all scarce resources and ecosystem services. So spoil away! There is no substitute for bee pollination, however, which means we are eating cheaply at the risk that future generations will not be able to eat some of these foods at all. I know almond growers in California who are having entire colonies of bees *flown* over from Australia in order to have their crops pollinated because Colony Collapse Disorder (CCD) has decimated domestic US hives. That might not make any sense – it certainly doesn't to the audiences I mention this to. But thanks to cheaponomics – and cheap oil in particular – it still makes cents.

Then there are cheap foods' links to climate change. It has been estimated that agriculture accounts for 10 to 12 percent of total global greenhouse gases (GHGs) or 60 percent of global nitrous oxide (N_2O), 50 percent of global methane (CH_4), and less than one percent of global carbon dioxide (CO_2).[97] If one accounts for emissions from land-use changes that arise from an expansion of agricultural land (such as through deforestation in Brazil and Indonesia), we find the sector to be responsible for as much as a third of total global anthropogenic GHGs.[98] And the carbon footprint of cheap food is only increasing. Global agricultural emissions increased by 17 percent from 1990 to 2005.[99]

Then there is all the food wasted. Researchers at the USDA estimate that the total value of food wasted at the retail and consumer levels in the United States in 2008 topped US$165.6 billion.[100] This loss translates into almost 124 kg (273 pounds) per person – that's an awful lot of food and embedded resources that could have been put to better use. US per capita food waste has increased by more than 50 percent since 1974.[101] The energy embedded in all this wasted food represents approximately two percent of the country's total annual energy consumption.[102] Americans are far from alone in their conspicuous wastefulness of calories. Canadians toss out about C$27 billion worth of food annually.[103] In the UK, the British discard approximately seven million tons of food – or roughly one-third of all food purchased by consumers – annually. At a retail cost of roughly UK£10.2 billion (US$19.5 billion), this waste has a CO_2 equivalent of 18 million tons – an amount equal to the annual emissions of one-fifth of the total car fleet in all of the UK.[104] Continuing our journey around the world: in India, roughly 30 percent of the country's fruits and vegetables and 30 percent of its grain are lost annually due to poor storage facilities.[105] In China, food waste has increased exponentially in recent years and now accounts for close to 70 percent of all household and commercial waste.[106] In South Korea, food waste increased roughly three percent annually between 2008 and 2012. Today, daily food waste in this country exceeds 17,100 tons.[107] While in Japan, household and food industries together waste about 17 million metric tons of edible food each year.[108]

The elephant in the room when discussing cheap food is the alternative, or more specifically the retail price of what I call affordable food. So let me put a little paint on this elephant so we can see it better, recognizing that I will return to this subject in later chapters when sketching out an outline of what an affordable society might look like. Does improving cost-internalization mean more expensive, retail price-wise, food? It is hard to say, as price increases due to cost-internalization will at least in part be offset by a reduction in the amount of food currently wasted. Reducing food waste is an obvious goal as we move toward affordable food. We could conceivably reduce the real cost of food while not having to worry too much about rapidly rising retail prices if we did a better job actually eating – and more fairly distributing – the food we produce. Let us also not forget that "expensive" is a relative term. A 5 percent increase, for example, in the price of any given food item affects households differently. My household, and I am far from "rich," could likely absorb the cost with little impact. The same could not be said, however, of someone living below the poverty level. Yet what if cheaponomics is partially responsible for the increasingly unhinged levels of inequality we are seeing around the world? (Cheaponomics *is* responsible for it, as I detail in the book's final chapters.) Cheap is not much good to households whose incomes are dropping faster than the price of food, which, sadly, represents the economic reality for millions – if not billions – on this planet. I recognize that once costs are better reflected in the retail price of goods those products are likely going to be priced a little higher than when they were "cheap." And I also recognize that food is unique, in the sense that while the price increase of many household commodities will be offset by the fact that those products will last longer (therefore you will not need to buy as many in the long run), food can only be consumed once. Yet because cheaponomics is responsible for keeping incomes for the vast majority of the world's population depressed we still have reason to hope as we struggle for an affordable prosperity. What matters is that the alternatives we collectively work toward lift incomes among the world's poor at rates that exceed any increases in the price of food.

But that's a topic for later chapters, where I discuss such issues as income inequality (Chapters 9 and 10), "full" employment (Chapters 7 and 10), and citizen (versus consumer) choice (Chapter 8).

Notes

1 This research eventually led to the publication of Carolan, Michael (2011) *Embodied Food Politics* (Burlington: Ashgate).
2 Maillot, M., N. Darmon, F. Vieux, and A. Drewnowski (2007) "Low energy density and high nutritional quality are each associated with higher diet costs in French adults," *American Journal of Clinical Nutrition*, 86(3), pp. 690–6.
3 Monivais, P., J. Mclain, and A. Drewnowski (2010) "The rising disparity in the price of healthful foods: 2004–8," *Food Policy*, 35(6), pp. 514–20.
4 Putman, J., J. Allshouse, and L. Kantor (2002) "US per capita food supply trends," *Food Review*, 25(3), pp. 2–15.
5 Carolan, Michael (2011) *The Real Cost of Cheap Food* (London and New York: Routledge/Earthscan); Carolan, Michael (2013) *Reclaiming Food Security* (London and New York: Routledge/Earthscan).

6 Welsh, R. and R. Graham (1999) "A new paradigm for world agriculture," *Field Crops Research*, 60, pp. 1–10.
7 Lappe, F. and J. Collins (1986) *World Hunger: Twelve Myths* (New York: Grove Weidenfeld, a Food First Book), p. 49.
8 Carolan, *The Real Cost of Cheap Food* (2011), p. 2.
9 Gardner, Bruce (1987) "Causes of US farm commodity programs," *Journal of Political Economy*, 95(2), pp. 290–310.
10 Carolan, Michael (2012) *The Sociology of Food and Agriculture* (New York and London: Routledge/Earthscan), p. 22.
11 Ibid., p. 22.
12 Carolan, *The Real Cost of Cheap Food* (2011), p. 68.
13 Ibid.
14 Wexler, Alexandra (2012) "Sugar users want US to ease import curbs," *Washington Post*, April 1, http://online.wsj.com/article/SB10001424052702303816504577314034112332296.html, last accessed December 31, 2012.
15 Harvie, A. and T. Wise (2009) "Sweetening the pot: Implicit subsidies to corn sweeteners and the US obesity epidemic, global development and environmental institute," Tufts University, Policy Brief No 09–01, February, www.ase.tufts.edu/gdae/Pubs/rp/PB09–01SweeteningPotFeb09.pdf, last accessed December 31, 2012.
16 Institute of Medicine (2004) "Advertising, marketing and the media: Improving messages," Institute of Medicine, Washington, DC, www.iom.edu/~/media/Files/Report%20Files/2004/Preventing-Childhood-Obesity-Health-in-the-Balance/factsheetmarketingfinaBitticks.ashx, last accessed December 31, 2012.
17 Carolan (2013), p. 166.
18 Mink, M., A. Evans, C. Moore, K. Calderon, and S. Deger (2010) "Nutritional imbalance endorsed by televised food advertisement," *Journal for the American Dietetic Association*, 110(6), pp. 904–10.
19 Harmon, Katherine (2012) "Global high fructose corn syrup use may be fueling diabetes increase," *Scientific American*, November 27, http://blogs.scientificamerican.com/observations/2012/11/27/global-high-fructose-corn-syrup-use-may-be-fueling-diabetes-increase/, last accessed July 7, 2013.
20 Starmer, E. and T. Wise (2007) "Feeding at the trough: Industrial livestock firms saved $35 billion from low feed prices," Policy Brief No 07–03, Global Development and Environment Institute, Tufts University, Medford, MA.
21 Starmer, E. and T. Wise (2007) "Living high on the hog: Factory farms, federal policy, and the structural transformation of swine production," Working Paper No 07–04, Global Development and Environment Institute, Tufts University, Medford, MA.
22 Carolan, *The Real Cost of Cheap Food* (2011), pp. 104–5.
23 See, for example, van Beers, Cees and C. van den Bergh (2009) "Environmental harm of hidden subsidies: Global warming and acidification," *AMBIO: A Journal of the Human Environment*, 38(6), pp. 339–41; Mayrand, Karel, Stephanie Dionne, Marc Paquin, and Lsaak Pageot-LeBel (2003) "The economic and environmental impacts of agricultural subsidies: An assessment of the 2002 US Farm Bill and Doha Round," North American Commission for Environmental Consequences, Montreal, Canada, www.wto.org/english/forums_e/ngo_e/unisfera_jully03_e.pdf, last accessed December 31, 2012; Myers, N. (1998) "Lifting the veil on perverse subsidies," *Nature*, 392, pp. 327–8.
24 van Beers and van den Bergh (2009).
25 FAO (2002) "Reducing poverty and hunger: The critical role of fi nuancing for food, agriculture and rural development," Food and Agriculture Organization, World Food Programme, Rome, ftp://ftp.fao.org/docrep/fao/003/Y6265E/Y6265E.pdf, last accessed January 1, 2013.

26 Prey, Leslie, Laura Pillsbury, and Maria Oria (2012) "Exploring health and environmental costs of food: Workshop summary" (Washington, DC: National Academy of Sciences), p. 6.
27 Carolan (2013).
28 Ibid., p. 137.
29 Ibid., p. 64.
30 Hawkes, C. (2005) "The role of foreign direct investment in the nutrition transition," *Public Health Nutrition*, 8(4), pp. 357–65.
31 Arroyo, P., A. Loria, and O. Mendez (2004) "Changes in the household calorie supply during the 1994 economic crisis in Mexico and its implications for the obesity epidemic," *Nutrition Reviews*, 62, pp. S163–S168.
32 Hawkes (2005).
33 Bhasin, Kim (2011) "15 facts about Coca-Cola that will blow your mind," *Business Insider*, June 9, www.businessinsider.com/facts-about-coca-cola-2011-6?op=1, last accessed January 1, 2013.
34 Rivera J., S. Barquera, T. Gonzalez-Cossio, G. Olaiz, and J. Sepulveda (2004) "Nutrition transition in Mexico and in other Latin American countries," *Nutrition Reviews*, 62, pp. S149–S157.
35 Clark, S., C. Hawkes, S. Murphy, K. Hansen-Kuhn, and D. Wallinga (2012) "Exporting obesity: US farm and trade policy and the transformation of the Mexican consumer food environment," *International Journal of Occupational and Environmental Health*, 18(1), pp. 53–65.
36 Hawkes (2005).
37 Cawley, J. and C. Meyerhoefer (2012) "The medical care costs of obesity: An instrumental variables approach," *Journal of Health Economics*, 31, pp. 219–30.
38 Finkelstein, Eric, Justin Trogdon, Joel Cohen, and William Dietz (2009) "Annual medical spending attributable to obesity: Payer and service specific estimates," *Health Affairs*, 28(5), pp. w822–w831.
39 Colditz, G. (1999) "Economic costs of obesity and inactivity," *Medical Science in Sports and Exercise*, 31, pp. S663–67.
40 Trogdon, J., E. Finkelstein, T. Hylands, P. Dellea, and S. Kamal-Bahl (2008) "Indirect costs of obesity: A review of the literature," *Obesity Reviews*, 9, pp. 489–500.
41 Ricci, J. and E. Chee (2005) "Lost productive time associated with excess weight in the US workforce," *Journal of Occupational Environmental Medicine*, 47, pp. 1227–34.
42 Wallinga, D., H. Schoonover, and M. Muller (2009) "Considering the contribution of US agricultural policies to the obesity epidemic: Overview and opportunities," *Journal of Hunger and Environmental Nutrition*, 4(1), pp. 3–19.
43 Foresight (2007) Tackling Obesity: Future Choices, UK Government's Foresight Programme, Government Office for Science, London, www.bis.gov.uk/assets/bispartners/foresight/docs/obesity/obesity_final_part1.pdf, last accessed January 2, 2013.
44 Hall, A. (2010) "Overweight people should pay 'fat tax' to cover healthcare costs, German MP says," *Telegraph*, July 22, www.telegraph.co.uk/news/worldnews/europe/germany/7904990/Overweightpeople-should-pay-fat-tax-to-cover-healthcare-costs-German-MP-says.html, last accessed January 2, 2013.
45 Levy, E., P. Levy, C. Le Pen, and A. Basdevant (1995) "The economic costs of obesity: The French situation," *International Journal of Obesity and Related Metabolic Disorders*, 19, pp. 788–92.
46 Colditz (1999).
47 Colagiuri, S., C. Lee, R. Colagiuri, D. Magliano, J. Shaw, P. Zimmet, and I. Caterson (2010) "The cost of overweight and obesity in Australia," *Medical Journal of Australia*, 192(5), pp. 260–64.

48 *Bloomberg Business Weekly* (2011) "Cost of obesity approaching $300 billion per year," *Bloomberg Business Weekly*, January 11.
49 Poplin, B., S. Kim, and E. Du Rusev (2006) "Measuring the full economic costs of diet, physical activity and obesity-related chronic diseases," *Obesity Reviews*, 7, pp. 271–93.
50 Ibid.
51 Kulkarni, S., A. Levin-Rector, M. Ezzati, and C. Murray (2011) "Falling behind: Life expectancy in US counties from 2000 to 2007 in an international context," *Population Health Metrics*, 9(1), pp. 1–12.
52 Ibid., p. 1.
53 Gryka, A., J. Broom, and C. Rolland (2012) "Global warming: Is weight loss a solution?" *International Journal of Obesity*, 36, pp. 474–6.
54 Quoted in Irfan, Umair and Climatewire (2012) "Global shift to obesity packs serious climate consequences," *Scientific America*, June 21, www.scientificamerican.com/article.cfm?id=global-shift-obesity-packs-serious-climate-consequences, last accessed January 2, 2013.
55 Roberts, Ian and Phil Edwards (2010) *The Energy Glut* (London: Zed Books).
56 Fairchild, Caroline (2012) "Gas milage, costs affected by driver's weight," *Huffington Post*, October 9, www.huffingtonpost.com/2012/10/09/gas-mileage-costs-affected-by-drivers-weight_n_1951174.html, last accessed January 2, 2013.
57 Guthman, Julie (2011) *Weighing In: Obesity, Food Justice and the Limits of Capitalism* (Los Angeles: University of California Press).
58 Laskawy, Tom (2012) "What does obesity have to do with climate change? Plenty, say some scientists," *Grist*, December 12, http://grist.org/food/what-does-obesity-have-to-do-with-climate-change-plenty-says-new-study/, last accessed January 2, 2013.
59 Drewnowski, Adam (2009) "Obesity, diets and social inequalities," *Nutrition Reviews*, 67(s1), pp. s36-s39.
60 Carolan (2013).
61 Hoekstra, Arjen (2013) *The Water Footprint of Modern Consumer Society* (New York: Routledge), p. 56.
62 Dune, N. (1994) "Why a hamburger should cost 200 dollars – the call for prices to reflect ecological factors," *Financial Times*, January 12, pp. 12–14.
63 Patel, Raj (2009) *The Value of Nothing: How to Reshape Market Society and Redefine Democracy* (New York: Picador), pp. 43–4.
64 Colorado State University Extension (2008) "On average, how many pounds of corn make one pound of beef?" Colorado State University, Fort Collins, CO, October 8, www.extension.org/pages/35850/on-average-how-many-pounds-of-corn-make-one-pound-of-beef-assuming-an-all-grain-diet-from-backgroundi, last accessed January 2, 2012.
65 CDC (2010) "2009 H1N1 flu: Situation update," www.cdc.gov/h1n1flu/update.htm, last accessed January 3, 2013.
66 Council on Foreign Relations (2005) Council on Foreign Relations Conference on the Global Threat of Pandemic Influenza, Session 1: Avian flu – where do we stand? Transcript, www.cfr.org/publication/9230/council_on_foreign_relations_conference_on_the_global_threat_of_pandemic_infl uenza_session_1.html, last accessed January 3, 2013.
67 Article reproduced at www.organicconsumers.org/Toxic/ecoli0702.cfm, last accessed January 3, 2013.
68 DOJ (United States Department of Justice) (2006) "Agroterrorism – why we're not ready," DOJ, Washington, DC, www.ncjrs.gov/pdffiles1/nij/214752.pdf, last accessed January 3, 2013, p. 1.
69 Sones, K. (2006) "Global trade in livestock: Benefits and risks to developing countries," *New Agriculturalist*, May, www.new-ag.info/focus/focusItem.php?a=1157, last accessed January 3, 2013.

70 WHO (2007) "The world health report 2007: A safer future – a global public health security in the twenty-first century," WHO, Geneva, Switzerland, p. 30.
71 Wang, B. (2010) "Free antibiotics hurt patients," *The Daily Targum*, September 26, www.dailytargum.com/opinions/free-antibiotics-hurt-patients-1.2343092, last accessed January 3, 2013.
72 FAO (2006) "Livestock's long shadow: Environmental issues and problems," Food and Agriculture Organization of the United Nations, Rome, Italy, www.fao.org/docrep/010/a0701e/a0701e00.HTM, last accessed July 22, 2013.
73 Pelletier, Nathan and Peter Tyedmers (2010) "Forecasting potential global environmental costs of livestock production, 2000–2050," *PNAS*, 107(43), pp. 18371–4.
74 Daley, C., A. Abbott, P.S. Doyle, G.A. Nader, and S. Larson (2010) "A review of fatty acid profiles and antioxidant content in grass-fed and grain-fed beef," *Nutritional Journal*, 9(10), pp. 1–12, p. 5.
75 Greger, M. (2007) "The long haul: Risks associated with livestock transport," *Biosecurity and Bioterrorism*, 5(4), pp. 301–11, p. 305.
76 Ibid.
77 Costa, L. (2009) "Short-term stress: The case of transport and slaughter," *Italian Journal of Animal Science*, 8(1), pp. 241–52, p. 241.
78 Mitloehner, F. and M. Schenker (2007) "Environmental exposure and health effects from concentrated animal feeding operations," *Epidemiology*, 18(3), pp. 309–11.
79 Donham, K., S. Wing, D. Osterberg, J. Flora, C. Hodne, K. Thu, and P. Thorne (2007) "Community health and socioeconomic issues surrounding concentrated animal feeding operations," *Environmental Health Perspectives*, 115(2), pp. 317–20.
80 Van Der Hoek, W., F. Konradsen, K. Athukorala, and T. Wanigadewa (1998) "Pesticide poisoning: A major health problem in Sri Lanka," *Social Science and Medicine*, 46(4), pp. 495–504.
81 Wesseling, C., L. Castillo, and C. Elinder (1993) "Pesticide poisonings in Costa Rica," *Scandinavian Journal of Work, Environment and Health*, 19(4), pp. 227–35; Garming, H. and H. Waibel (2009) "Pesticides and farmer health in Nicaragua: A willingness-to-pay approach to evaluation," *The European Journal of Health Economics*, 10(2), pp. 125–33.
82 Williamson, S. (2005) "Breaking the barriers to IPM in Africa: Evidence from Benin, Ethiopia, Ghana, and Senegal," in *The Pesticide Detox*, edited by J. Pretty (London: Earthscan), pp. 165–80.
83 See, for example, Harrison, Jill (2011) *Pesticide Drift and the Pursuit of the Environmental Justice Movement* (Cambridge, MA: MIT Press).
84 Liu, Yvonne, and Dominique Apollon (2011) *The Color of Food* (New York: Applied Research Center).
85 Domina, D. and C.R. Taylor (2010) "The debilitating effects of concentration markets affecting agriculture," *Drake Journal of Agricultural Law*, 15(1), pp. 61–108.
86 Carolan (2012), p. 106.
87 Donham *et al.* (2007).
88 Mirabelli M., S. Wing, S. Marshall, and T. Wilcosky (2006) "Asthma symptoms among adolescents who attend public schools that are located near confined swine feeding operations," *Pediatrics*, 118(1), pp. 66–75.
89 Wright, Wynne, Cornelia Flora, Kathy Kremer, Willis Goudy, Clare Hinrichs, Paul Lasley, Ardith Maney, Margaret Kronma, Hamilton Brown, Kenneth Pigg, Beverly Duncan, Jean Coleman, and Debra Morse (2001) "Technical work paper on social and community impacts," prepared for the Generic Environmental Impact Statement on Animal Agriculture and the Minnesota Environmental Quality Board.

90 Lobao, Linda and Curtis Stofferahn (2008) "The community effects of industrialized farming: Social science research and challenges to corporate farming laws," *Agriculture and Human Values*, 25(2), pp. 219–40.
91 Tegtmeier, E. and M. Duffy (2004) "External costs of agricultural productivity in the United States," *International Journal of Agricultural Sustainability*, 2, pp. 1–20.
92 Pretty, J., A. Ball, T. Lang, and J. Morison (2005) "Farm costs and food miles: An assessment of the full cost of the UK weekly food basket," *Food Policy*, 30, pp. 1–19.
93 Pimentel, D. (2005) "Environmental and economic costs of the application of pesticides primarily in the United States," *Environment, Development and Sustainability*, 7, pp. 229–52.
94 Allsopp, M., W. de Lange, and R. Veldtman (2008) "Valuing insect pollination services with cost replacement," *PLoS One*, 3(9), pp. 1–8.
95 Pimentel (2005).
96 Allsopp *et al.* (2008).
97 Smith, P., D. Martino, Z. Cai, D. Gwary, H. Janzen, P. Kumar, B. McCarl, S. Ogle, F. O'Mara, C. Rice, B. Scholes, and O. Sirotenko (2007) "Agriculture," in *Climate Change 2007: Mitigation. Contribution of Working Group III to the Fourth Assessment Report of the Intergovernmental Panel on Climate Change*, edited by B. Metz, O.R. Davidson, P.R. Bosch, R. Dave, and L.A. Meyer (Cambridge and New York: Cambridge University Press), www.ipcc.ch/publications_and_data/ar4/wg3/en/ch8.html, last accessed January 4, 2013.
98 Bellarby J., B. Foereid, A. Hastings, and P. Smith (2008) *Cool Farming: Climate Impacts of Agriculture and Mitigation Potential* (Amsterdam: Greenpeace International).
99 Smith *et al.* (2007).
100 Buzby, Jean and Jeffrey Hyman (2012) "Total and per capita value of food loss in the United States," *Food Policy*, 37, pp. 561–70.
101 Hall, K., J. Guo, M. Dore, and C. Chow (2009) "The progressive increase of food waste in America and its environmental impact," *PLoS One*, 4(1), pp. 1–6.
102 Cuéllar, A. and M. Weber (2010) "Wasted food, wasted energy: The embedded energy in food waste in the United States," *Environmental Science and Technology*, 44 (16), pp. 6464–9.
103 Gooch, M., A. Felfel, and N. Marenick (2010) "Food waste in Canada," George Morris Center, University of Guelph, Guelph, Canada, www.vcmtools.ca/pdf/Food%20Waste%20in%20Canada%20120910.pdf, last accessed January 4, 2013.
104 Desrochers, P. and H. Shimizu (2008) "Yes, we have no bananas: A critique of the 'food miles' perspective," Policy Primer No 8, Mercatus Center, George Mason University, Washington, DC.
105 Mukherji, B. and B. Pattanayak (2011) "New Delhi starts drive to root out hunger," *Wall Street Journal*, June 8, http://online.wsj.com/article/SB10001424052702304259304576372813010336844.html, last accessed January 4, 2013.
106 Xin, Z., W. Kaihao, and C. Anqi (2012) "Waste not, want not," *China Daily*, www.chinadaily.com.cn/cndy/2012-01/19/content_14472383.htm, last accessed January 4, 2013.
107 Hou, Lisa (2013) "You waste, you pay," *Common Wealth: English Edition*, April 11, http://english.cw.com.tw/article.do?action=show&id=14131, last accessed April 30, 2013.
108 Venkat, K. (2011) "The climate change and economic impacts of food waste in the United States," *International Journal of Food System Dynamics*, 2(4), pp. 431–46.

Part II

Cheap economies and communities

Chapter 5

The real cost of automobiles and car-munities

"If people didn't want to drive they won't. People choose to use their car because it's the cheapest, most efficient mode of transportation out there. Period!" It was the spring of 2012 and I was conducting a focus group on public perceptions of electric, hybrid, and biofuel-powered automobiles. About halfway through our session, conversation steered to the very premise of alternative fuels and whether this framing, as a solution to things like climate change, peak oil, and energy dependence, inadvertently (or perhaps advertently) keeps us from searching for viable alternatives to fuel. Not long thereafter two participants starting criticizing what one referred to as our "auto-centric culture," evoking the wrath of another seated at the table. According to this individual, to criticize the car is to criticize democracy itself: "We vote with our pocketbooks and with our feet in the United States and in either case the choice is clear: we've chosen the car." The unexpected outburst ended with the words that open this chapter.

These sentiments are far from novel. I hear them all the time. The logic is so simple it is easy to be seduced into accepting its conclusion – that cars are handily winning the vote in the democracy that is the market – as valid. People are not mindless dolts. The car is the dominant mode of transportation in most parts of the world. Hence: people are willfully choosing the car. This is why it is important to look for the general in the particular. If you look at individuals in asocial isolation you see one thing: people autonomously selecting automobility over the alternatives. But there is a problem with this perspective. And it is a big one. We are not asocial. We do not live in a vacuum. We are social creatures, who shape, *and who are shaped by*, the world within which we are embedded. Once you understand this, the aforementioned logical house of cards comes tumbling down.

For markets to do their thing, which is to efficiently allocate resources, price needs to accurately represent the actual – which is to say *total* – costs associated with any decision. Accurate price signals ensure that neither over-spending nor under-spending on resources occurs. When accurate prices are not charged we have what is called a market failure. Market failures describe situations where the so-called invisible hand fails to allocate resources in a socially desirable manner that maximizes aggregate well-being. Leaving aside for later chapters the fact that most (all?) of today's markets are failed ones – after all, today's economy actively encourages the socialization of costs – the focus of this chapter will be on the various distorted signals that underlie decisions about whether or not to drive. Drivers, as I will show, are paying for a fraction of one percent of the real cost of the cars they drive. That is not a market failure. That is market malpractice.

A Mercedes in everyone's garage

The AAA's (formally known as the American Automobile Association) annually-calculated "Your Driving Costs" places the average yearly cost to own and operate a car in the United States at US$8,946. That breaks down to 59.6 cents per mile based on 15,000 miles of driving per year (roughly the distance driven annually by the average American).[1] This calculation assumes full ownership of the automobile so it does not include the interest paid by those making monthly car payments. When I ask students to name the largest out-of-pocket cost of their automobile the first thing that comes most often to mind is fuel. But according to the AAA, fuel costs make up only 24 percent of the US$8,946 (or US$2,130). Other figures going into the AAA's annual calculation include tire, depreciation, maintenance, and insurance costs.

There are roughly two vehicles and two licensed drivers per household in the United States.[2] That means each US household, according to the AAA, spends on average US$17,892 annually to drive a car. The median household income in 2011 was US$50,054.[3] Therefore the average household in the United States spends 36 percent of its annual income on automobiles – *36 percent*! And that only takes into account direct out-of-pocket expenses. Americans are also, on average, holding onto their vehicle 57 months (71.4 months for new vehicles and 49.9 months for used) before trading it in for something else – or just under five years.[4] In short, if you happen to be an "average American," you will have spent roughly US$89,460 (US$17,892 x 5) for those two cars in your garage by the time you get rid of them. That's the price of a luxury sedan.

The person that could walk faster than a car: YOU!

Mark Twain was a brilliant man, a gifted author, and an eloquent speaker. A shrewd business investor, however, he was not. That is at least what conventional wisdom tells us. Mr. Twain, you see, was the money behind the Paige Compositor, an invention developed by James W. Paige in the late 1800s. It was conceived to replace the human typesetter of a printing press with a mechanical arm thus making the printing process faster and, in the end, cheaper. Mark Twain invested US$300,000 (more than US$8 million today) in the failed venture, driving the Twain family to the brink of bankruptcy.[5]

The machine failed to sell because it required continuous adjustment. Mark Twain's favorable view of the machine was no doubt a product of choosing to focus on only those moments when the machine was working properly. Yet the immense complexity of the machine, and its 18,000 parts, meant that the adjustment process was a normal part of what it meant to be "working properly." After factoring in for all this downtime the Paige Compositor suddenly looked like an overpriced waste of time.

The automobile is our Paige Compositor and we are its Mark Twain. Sure, cars are all designed to travel at speeds in excess of 100 mph, far faster than what is possible on foot or bike. That is our Mark Twain moment, viewing the car's capabilities in abstraction. In the real world, however, there are stop lights, tight corners, speed limits, pedestrians, and, most significant of all, *traffic*. A "race" was held in New York in 2008 between a bike, car, and bus/subway to see who could cover the 4.5 miles from Brooklyn's Fort Greene to Manhattan's Union Square the fastest. The bicycle won handily, taking just over 16 minutes to finish the trip; the car took 22 minutes; and the public transit rider, 29 minutes. The carbon footprint of each was also calculated: the bike came in at zero; the transit rider, one pound; and the car, six pounds. I am sure many of us can relate to the outcome of this race, particularly in light of these statistics: 25 percent of all trips by automobile are made within a mile of the home; 40 percent of all trips by automobile are made within two miles of the home; 50 percent of the working population commutes five miles or less to work.[6] I know I can. I live about a mile from where I work. By car the commute can be as long as 15 minutes, especially when factoring in time spent looking for a place to park. By bike: three minutes. Even though experience ought to tell them otherwise, research indicates that the public often overestimates the financial and time costs of alternative modes of transportation while simultaneously underestimating those associated with the automobile.[7]

This brings me to what is known as "effective speed."[8] Effective speed is, in some respects, calculated very conventionally: speed equals distance divided by time. The novelty lies in the fact that *all* time costs are considered. For car drivers, a significant – though typically invisible – time cost is the time spent at work to earn the money to pay for all the aforementioned expenses associated with this very costly mode of transportation. Key variables needed to calculate effective speeds for any mode of transportation are average trip speed; the direct and indirect costs of the mode of transportation; the average income of the population (which determines how much time is devoted to earning the money to pay the costs); and any other time devoted to the mode of transportation besides travel (such as time spent filling a vehicle with fuel).

The ideas behind effective speed have been around some time. As Paul Tranter, one of the concept's main champions, points out, its spirit goes back to at least Henry David Thoreau. In *Walden*, first published in 1854, Thoreau compares his own speed with that of a fellow traveler who plans to go by train to a nearby town:

> I start now on foot, and get there before the night. You will in the meanwhile have earned your fare, and arrive there some time tomorrow, or possibly this evening, if you are lucky enough to get a job in season. Instead of going to Fitchburg, you will be working here the greater part of the day. And so, if the railroad reached around the world, I think that I should keep ahead of you.[9]

These thoughts were echoed, though cast in terms more likely to resonate with contemporary readers, over a century later (in 1974) by Ivan Illich in *Energy and Equity*.[10] "The typical American male devotes more than 1,600 hours a year to his car," Illich wrote, at a time when, it is worth noting, we drove considerably less.

> He sits in it while it goes and while it stands idling. He parks it and searches for it. He earns the money to put down on it and to meet the monthly installments. He works to pay for petrol, tolls, insurance, taxes and tickets. He spends four of his sixteen waking hours on the road or gathering his resources for it.[11]

And this time, Illich continues:

> does not take into account the time consumed by other activities dictated by transport: time spent in hospitals, traffic courts and garages, time spent watching automobile commercials or attending consumer education meetings to improve the quality of the next buy. The model American puts in 1,600 hours to get 7,500 miles: less than five miles per hour.[12]

Recent research has looked at effective speeds of cyclists in different cities, calculating how slow cyclists could travel and still be effectively faster than a car.[13] If only out-of-pocket costs are considered, then the fastest that a cyclist would need to travel, among the cities studied, would be 13.3 mph in Canberra, Australia; the slowest, 1.9 mph, in Nairobi, Kenya. (The car's near-standstill effective speed in Kenya is largely a product of the country's abysmally low average income which makes car ownership a very time-consuming activity.) If external costs are also considered, cyclists in Canberra would need to average only 11.3 mph to be faster than a car driver. In New York, Los Angeles, Tokyo, and Hamburg cyclists would not need to travel faster than 8 mph to outrun an automobile.

The idea of effective speed points to a "speed paradox" of sorts when it comes to the motor vehicle: the "faster" one tries to go with this mode of transportation the slower it becomes. Increasing trip speeds has little impact on effective speed because the main time cost is not driving but the time spent earning money to pay for the costs of driving. Indeed, driving faster could further reduce effective speed by causing those costs to go up, such as by reducing gas mileage, increasing the rate of tire wear, and perhaps even resulting in a costly accident. There is also little that governments can do to reduce the car's effective speed. The costs of building wider roads, for instance, more than offset any reductions in travel time. In fact, the data supporting what is known as the fundamental law of road congestion quite convincingly demonstrate that more roads lead to more traffic and in the end *increased* road congestion.[14] After converting these immense costs to a time measure – costs that are paid for by taxpayers – we find the effective speed of automobiles to be further slowed.

And we have yet to even start talking about the car's exponentially larger costs to public health and the environment; costs so large they cannot be worked off in a lifetime. In other words, from an effective speed standpoint, when *all* costs of the car are tallied this mode of transportation not only places us at a standstill but future generations as well.

Costs to public health and the environment

In the time it takes to read this chapter 75 people from around the world will have lost their lives in a road traffic crash (assuming one reads straight through and at a pace of about 300 words per minute). That adds up to more than 1.3 million fatalities annually.[15] Let me put this into some perspective. The World Health Organization (WHO) estimates that smoking kills about five million people per year. This figure includes the more than 600,000 non-smokers who will die from exposure to second-hand smoke.[16] But there are approximately 1.3 billion smokers worldwide, compared to fewer than 650 million licensed drivers. (While there are about one billion registered cars in the world there are numerous countries – like the United States – that have far more vehicles than operators.[17]) Vehicles are the leading cause of death in the United States among ages 5 to 34. This is not too far off from global fatality statistics, as road crashes are the leading cause of death worldwide from ages 15 to 29 and the second leading cause of death from ages 5 to 14.[18] While road traffic injuries are currently the tenth leading cause of death worldwide the WHO estimates that by 2030 that ranking will be fifth.[19] In light of these statistics health professionals are starting to question, quoting the title of a recent article in the *Journal of Public Health*, "are cars the new tobacco?"[20]

Those of us living in high-income countries can perhaps be partially forgiven for not fully appreciating the carnage brought on by car accidents. In countries like the United States, fatalities are decreasing. For instance, in 2003 there were a total of 42,643 deaths. This number decreased to 33,808 by 2008. Yet even this represents a cost we cannot afford, after all we are talking about lives lost which is an incalculable cost that you cannot put a price on. Though some have tried: these fatalities, when combined with the roughly three million car-related injuries total costs (deaths plus injuries), approximate roughly 2.5 percent of the US national GDP.[21] The risk of dying on the road is considerably higher in low and middle-income countries, where fatality rates lie somewhere between 21.5 and 19.5 (per 100,000), respectively. In high-income countries, the rate is 10.3 (per 100,000). This disparity explains why more than 90 percent of the world's road fatalities occur in less affluent countries, even though they have only 48 percent of the world's registered vehicles.[22]

While the equivalent of a 9/11 is happening almost every month in the United States at the wheels of the automobile some countries are experiencing all-out war on their roads. In Vietnam, for instance, more than 4,000 children die in traffic accidents a year – or 11 a day.[23] That is a death rate approaching estimates of children killed every year during the Vietnam War (or the American War, for those living in Vietnam). These already-stark differences between countries, in terms of road fatalities, are only becoming amplified. From 1975 to the turn of the century car-fatality rates in Canada and the United States declined by 63 percent and 27 percent, respectively, while China's rate increased by 234 percent and Botswana's by 383 percent.[24] And we can only assume that these asymmetries are in actuality greater than the statistics depict, as we know that underreporting – of basically everything – is endemic in poorer countries.

Who are these people dying and being injured on the world's roads? That depends on where in the world we direct our gaze. In the United States and Canada, for instance, 65 percent of reported road deaths involve vehicle occupants. Conversely, in low- and middle-income countries of the Western Pacific Region (one of the six regions according to the WHO), 70 percent of reported road fatalities are among what are known as "vulnerable road users," namely, pedestrians, children, cyclists, and users of motorized two-wheel vehicles.[25] Looking specifically at pedestrians: while accounting for 12 percent of road traffic deaths in the United States they constitute 50 percent, 45 percent, and 35 percent in Ethiopia, Kenya, and Malawi, respectively. While only adults drive, the automobile does not discriminate according to age. A quarter of traffic-related pedestrian deaths in the United States occur among children up to the age of 14.[26] Among children aged from 5 through 14, the vehicle crash death rate is more than five times that of drowning, the second most common cause of unintentional injury.[27]

When looking for ways to reduce these car-related fatality rates we have to be careful not to merely be substituting one lethal problem for another. For example, the rate of pedestrian injury and death has decreased in recent decades among Mexican adolescents. Yet research indicates this is largely due to an overall decrease in general physical activity compared to previous generations.[28] In other words, children are being pushed out of the street to make way for the car. The problem, however, is that without alternative safe outdoor play spaces children are heading indoors in droves. Death by car or by social media, cheap food, and inactivity? In many instances the latter is merely being substituted for the former.

What do the data say on this point? Are cars making us fat? While drawing a direct causal link between car prevalence in a society and obesity rates is next to impossible ("correlation does not imply causality," as I repeatedly tell my students), the evidence pointing to a correlation between the two is overwhelming. One study found that each additional kilometer walked per day lowers an individual's likelihood of becoming obese by 4.8 percent, whereas each additional hour spent in a car per day is associated with a six percent increase in obesity.[29] Another study examining urban sprawl in US metropolitan areas between 1970 and 2000 calculates that had those areas held to 1970 levels of urban density then rates of obesity would be 13 percent lower than what they are at the present.[30]

Obesity and road accidents and fatalities are not our only public health concerns attributable to the automobile. There is also a growing stack of studies pointing to a positive association between exposure to road traffic and aircraft noise and high blood pressure and heart disease, including myocardial infarction (aka heart attacks).[31] The WHO recently calculated disability-adjusted life-years (DALYs) due to noise pollution for all of Europe, recognizing that the majority of the noise comes from road traffic and airplanes. According to the WHO, DALYs is "the sum of years of potential life lost due to premature mortality and the years of productive life lost due to disability."[32] It was estimated that DALYs lost in Europe from environmental noise equated to 61,000 years for ischemic heart disease, 45,000 years for cognitive impairment of children, 903,000 years for sleep disturbance, 22,000 years for tinnitus, and 654,000 years for annoyance. In total, more than one million healthy life years are lost annually in Europe due to automobile and airplane noise.[33]

Maybe cars really are the new tobacco and car exhaust the new second-hand smoke. Thanks to high levels of smog, merely living in any of Spain's major metropolitan areas — such as Madrid, Barcelona, and Seville — has an equivalent negative effect on one's lungs as smoking half a pack of cigarettes a day.[34] Researchers at the University of California Berkeley School of Public Health found that a child riding inside any one of the state's 25,000 diesel school buses may be exposed to up to four times the level of toxic diesel exhaust as someone riding in a car in front of it.[35] We also know that living in proximity to a major roadway increases one's risk of acquiring a respiratory disease. One study looking at communities in Southern California found that children living within a quarter of a mile of a freeway had an 89 percent greater risk of developing asthma than those who lived a mile away.[36]

Just 1 percent of China's 560 million urban dwellers breathe air considered safe by European Union (EU) standards. The United States has determined as unsafe any reading above 40 micrograms of particulate matter (fine dust, soot, and aerosol particles) less than 10 microns in diameter. At this diameter, particles can pass through the throat and nose and enter the lungs. After being inhaled, they can affect the heart and lungs and cause serious health problems.

98 Cheap economies and communities

In 2006, Beijing's average (of particulate matter less than 10 microns in diameter) was 141 micrograms.[37] The World Bank calculated that outdoor air pollution in China was so extreme that it is prematurely killing 350,000 to 400,000 city dwellers *annually*.[38] While China clearly has an industrial pollution problem – being the world's leading producer and consumer of coal doesn't help – the report also implicates automobile emissions; a level of culpability that will only increase as half of the global growth in auto production in 2012 was attributed to rising demand in this single country.[39]

Then there is climate change, arguably the largest public (and environmental) health threat of all. According to the US Environmental Protection Agency, roughly 20 percent of total US emissions of CO_2 are from passenger vehicles, namely, cars and light trucks.[40] Yet this is only the tip of the tailpipe. Lest we forget, cars do not exist in a socio-technical vacuum. A life cycle analysis of energy consumption and emissions linked to parking infrastructure is revealing, as it shows a truer picture of the car's ecological footprint – after all, if there were no cars there would be no need for parking. Specifically, this study conducted an inventory of greenhouse gases, carbon monoxide (CO), sulfur dioxide (SO_2), mono-nitrogen oxides (NO_x), volatile organic compounds (VOCs), and PM10 (PM: particulate matter) from the point of raw material extraction, to transport, asphalt and concrete production, construction, and maintenance for the hundreds of millions of parking spaces in the United States. (This was arguably a conservative analysis as it did not include the ubiquitous home driveway and garage.) The authors found that total energy consumption for cars increased 65 percent while total greenhouse gas emissions increased 61 percent, compared to the levels when just the automobile's life cycle was examined.[41]

The car was initially praised by public health officials and politicians for saving early-twentieth-century urban dwellers from a major environmental ill, specifically, the horse manure that at the time blanketed city streets. It is a bitter irony that the very thing initially heralded for its positive public health "benefits" would eventually be responsible for a level of environmental havoc that makes the previous problem quaint by comparison. In retrospect, I think we would all have been better off with the manure.

They paved paradise and put up a parking lot[42]

To drive or not to drive? That all depends on whether there is a place to park. At the present moment, there are places; plenty in fact and most of them "free." Estimates place the total number of parking spaces in the United States at between 500 million and 2 billion – again, *just in the United States*.[43] Wide discrepancies in such estimates are inevitable, as a "parking space" can be defined and measured in a variety of different ways. Does one look at only off-street parking or should all on-street parking also be included in this calculation? What about temporary event parking, such as large grassy fields and open gravel lots located next to stadiums? And what about private driveways and the country's millions of attached and detached garages? The more you say "yes" to these questions the closer you get to that two billion figure.

Some brave soul actually tried to put a price tag on all these spaces. According to their calculation, the total subsidy in the United States for off-street parking in 2002 was as much as US$374 billion. US taxpayers are paying more than a third of a trillion dollars a year so folks in that country can park for free. And, again, this figure does not even take into consideration the millions of (mostly free) miles of on-street parking. That comes out to be more than the US government (in 2002) spent on either Medicare (US $231 million) or national defense (US$349 million).[44] There were roughly 190 million licensed drivers in the United States in 2002. That US$374 billion translates into a US$2,000 government handout to each registered driver in the country.

The world-renowned twentieth-century architect and planner Victor Gruen estimated back in the 1960s that every car in the United States has at least one parking space at home (today the figure is more than two) and three or four more lying elsewhere in reserve.[45] Among that standing reserve, at least one is at work. Nationwide, 95 percent of all commuters park free at their place of employment.[46] It has been estimated that "free" parking reduces the cost of commuting by car by 71 percent.[47] In light of such overwhelming incentives to drive, we can see how driving a car is, for many, about as much of a "choice" as doing taxes.

This automobile welfare – we might as well call it what it is – is rooted in our understanding of "proper" land use planning. Federal, state, and local government tax policies are often biased in favor of vehicle use. For example, fuel is exempt from general taxes in many jurisdictions, land devoted to public roads and parking facilities is exempt from rent and taxes, and fuel (and bio-fuel) producers are showered with significant tax exemptions and subsidies.[48] Large taxpayer-funded roads represent a significant portion of land that cannot be taxed, while being of benefit primarily to private motorists. Similarly, private lands are typically taxed at a lower rate when paved over to make a parking lot.[49] Many current zoning codes also favor automobile-oriented land-use patterns, which include things like density restrictions, single-use zoning, and, yes, minimum parking requirements.[50] You read that right: thanks to existing zoning codes it is essentially *illegal* to make mixed-use walkable communities and to not provide free parking. The result is a self-fulfilling prophecy: more car-oriented land use and reduced travel alternatives lead to more driving and more socialized costs.

Below are some other costs not included in that US$374 billion a year figure.

- Environmental: a one-acre paved parking lot produces roughly 16 times the volume of runoff compared to a similarly sized meadow.[51] Moreover, as that runoff flows across a paved automobile-driven surface water

temperature rises and pollutants, such as oil and metals, are carried into waterways threatening the health of the watershed.
- Heat: the term urban jungle is apt as parking lots can get hot – *really* hot. The temperature of the paved surface itself can be 68 to 104°F (20 to 40°C) higher than a vegetated surface in the same location.[52] This "heat island effect" can also produce differences in evening temperatures between city and the countryside, as this solar energy is released back into the atmosphere – a difference in atmospheric temperatures as high as 22°F (12°C).[53] Heat islands increase summertime peak energy demands, air-conditioning costs, greenhouse gas emissions, and heat-related illness and mortality.
- Energy (lighting) costs: the land of the never setting sun. The fact that parking lots are always lit (sometimes even more brightly at night than during the day) means they consume tremendous amounts of energy. And now the light itself is being defined as a pollutant: light pollution.

As any economist will tell you, when calculating the costs of a given decision we also have to include what was sacrificed by not going with the next best alternative – what is known in economic parlance as opportunity costs. Typically, opportunity costs are measured very myopically, in very short and easily monetized terms. Which is why, for instance, there are density restrictions, single-use zoning, and, yes, minimum parking requirements. That is because the opportunity cost of not having free parking is not having as many people on the road, which has mistakenly been viewed as a bad thing as far as "development" and "progress" are concerned. As a sociologist I tend to view opportunity costs more broadly, which is why I prefer the term social opportunity costs. Social opportunity costs take into consideration the resources – social and material – used to produce a particular good or service, recognizing that they are no longer available for other purposes. When thinking about the social opportunity costs of parking spaces – two billion of them! – we are not only talking about the actual materials used to construct and maintain them, though these by themselves are significant. We also need to think about all the other socially valuable things that this space could be were it not a well-lit, impervious, oil-covered concrete jungle: think playgrounds, urban gardens, pedestrian walkways, and bike paths. Food for thought: if we were to cover those two billion parking spaces with solar panels they could generate around 50 billion kWh per day. That is enough electricity to power 50 billion US households for one month.[54] Or if we instead covered that area with trees we would remove 10,086,440 metric tons of CO_2 per year.[55] While that is only a fraction of the more than one billion metric tons of CO_2 that global vehicle transport emits each year, we cannot forget that by removing off-street parking we would also greatly disincentivize car use. Thus, while growing (literally) world CO_2 sink capacity by replacing off-street parking with trees we could also expect a tremendous decrease in CO_2 emissions due to people driving less.

The costs of car-munity

I will admit this much: urban (and certainly rural) environments are such that we often need vehicles like the car to get around. In places such as Los Angeles or Mexico City one would have to be extremely brave (perhaps even suicidal) to travel great distances by, say, bike. In the small rural town in Iowa where I grew up (population 350), which is 15 miles from the nearest "city" and its 12,000 people, the car is the only transportation option for those looking to venture beyond its borders (though I have known of the occasional tractor being used for this end). Yet while conventional wisdom sees in this admission a rationale for more cars, roads, and parking spaces I see just the opposite. The reason for my position is quite simple. Urban and community patterns have taken the shape they have in large part *because of* available transportation systems. The automobile made certain patterns of urbanization possible; patterns that, not surprisingly, are found today to be difficult to service under alternative transportation forms. So while many would like us to think that the car's rise is the outcome of consumer democracy – where you vote with your wallet – an honest look at history shows that the "election" was rigged. After all, the question we are essentially voting on is "What mode of transportation would you choose in a society that's specifically designed for the automobile?" So what are the types of urban environments produced by the automobile and what are their associated costs? In answering this question we find that the communities made in the car's shadow – these *car*-munities – are incredibly expensive, in terms of their cost to human well-being, social cohesion, and, even, democracy itself.

Writers, academics, and activists have been critical of the car's social impact for decades. For example, Jane Jacobs, author of *The Death and Life of Great American Cities*, argued repeatedly that we are building cities for cars rather than for people and passionately noted the consequences of this choice.[56] Standing on the shoulders of these earlier critics, scholars today have at their disposal new data that even hard-headed, pro-automobile empiricists cannot ignore. "Show me the evidence that cars are bad for community," they would demand. Now we can oblige.

An obvious place to start is with Robert Putman's famous book *Bowling Alone*.[57] While empirically compelling, this book, perhaps more than any other in recent years, got the public talking and thinking about how things like sprawl and long commutes negatively impact community. One of Putman's conclusions: "the car and the commute ... are demonstrably bad for community life." He goes on by explaining that "each additional ten minutes in daily [car] commuting time cuts involvement in community affairs by ten percent – fewer public meetings attended, fewer committees chaired, fewer petitions signed, fewer church services attended, less volunteering, and so on."[58]

Putman's conclusions have fared well in light of more recent research. High dependence on the automobile is positively associated, at statistically significant levels, with weakened neighborhood social ties.[59] We know that the emotional and intellectual development of children is enhanced in more walkable, mixed-use communities, most likely due to a combination of increased opportunities for physical activity, independence, and community cohesion.[60] Automobile dependence is also shown to have a strong negative impact on whether an individual visits friends or participates in out-of-home sports and cultural activities and a positive effect on in-home (and largely asocial) "activities" like watching television and playing video games.[61]

A particularly extensive study to examine the links between automobile use and community health comes out of Harvard University's Department of Government.[62] Based on approximately 30,000 interviews from 40 different US geographical settings, this research paints a clear picture of the car's costs to civic disengagement and community cohesion more generally. The following are just some of the findings to come out of this extensive dataset.

- The lower the percentage of solo commuters in one's ZIP code the more likely an individual is to belong to a political organization, attend a partisan political meeting, attend a demonstration, sign a petition, or vote.
- Living in a high-density area is a positive predictor of membership in a political organization, attendance at demonstrations, and signing a petition (even after controlling for central-city residence status and an individual's interest in politics).
- Residence in a very high density area is associated with membership in a local reform group.
- Residents of neighborhoods built before 1950 (which is a strong predictor of being a walkable neighborhood) are significantly more likely to belong to a political organization, attend a partisan political event, attend a march or demonstration, vote in a national election, or attend a public meeting (even after controlling for central-city residence status).
- A long commute is a strong predictor of having a reduced number of friends and a low attendance at public meetings and a modest predictor of reduced social trust and reduced membership in groups.
- Neighborhood-level (ZIP code) commuting time is a strong predictor of reduced social trust and even a stronger predictor than individual commuting time (if your neighbors are stuck in traffic every day the fact that your commute is short isn't going to do much to increase your social interaction with them).
- Commuting time is inversely associated with an individual's subjective levels of personal happiness as well as their levels of happiness toward their community.

In light of these findings, the study's author explains that "there is good reason, from a civic point of view, to encourage forms of community design that reduce commuting time and to encourage the preservation and increased livability of both our older neighborhoods and our central cities." Yet, in the end, "the biggest payoff, at least from a political participation point of view, appears to be in getting Americans out of their cars".[63]

And the total is ...

Conventional economic theory wants us to believe that recent urban development patterns are the result of market forces and are therefore natural, inevitable, and, because there is a tinge of religiosity in free-market doctrine, good. The argument goes something like this: sprawl is driven by rising real incomes and decreasing transportation costs, which have allowed households and places of work and play to be located farther apart, typically resulting in more land consumed per capita the further one gets from central cities. "Thus," to quote Samuel Staley, a well-known cheerleader of market-based societies, "markets transform land from one use to another using the price system to guide buyers and sellers."[64] Unfortunately, Staley fails to mention that the pricing system is more distorting than the mirrors in a fun house. The travel costs alone of commuting 31 miles (each way) have been calculated to be about US$10,000 annually.[65] I can think of quite a few households where both adults commute at least that distance. That is US$20,000 a year. If they are living where they are merely to access cheaper housing they would be better off moving to the community where they work allowing them to spend more time at home with family and friends. At today's low interest rates, that US$20,000 a year could buy them roughly US$200,000 of an additional mortgage. If the pricing system really worked I doubt so many people would be sitting idly watching (and smelling) much of their savings go up in exhaust fumes.

Cheaponomics proponents like Staley are correct in saying that the price of transportation is decreasing but its *costs* most assuredly are not. The price is also terribly wrong when it comes to land, though you would never know it reading the writings of sprawl apologists. Jan K. Brueckner, Professor of Economics at the University of California, writes:

> Concerns about loss of "scarce" farmland, often enunciated by critics of sprawl, are also misplaced. Because the value of farm output is fully reflected in the amount that agricultural users are willing to pay for the land, a successful bid by urban users means that society values the houses and other structures built on the land more than the farm output that is forgone. If farmland became truly scarce and in need of preservation its selling price would be high, making the land resistant to urban encroachment.[66]

There are a number of problems with this statement. First, individual consumer decisions, even in the aggregate, do not equate to statements of what society values. If they did, society could only value things that could be monetized and commodified. What an unfortunate world it would be if that were true, as most of the things that we really value cannot be imprinted with a price tag – precisely because they are so valuable to us! That is why markets, when left to their own devices, do a terrible job at recognizing *social* value. The market price for a pickup load of logs, for example, says absolutely nothing about the value they had in a previous life for things like flood control, water purification, habitat, and carbon sinking. As William Rees, founding member and former president of the Canadian Society for Ecological Economics, correctly points out, "This is why the consumer purchasing a board foot of lumber – or just about anything else – doesn't come close to paying the full social cost of production."[67]

When we chop down trees and pave over farmland to build suburbs and additional roads societal value is lost. These costs are not reflected in the price of land. Moreover, there are many costs, as we have seen, that come with car-centric development that also go unaccounted for by the land-market: congestion, pollution, obesity, accidents, and the erosion of community and civic engagement, to name just a few.

Finally, in light of what was discussed in the previous chapter about cheap food, and having grown up in Iowa and seeing this happen first-hand, I must take particular issue with Brueckner's characterization of why farm land is lost to sprawl:

> Because the value of farm output is fully reflected in the amount that agricultural users are willing to pay for the land, a successful bid by urban users means that society values the houses and other structures built on the land more than the farm output that is forgone.[68]

Wrong. The pricing signals at work in the agrifood system – thanks to things like subsidies, cheap oil, and the increasingly empty nature of the calories produced – are as wildly distorted as those driving automobile-dependent sprawl. The agro-ecological value of farmland is incalculable. And because of that it is penalized in the marketplace by being woefully underpriced. Our only recourse, following conventional economic wisdom, is to cross our fingers and hope that substitutes will eventually be found for all those invaluable services lost due to sprawl.

I have avoided giving "grand totals" in this book, as doing so gives an answer to the wrong question. As I tell my students, "If they can get you asking the wrong questions, they don't have to worry about answers." The question is not "what is the correct price" because that assumes there is one. Yet in this case I will break that rule, as the total, if one were forced to play the pricing game, is so ridiculously high.

Mark Delucchi is a research scientist at the Institute of Transportation Studies at University of California, Davis. No one has spent more time trying to put an accurate price on our car-centric culture – an ambition culminating in a 21-volume, 2,000-plus page analysis of all of the social costs of motor-vehicle use in the United States.[69] This analysis factors in such things as pollution, negative impacts to human health, "free" parking, accidents, road congestion/delays, and the costs for building and maintaining infrastructure and the services to patrol it. While much of the analysis was conducted in the late 1990s the data are from 1991. Dr. Delucchi calculates that the total social cost of the automobile for Americans in 1991 was as high as US$3.3 trillion – the equivalent of roughly US$5.1 trillion in today's dollars (or one-third of the country's entire GDP). There were "only" 188 million registered vehicles on the road in the United States in 1991. Today, that figure exceeds 250 million, which means that the US$5.1 trillion figure is undoubtedly too low to accurately reflect present costs. If you think that number is absurdly high there is also an analysis by Todd Litman. Litman is the founder and Executive Director of the Victoria Transport Policy Institute and incidentally the person arguably in second place for spending the most amount of time calculating the real cost of the automobile. He has independently come up with a figure almost equally as mind-blowing: US$3.4 trillion.[70]

If we were to fold those costs into, for example, the price of gasoline, that works out to a tax of between US$25.40 per gallon (for the US$3.4 trillion figure) and US$38.10 per gallon (for the US$5.1 trillion figure).[71] In the end, the *actual* price is academic because it seeks to answer the wrong question. All we need to know is that the true costs of the automobile are high; too high for us to allow it to remain our dominant mode of transportation. Then there is the other side of the cost coin: social opportunity costs – aka opportunities missed. Think of all the things we could be doing if we were not paying those considerable socialized costs. Education, healthcare, poverty alleviation, eliminating hunger, adapting to and mitigating for climate change: you can do a lot with a couple trillion dollars.

Peak car and choosing choice

In the aggregate, the data indicate we have a long way to go in laying off the gas as it appears many countries are accelerating wildly. While few nations can compete with the United States as far as love of automobility is concerned, global trends suggest that others are on the verge of an elopement. Indeed, those same data indicate that drivers in the United States might be growing tired of this, up until now, largely monogamous relationship. Though the United States still has, by far, the most passenger cars, auto sales in China overtook those in the United States in 2011. In fact, the number of cars per 1,000 persons in the United States has been *declining* since 2006 – from 453 cars per 1,000 in 2006 to 423 cars per 1,000 in 2010 (I'll be returning to this point in a moment). Those countries accelerating include China (where the accelerator is poised against the floorboard), which saw its "cars per 1,000" figure increase from 18 in 2006 to 44 in 2010. That's more than a 100 percent increase in four years. Other nations racing alongside China include (based on 2006 to 2010 increases in cars per 1,000 people): Jordan, increasing from 87 to 123; Syria, from 18 to 36; Bulgaria, from 230 to 345; and Poland, from 351 to 451.[72] There remains one thing Americans apparently still love far more than any other nation: poor fuel economy – a particularly egregious example of cost socializing, as already detailed. Japan, the European Union, and India have far stricter limits on automobile carbon emissions than what's allowed in the United States. Even China: while car emission standards there are roughly the same as in the United States, after adding other light-duty vehicles Chinese standards are considerably better.[73]

So: trends, in the aggregate, are troubling. Yet there remain particular instances that should give us hope. Citizens in countries throughout Western Europe as well as in Japan and, increasingly, China, for example, have far more of a choice when it comes to selecting methods of mobility. They've accomplished this not by adopting policies that reject the car (as plainly evident with China) but by adopting policies that do *not* reject other methods, such as through subsidies for public transportation and by having dedicated cycling lanes; though it certainly doesn't hurt to also adopt policies that reduce the level of costs socialized by the automobile, like by eliminating "free" parking and by having higher gas taxes.

And what's this talk about "peak car" – a phenomenon taking place in the United States, UK, France, and New Zealand where car use is either flattening out or in decline?[74]

Importantly, according to these studies, trends predate 2008, so we can't explain them away with talk of the global recession. Rising fuel costs and road congestion are two explanations, but not the only ones. Other likely variables at work include stagnating wages among the middle class, growing income inequality, and increasing vehicle operating costs.[75] We also know that younger people today are less enamored with, and monogamous toward, private car ownership than generations past. One survey found that 46 percent of American drivers aged 18 to 24 said they would choose having access to the internet over owning a car.[76] The so-called Millennials, those born in the 1980s through the early 2000s, in particular, are logging fewer miles behind the wheel. They are also waiting longer before obtaining their driver's licenses and using alternative transportation more often.

Younger people are showing a greater desire to move back to urban centers where cars are increasingly a hindrance. In central London, for example, the average car speed is roughly ten miles per hour – the approximate speed of a running chicken! Experiencing first-hand the freedom of having a real choice in transportation (or at least more of a choice than those trapped in car-munity suburbia), these individuals are also privy to the benefits that come with having true alternatives to the automobile. Countries, for example, which have intentionally invested heavily in these alternatives, such as walking,

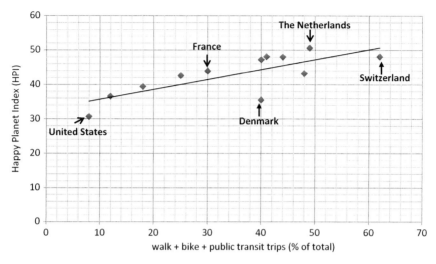

Figure 5.1 Relationship between Happy Planet Index and percent of total trips by walking, biking, or public transit for select high-income nations

cycling, and public transport, tend to score higher, as noted in Figure 5.1, on the Happy Planet Index (HPI) than those that do not.

The HPI is discussed in greater detail in Chapter 9. For the moment, it is only important to know that the HPI is a prosperity metric that takes into consideration a country's life expectancy at birth, general life satisfaction score, and ecological footprint. A high HPI score, in other words, reflects a society with high life expectancy, high life satisfaction, and low ecological footprint. While correlation does not equal causation, as statisticians are fond of saying, it sure is a hint. And one of the things hinted at by the figure is yet another cost of automobile dependency: reduced prosperity.

Notes

1 Pritchett, Ginnie (2012) "Cost of owning and operating vehicle in US increased 1.9 percent according to AAA's 2012 'Your Driving Costs' Study," AAA News Room, AAA, Orlando, FL, http://newsroom.aaa.com/2012/04/cost-of-owning-and-operating-vehicle-in-u-s-increased-1-9-percent-according-to-aaa%E2%80%99s-2012-%E2%80%98your-driving-costs%E2%80%99-study/, last accessed January 14, 2013.
2 US Department of Energy (2010) "Vehicles per household and other demographic statistics," US Department of Energy, Washington DC, April 12, www1.eere.energy.gov/vehiclesandfuels/facts/2010_fotw618.html, last accessed January 14, 2013.
3 Luhby, Tami (2012) "Median income falls, but so does poverty," *CNN Money*, September 12, http://money.cnn.com/2012/09/12/news/economy/median-income-poverty/index.html, last accessed January 14, 2013.
4 Kelly Blue Book (2012) "Average length of US vehicle ownership hit an all-time high," Kelly Blue Book, February 23, www.kbb.com/car-news/all-the-latest/average-length-of-us-vehicle-ownership-hit-an-all_time-high/2000007854/, last accessed Jsanuary 15, 2013.

5 The Mark Twain House and Museum (n.d.) www.marktwainhouse.org/museum/our_collection.php, last accessed January 15, 2013.
6 LAB (n.d.) *Ride for the Environment* (Washington, DC: League of American Bicyclists), www.bikeleague.org/resources/why/environment.php, last accessed January 15, 2013.
7 RACWA (2007) *Vehicle Running Costs*. (Perth, WA: Royal Automobile Club of WA), http://rac.com.au/go/motoring/buying-a-car/operating-costs, last accessed January 12, 2013.
8 This discussion draws heavily on Tranter, Paul (2012) "Effective speed: Cycling because it's 'faster'," in *City Cycling*, edited by John Pucher and Ralph Buehler (Cambridge, MA: MIT Press), pp. 57–74.
9 Walden, Henry David (1910) *Walden* (New York: Thomas T. Crowell and Company), p. 68.
10 Illich, Ivan (2000) *Energy and Equity* (New York: Marion Boyars Publishers).
11 Ibid., p. 18.
12 Ibid., pp. 18–19.
13 Tranter (2012).
14 Duranton, G. and M. Turner (2009) "The fundamental law of road congestion: Evidence from US cities," Cambridge, MA, National Bureau of Economic Research, NBER Working Paper no. 15376, September, www.nber.org /papers/w15376.pdf, last accessed January 15, 2013.
15 Douglas, Margaret, Stephen Watkins, Dermot Gorman, and Martin Higgins (2011) "Are cars the new tobacco?" *Journal of Public Health*, 33(2), pp. 160–9.
16 World Health Organization (2012) "Tobacoo, fact sheet number 339," World Health Organization, May, www.who.int/mediacentre/factsheets/fs339/en/index.html, last accessed January 17, 2013.
17 Short, John and Luis Pinet-Peralta (2010) "No accident: Traffic and pedestrians in the modern city," *Mobilities*, 5(1), pp. 41–59.
18 WHO (2009) "Global status report on road safety: Time for action" (Geneva: World Health Organization), http://whqlibdoc.who.int /publications /2009/9789241563840 eng.pdf, last accessed January 17, 2013.
19 Ibid.
20 Douglas *et al.* (2011).
21 Ibid.; Short and Pinet-Peralta (2010).
22 Carolan, Michael (2013) *Society and the Environment: Pragmatic Solutions to Ecological Issues* (Boulder: Westview Press).
23 Short and Pinet-Peralta (2010).
24 Peden, M., R. Scurfield, D. Sleet, D. Mohan, A. Hyder, E. Jarawan, and C. Mathers (2004) *World Report on Road Traffic Injury Prevention: Summary* (Geneva: World Health Organization).
25 WHO (2009).
26 Freeman, V., E. Shanahan, and P. Guild (2004) "Reducing mortality from motor-vehicle crashes for children 0 through 14 years of age: Success in New York and North Dakota," Cecil G. Sheps Center for Health Services Research, University of North Carolina at Chapel Hill, Chapel Hill, NC.
27 Short and Pinet-Peralta (2010).
28 Ibid.
29 Frank, L., M. Andresen, and T. Schmid (2004) "Obesity relationships with community design, physical activity, and time spent in cars," *American Journal of Preventative Medicine*, 27, pp. 87–96.
30 Zhaoa, Z. and R. Kaestnerb (2010) "Effects of urban sprawl on obesity," *Journal of Health Economics*, 29, pp. 779–87.

31 WHO (2011) "Burden of disease from environmental noise: Quantification of healthy life years lost in Europe" (Geneva: World Health Organization), www.euro.who.int/data/assets/pdffile/0008/136466/e94888.pdf, last accessed January 7, 2013.
32 WHO (n.d.b) "WHO definition of health" (Geneva: World Health Organization), www.who.int /about /definition /en /print.html, last accessed January 19, 2013.
33 WHO (2011).
34 Ham, Anthony (2006) "Spain chokes under grey beret," *The Age*, February 11, www.theage.com.au/news/world/spain-chokes-under-grey-beret/2006/02/10/1139542406209.html, last accessed January 18, 2013.
35 Solomon, Gina, Todd Campbell, Gail Ruderman Feuer, Julie Masters, Artineh Samkian, and Kavita Ann Paul (2001) *No Breathing in the Aisles: Diesel Exhaust Inside School Buses* (Washington, DC: National Resources Defense Council), www.nrdc.org/air/transportation/schoolbus/schoolbus.pdf, last accessed January 18, 2013.
36 Tamminen, Terry (2006) *Lives Per Gallon: The True Cost of Our Oil Addiction* (Washington, DC: Island Press), p. 21.
37 Kahn, J. and J. Yardley (2007) "As China roars, pollution reaches deadly extremes," *New York Times*, August 26, www.nytimes.com/2007/08/26/world/asia/26china.html?pagewanted=print, last accessed January 18, 2013.
38 World Bank (2007) "The cost of pollution in China" (Washington, DC: World Bank), http://siteresources.worldbank.org/INTEAPREGTOPENVIRONMENT/Resources/ChinaCostofPollution.pdf, last accessed January 18, 2013.
39 PWC (2011) "PWC's autofacts forecasts 2012 global automotive assembly to increase to 83.5 million units," August 3 (New York: PricewaterhouseCoopers), www.pwc.com/us/en/press-releases/2011/pwcs-autofacts-forecasts-2012.jhtml, last accessed January 18, 2013.
40 CBO (2008) "Climate change policy and CO_2 emissions from passenger vehicles, Congressional Budget Office," Economic and Budget Issue Brief, October 6, www.cbo.gov/sites/default/files/cbofiles/attachments/10-06-ClimateChange_Brief.pdf, last accessed January 18, 2013.
41 Chester, Mikhail, Arpad Horvath, and Samer Madanat (2010) "Parking infrastructure: energy, emissions, and automobile life-cycle environmental accounting," *Environmental Research Letters*, 5, pp. 1–8.
42 Reference to famous line in the Joni Mitchell song "Big Yellow Taxi" (1970).
43 Chester *et al.* (2010).
44 Shoup, Donald (2004) *The High Cost of Free Parking* (Washington, DC: American Planning Association).
45 Ibid., p. 209.
46 Ibid., p. 211.
47 Ibid., p. 212.
48 Litman, Todd (2005) "Transportation costs and benefit analysis," Victoria Transport Policy Institute, www.vtpi.org/tca, last accessed January 19, 2013.
49 Litman, Todd (2010) "Community cohesion as a transport planning objective," Victoria Transport Policy Institute, Victoria, BC, April 15, www.vtpi.org/cohesion.pdf, last accessed January 19, 2013.
50 Ibid.
51 Ben-Joseph, Eran (2012) *Rethinking a Lot: The Design and Culture of Parking* (Cambridge, MA: MIT Press), p. 32.
52 Ibid., p. 32.
53 Carolan (2013), p. 19.
54 Ben-Joseph (2012), p. 18.
55 Ibid., p. 19.

56 Jacobs, Jane (1961) *The Death and Life of Great American Cities* (New York: Random House).
57 Putnam, Robert (2001) *Bowling Alone* (New York: Simon & Schuster).
58 Ibid., p. 213.
59 Litman (2010).
60 Gilbert, R. and C. O'Brien (2005) "Child- and youth-friendly land-use and transport planning guidelines," (Plymouth, UK: University of Plymouth, Centre for Sustainable Transportation), http://cst.uwinnipeg.ca/documents/Guidelines_ON.pdf, last accessed January 20, 2013.
61 Litman (2010).
62 Williamson, T. (2002) "Sprawl, politics, and participation: A preliminary analysis," *National Civic Review*, 91(3), pp. 235–44.
63 Ibid., p. 243.
64 Staley, Samuel (1999) "The sprawling of America: In defense of the dynamic city," Policy Study No 251, Reason Foundation, Washington, DC, http://reason.org/files/ed09db5e026808f5a16e1e56cf28aad3.pdf, last accessed January 20, 2013, p. 9.
65 Blais, Pamela (2010) *Perverse Cities: Hidden Subsidies, Wonky Policy, and Urban Sprawl* (Vancouver: UBC Press), p. 39.
66 Brueckner, Jan (2001) "Urban sprawl: Lessons from urban economics," *Brookings-Wharton Papers on Urban Affairs*, 1, pp. 65–97, p. 70.
67 Rees, W. (2009) "True cost economics," in *Berkshire Encyclopedia of Sustainability*, edited by C. Laszlo (Great Barrington, MA: Berkshire Publishing Group), pp. 468–71, p. 470.
68 Brueckner (2001), p. 70.
69 Delucchi, Mark A. (2004) "Summary of theory, data, methods, and results: Report #1 in the series: The annualized social cost of motor-vehicle use in the United States, based on 1990–91 Data," Institute of Transportation Studies, University of California, Davis, Research Report UCD-ITS-RR-96-03(01)_rev1.
70 Litman, Todd (2011) "Transportation cost and benefit analysis techniques, estimates and implications," Victoria Transport Policy Institute, Victoria, Canada, www.vtpi.org/tca/tca00.pdf, last accessed January 21, 2013.
71 According to the US Energy Information Administration, in 2011 the United States consumed about 134 billion gallons (or 3.19 billion barrels) of gasoline (see, www.eia.gov/tools/faqs/faq.cfm?id=23&t=10). I divided each of the total cost estimates by 134 billion.
72 World Bank (n.d.) "Passenger cars (per 1,000 people)," World Bank, Washington, DC, http://data.worldbank.org/indicator/IS.VEH.PCAR.P3, last accessed July 23, 2013.
73 Snyder, Tanya (2013) "Car ownership may be down in the US, but it's soaring globally," *DC.Streets*, July 5, http://dc.streetsblog.org/2013/07/05/car-ownership-may-be-down-in-the-u-s-but-its-soaring-globally/, last accessed July 23, 2013.
74 See, for example, Goodwin, P. (2012) "Three views on peak car," *World Transportation Policy and Practice*, 17(3), pp. 8–17.
75 Cohen, Marie (2012) "The future of automobile society: A socio-technical transitions perspective," *Technology Analysis and Strategic Management*, 24(4), pp. 377–90.
76 Chozick, A. (2012) "To draw reluctant young buyers, G.M. turns to MTV," *New York Times*, March 22, www.nytimes.com/2012/03/23/business/media/to-draw-reluctant-young-buyers-gm-turns-to-mtv.html?pagewanted=all&_r=0, last accessed July 23, 2013.

Chapter 6

Retail concentration and rock-bottom prices ... but at what cost?

We have all heard the comparison, or something like it: if Walmart were a country, its GDP (roughly US$470 billion) would rival that of Norway's (approximately US$480 billion). Or, to look at it another way, if it were a sovereign nation it would be China's sixth-largest market. At some level, this chapter is less about Walmart per se and more about what happens when giant firms begin rivaling affluent nations, particularly in terms of their respective global reach and influence. Yet, similarly, it is impossible to not personalize this chapter given the firm's standing in the global economy. Three of the world's four largest companies in 2013 are petroleum firms. Guess who's leading the pack? Walmart. In comparison to other retail giants, Walmart stands alone. The combined sales of its three largest competitors – Carrefour (US$112.6 billion), Tesco (US$96.8 billion), and Metro (US$90.5 billion) – do not come anywhere close to Walmart's annual sales figures, which, again, are approaching half a trillion dollars.

Walmart: a poster child of sorts for cheaponomics; a firm emulating a model of "success" that others – many others – are seeking to emulate. This chapter is ultimately about that model and how the currency of macroeconomics, economies of scale, and growth are acting as a smokescreen of sorts to the lived experiences of billions as communities, social relationships, and households are being bankrupted in the name of progress. Walmart merely provides me a way to give that business model a familiar face.

Wal-fare

Politicians and the general public frequently misidentify who the real recipients of welfare are. The term "welfare queen" is certainly fitting, as the largest beneficiaries of government support have incomes that would make a monarch blush. But we are way off base when it comes to *who* we assign this label to. A calculation of federal government expenditures reveals that US taxpayers paid out roughly US$59 billion in 2006 to support traditional social welfare programs like housing assistance and food stamps, whereas US$92 billion went to corporations.[1] (The Cato Institute conducted a similar analysis in 2002 and concluded US$93 billion was spent on corporate welfare for the year.[2]) Almost all of the US$92 billion goes to firms in the energy and agriculture sectors. Yet, as I will explain, this US$92 billion is a conservative estimate. Hundreds of millions of additional dollars are transferred annually from taxpayers to firms, most notably through federal programs which many of their workers qualify for as a result of being paid a pittance while receiving little to no employee benefits. Walmart is the largest benefactor of this subsidized "cheap" labor.[3] Then there are the billions of dollars in tax breaks at state and local levels – which are essentially subsidies because they represent lost tax revenue – that firms like Walmart (and Walmart *in particular*) receive.[4]

A study from 2004 estimates that California taxpayers were annually subsidizing Walmart to the tune of US$86 million – which in today's (2013) dollars comes out to well over US$100 million – providing healthcare and other public assistance such as food stamps and subsidized housing to the state's 44,000 Walmart employees. As salaries and healthcare coverage levels among Walmart "associates" are below the industry average, the study further calculated what it would cost the citizens of California if competing retailers were to adopt similar wage and benefit levels. The bill to taxpayers would increase by US$410 million (or what is equal to US$500 million today).[5]

According to a 2005 *Tampa Bay Times* story, Walmart topped all companies operating in Florida in terms of the number of employees and family members eligible for Medicaid while coming in second for dependents enrolled in Florida Healthy Kids (a program offering health insurance for children ages 5 to 18).[6] A 2006 *Philadelphia Inquirer* investigation revealed that the company had the highest percentage of employees enrolled in Medicaid in Pennsylvania. One out of every six of the state's 48,000 Walmart employees were enrolled in Medicaid, according to this report, at a cost of roughly US$15 million annually; a figure that *excludes* the millions of dollars spent covering employees' dependents on Medicaid or any of the other public assistance (such as food stamps or subsidized housing) these individuals qualify for.[7] Twenty-one of the 23 states that have disclosed information have Walmart at the top of their list with the largest number of employees qualifying for federal poverty alleviation programs.[8]

The *New York Times* reported on a 2005 internal memo from a Walmart executive indicating that the company is well aware that many of its associates and their children qualify for publicly funded programs. What is most remarkable about the memo, however, is that it admits that its associates qualify for these programs at levels that are above the national average.[9] For instance, it acknowledged that 46 percent of associates' children are uninsured or on Medicaid. This compares to an industry average of 29 percent among large retailers and 32 percent for all retailers.[10] Digging through these reports we further learn that *qualifying* for health benefits through Walmart does not necessarily mean you *receive* them, as few can actually afford what the company

Retail concentration and rock-bottom prices   113

offers. It is almost as if Walmart *expects* taxpayers to provide healthcare for its employees. The 2012 Associate Benefits Book, distributed to all Walmart employees, lists contact information for assistance programs like Medicaid and CHIP (Children's Health Insurance Program). That way, even those eligible for the company's health insurance but who are "unable to afford the premiums" can receive quality healthcare ... from Uncle Sam.[11]

In late 2012 Walmart announced it will roll back even further its benefit levels. Under this policy, slated to take effect in 2013, Walmart also reserves the right to eliminate healthcare coverage for certain workers if their average work week falls below 30 hours. Why this blatant attempt at further cost socialization? The decision seeks to take advantage of recent US national healthcare reform – commonly known as Obamacare. A key feature of this reform is an expansion of Medicaid.[12] The company figures, why pay for something that the government is providing for "free." Free to them, perhaps; terribly costly, however, to the rest of us.

What makes this all the more remarkable is that, while Walmart profits handsomely from these various indirect subsidies it has managed to avoid paying its fair share into public coffers. Limited disclosure requirements make it difficult to conduct a comprehensive national inventory on just how much Walmart saves through taxes. After reviewing what data are available one report concludes that the public sector is losing more than US$1 billion annually to Walmart through various tax cuts, diversions, and loopholes.[13]

Big-box critics often claim that even the mention of building a new Walmart drives down property values in surrounding neighborhoods. As it turns out, Walmart actually agrees with them. Once a store is in operation for a year or two, headquarters commonly challenges the assessed value that local officials assign to the new store for tax purposes. An analysis found that the cumulative tax savings achieved by this strategy, from 1997 through 2007, was roughly US$30 million (or US$3 million a year).[14] It could be pointed out that that figure is but a fraction of the US$450 billion in sales the company made in 2012. That is the wrong way of looking at it. While little more than petty cash for this corporate giant, US$30 million is a princely sum for the communities that should have received this revenue. To make up for it, then, cities and counties had to either raise taxes on everyone else or cut services, such as to education, police and fire departments, and/or road construction and maintenance. In either case, the communities paid dearly.

As for the rest of that US$1 billion, it is lost to Walmart in many different ways.[15]

- Infrastructure subsidizes: taxpayers frequently pay for the roads, water and sewer lines, and other infrastructure on land sited for a Supercenter.
- Property tax breaks: county and local governments often agree to forgo revenues that the company would be required to pay in property taxes in order to entice firms to the area.

- State corporate income tax credits: these are economic development subsidies that make it possible for firms to reduce their tax liabilities by allowing them to deduct certain expenses.
- Sales tax rebates: this allows retailers to retain some of the sales tax it collects. It has been estimated that Walmart collects roughly US$60 million a year in the 26 states that provide these payments.[16]
- Enterprise zone status: special economic districts created by governments that seek to encourage investment by providing a variety of subsidies, such as property tax abatements, sales tax exemptions, reduced utility rates, and low-interest financing.
- General grants: an outright grant of public money to the company.

As outlined above, taxpayers give generously to Walmart and do so often quite willingly. They do this thanks to promises of a substantial return on their investment, in terms of more jobs and economic development. Walmart is presented as a goose that lays golden eggs. It turns out, that the goose was there all along and Walmart is what killed it.

Walmart math

Some might respond to the above figures arguing that all those associates qualifying for Medicare and other government assistance programs would still be doing so were it not for their jobs at Walmart; only under this scenario they would be unemployed. A low-paying job at Walmart is better than no job at all, right? Another argument I hear frequently defends the aforementioned taxpayer-funded giveaways on the grounds that the benefits far outweigh the costs. In other words, the subsidies, tax credits, and grants more than pay for themselves in terms of new jobs and simulative economic activity in the region. Both points, however, rest on faulty accounting. If the benefits outweigh the costs, that is only because the latter are being socialized.

Considerable evidence indicates that Walmart does not just pay its employees on average less than its competitors but that a store's presence depresses wages for the *entire region*. One study out of the University of California, Berkeley, found that counties that had opened a Walmart store between 1992 and 2000 saw a one percent decrease in wages across the entire general merchandise sector. In the grocery store sector, wages were reduced by an average of 1.5 percent.[17] Studies like this help explain the stunning conclusions reached by Stephan Goetz, co-author and Professor of Agricultural Economics at Pennsylvania State University.[18] The findings of this research were not those expected, as they draw a highly incriminating arrow from Walmart's presence in a county to the region's poverty rate. "I was sure," Goetz explains, "that after we controlled for all those other long lists of factors that cause poverty, there would be nothing left to explain, no poverty left over."[19]

Examining family poverty rates in every US county from 1989 to 1999, while controlling for everything known to cause poverty – variables like education level, age, and single heads of household – the data could not be more clear: counties with Walmart had higher poverty rates than those without.[20] While correlation does equal causation the fact that Goetz and his co-author, Hema Swaminathan, account for everything else can only mean one thing. "There is an effect," according to Goetz, "that we can only explain by Walmart's presence."[21] The study concludes noting that the firm is "not bearing the full economic and social costs of its business practices" but instead "transfers income from the working poor and from taxpayers, though welfare programs directed at the poor, to stockholders and the heirs of the Wal-Mart fortune, as well as to consumers." "These transfers," as the paper further notes, "are in addition to the public infrastructure subsidies often provided by local communities."[22]

In addition to its associations with lower wages Walmart has been linked to job losses in a region after the opening of new stores. We have all heard the promise: "This new store will bring with it hundreds of new jobs!" What is not mentioned are the number of jobs inevitably *lost* after the store opens its doors. According to one national-level study, Walmart store openings reduce county-level retail employment across the country by, on average, 150 workers.[23] This translates into a ratio of 1.4 retail sector jobs lost for every Walmart job gained. Do not be fooled by Walmart math: 1 (job gained) minus 1.4 (jobs lost) does not equal 1.

Returning to the question frequently parroted by the firm's proponents: isn't a job at Walmart better than no job at all? The problem with this question is that it is not the one we ought to be asking. Recall my warning from the previous chapter: if they can get you asking the wrong questions they need not worry about the answers. We should be inquiring instead about net jobs gained and well-being created, especially in light of what has been said about how the jobs being created are typically fewer in number than those replaced *and* lower paying.

Let us get something else clear: we are not just talking about an erosion of good paying *retail* jobs. Another sector, which often gets ignored in all of this, getting squeezed by large national chains are local, independent banks. National chains have no use for local banks. Nearly everyone else, however, does, especially in some of the smaller communities where Walmart operates. When small businesses start going under those independent banks lose customers, deposits, and investment options. Lose enough of these small businesses and the local bank's existence becomes threatened. If it were to go under the community not only loses still more jobs but an important – in some cases *the only* – source of local investment capital. The trust and social capital built up between residents and the managers of these local banks, who are often from the communities they serve, historically has often substituted for the more formulaic metrics used by managers of national banks, such as, for example, when assessing loans for small businesses. In addition to using independent banks, local retailers often buy locally when it comes to the services of attorneys, accountants, graphic designers, carpet cleaners, window washers, and marketing firms, just to name a handful of businesses that exist symbiotically with successful local, independent vendors. Large chains, conversely, handle many of these services internally, keeping local spending to an absolute minimum – a point I will return to shortly.

What would happen if Walmart decided to pay its associates a wage more in line with its competitors? Say, for the sake of argument, Walmart decided to pay its associates an average of US$12 an hour – a rate much higher than the US$9 to US$10/hr most associates currently earn. For those inclined to view such mandatory pay hikes (even hypothetical ones) as somehow "anti-free market" you can still sleep well at night. Think of it less as a raise and more as honest accounting, for such a pay increase would simply be internalizing costs that are otherwise socialized to taxpayers, society writ large, and, of course, the Walmart associates (as the suffering that goes with living in poverty is a grave cost to those experiencing it). So what would a wage increase do to the retail price of the firm's "cheap" goods? That is precisely the question asked by a team of scholars at the University of California, Berkeley.[24] They found that even if Walmart were to pass 100 percent of the wage increase onto consumers, prices in the store would increase roughly 1.1 percent. That translates into an additional US$13 a year for the average consumer who spends approximately US$1,187 annually at Walmart. And this is the worst-case scenario for consumers, as a portion of these costs could easily be absorbed through lower profit margins; something Walmart could certainly afford as their annual profits consistently exceed US$50 billion.

Walmart argues that the poor disproportionately benefit from the firm's cheap prices because those households spend a greater share of their annual incomes on food and other essentials compared to the more affluent. This may be true but it ignores that lower-income households are also overwhelmingly employed by Walmart and thus suffer disproportionately from their lower wages and poor benefit packages. When you add these up, the costs far exceed the benefits for lower-income households. While Walmart shoppers disproportionately have lower incomes the customers who spend most at the store are more likely to come from middle-class households. Thus, while 28.1 percent of the total retail price increase from higher salaries would be borne by consumers in families below 200 percent of the federal poverty level those same households would receive 41.4 percent of the benefits associated with an average hourly wage increase to US$12. This means low-income Walmart employees would see a raise of between US$1,670 and US$6,500 per year, while the average Walmart shopper would spend an additional $13 annually. That is a cost almost every one of us can afford, regardless of income bracket.

People don't live (or work) in the "macro" economy

The world, as seen through the disciplinary eyes of economics, is full of contradictions. When first introduced to the field you are pointed in two directions: up (and out) or down. The former is call "macro" economics; the latter, "micro." While initially presented as two sides of the same coin, closer inspection suggests these fields are describing distinct and separate worlds. Billions can be perfectly miserable in a world performing admirably (in the eyes of a cheaponomist) at the macroeconomic level. Just look around. I return to this point in the book's final chapters, as I tease out why this is and how we might be able to adjust our view of "the economy" to better account for the actual lived experiences of people.

I want to introduce this point here because firms such as Walmart place in particularly sharp relief the abovementioned contradictions and raise profoundly important questions about what we as a society value. While people do not live or work in the "macro" economy it could be said that Walmart does. Walmart employs more than 2.1 million people worldwide – more than the population of the city Houston. In the United States alone, the firm employs 1.4 million – that's one percent of the country's 140 million working population.[25] Its annual global sales are approaching half a trillion US dollars. Each week, Walmart serves more than 200 million customers in retail outlets located in 28 different countries.[26] Eight cents of every US dollar spent (in the United States) is done so at one of its retail stores.[27] The most frequent destination typed into Telenav GPS navigator is "Walmart."[28] In the aggregate, at the macro level, a growing Walmart is said to be unequivalently "good" for the economy. What's good for Walmart is good for, well, *everyone*, or so you would believe listening to its proponents:

> Therefore when Walmart decides to build 1,170 new stores that means that they are going to order billions of items from manufacturers. This act alone will spur economic activity for the economy as a whole. One example may be that they will place an order for 58,500 new Keurig coffee makers (50 per store) from Green Mountain Coffee Roasters.[29]

Arguments such as this one, however, rest on an ecological fallacy, in that the conclusions are based on false inferences about local and regional activities deduced from macro-level trends. New Walmart stores and jobs do not emerge *ex nihilo* – "out of nothing." As we have seen, they do their fair share of replacing (and downgrading). So rather than focusing exclusively on the 1,170 new stores, to pull a figure from the above quote, we need to also be asking, "*minus* how many existing stores and better paying jobs?" Doing this also helps us stay grounded to the ever-important lived concerns *of people*, recognizing that we do not experience the world in rarefied "macro" terms. From here, the costs of Walmart really start adding up. Drilling down allows for the identification of costs that are otherwise unidentifiable at the macro level. I have already identified some of them, such as Walmart's downward pull on wages and benefit levels after entering into a locality. Let's look at some more.

With their gaze locked exclusively on the global circulation of capital, macro-level analyses tell us absolutely nothing about the movement of these resources at local and regional scales: the levels that actually matter for the vast majority of the world's population. A study from the Maine Center for Economic Policy, for example, found that every US$100 spent at locally-owned businesses generates an additional $58 in local impact as a result of those store owners spending revenue within the community – what economists call a multiplier effect. By comparison, US$100 spent at national chain stores generates only US$33 in local impact. In other words, money spent at local businesses could generate a 76 percent greater return to the local economy than money spent at big-box stores.[30] This brings us back to a point made earlier when I briefly discussed the symbiotic-like relationship local businesses have with each other, whereas national chains rarely have any reason to buy local goods and services.

Returning to that Maine study: a 10 percent shift in consumer spending in Cumberland County (where that state's capital, Portland, is located), from national chains to locally-owned businesses, would inject into the regional economy an additional US$127 million and 874 new jobs generating over $35 million in wages – an economic tsunami that may not even register as a ripple at the macro level.[31] These findings mirror research looking at Salt Lake City, Utah. Independent and locally-owned retailers and restaurateurs were found to return a total of 52 percent and 78.6 percent, respectively, of all revenue to the local economy. The four major national retail chains included in the study, namely, Barnes & Noble, Home Depot, Office Max, and Target, recirculate an average of only 13.6 percent of their revenue locally. As for the three major restaurant chains examined – Darden, McDonald's, and P.F. Chang's – they recirculate an average of 30.4 percent of revenue back into the regional economy.[32] Based on 2007 retail figures, these findings indicate that a 10 percent shift from retail chains to independent, locally-owned stores would redirect US$362 million back into the community's economy every year. With the restaurants, a 10 percent shift in consumer spending would keep US$125 million in the regional economy.[33]

Regardless of where you look the story is almost always the same. Large national chains like Walmart cost local and regional economies dearly as evidenced by how even a small shift in consumer spending habits, toward independent businesses, could dramatically reinvigorate an otherwise fragile local economy. A 10 percent increase in the market share held by independent businesses in San Francisco, California, would generate an estimated additional US$200 million in annual economic impact and create 1,300 jobs with more than US$70 million in payroll.[34] In Grand Rapids, Michigan, such a shift in consumer purchasing would infuse the local economy with an additional US $137 million, plus 1,600 jobs generating US$53 million in wages.[35] The same holds for New Orleans, Louisiana.[36] To quote the authors of a study that looked at the impact of national chains on economic activity in the Big Easy:

> If Orleans Parish consumers, including residents, institutions, and visitors, were to shift just 10 percent of all retail activity from chains to local merchants, the result would be equivalent to injecting an additional $60 million annually into the local economy. At the metropolitan level, the same 10 percent shift would inject an additional $235 million into the regional economy every year.[37]

Dollars and jobs, however, are just the tip of the economic iceberg, lest we forget that the word "economics" is derived from the Greek word for management of the household – *oikonomia*. In the truest sense of word, the economy is composed of two interrelated systems. One involves money and market transactions. This is what we tend to focus on today when thinking of the term. But there is another system. One which Aristotle felt was even more important than markets because without it there could be no production or consumption: the household – aka non-market exchange relationships built on trust, mutual respect, and a sense of community. This brings me back to my earlier point about how billions can be perfectly miserable in a world "prospering" at the macroeconomic level. While the market tells us how much something costs – and, sadly, it doesn't even do this very well – non-market exchange relationships are what give life *value*.

There is tentative evidence incriminating Walmart as being partially responsible for the erosion of the productive base that makes market relations possible. David Brown, Professor of Political Science at the University of Colorado, finds the presence of Walmart stores in a community to be correlated, at statistically significant levels, with decreasing voter turnout, lower participation in political activities, less philanthropy, and declining social capital. This pattern was observed in four different datasets based on county and individual level data.[38] "The results," as described by Brown, "imply Walmart has a measurable impact on communities in the United States that reaches beyond prices, income, and employment. Big box retail, it seems, comes at a cost. Lower prices and all that comes with them hold important consequences for political participation."[39] This research corroborates the findings of a 2006 article in the *American Journal of Agricultural Economics* which concludes that the presence of Walmart stores decreases social capital stock in counties hosting the retail giant.[40]

Why might the presence of Walmart in a community erode those ever-important non-market exchange relationships – the very things, again, that give life value? To answer this question let us think about the *type* of community big-box stores like Walmart create. For one thing, they foster car-munities, to evoke a term introduced in the previous chapter. They encourage driving by wiping out locally-owned Main Street options, which by nature of their centralized location are more easily accessed by bike and foot. A big-box store, conversely, especially in smaller cities, is typically confined to a community's outskirts – the only place where its enormous footprint could fit. Moreover, the decline of downtowns and other neighborhood business districts that tend to come at the hands of Walmart – spaces that have long served to help build community – strip towns of the very thing that make them vibrant and which enhance the well-being of residents.

This brings up some significant *social* costs incurred when a region's public services are slashed to pay for the taxpayer-funded giveaways mentioned earlier in the chapter; cuts further compounded by the fact that chain stores do not inject as much of their revenues back into the local economy compared to the stores they put out of business. A vicious cycle is therefore all-too-often set into motion: cuts to "hard" infrastructure, in terms of schools, roads, and other publicly funded services, further erodes a community's "soft" infrastructure, such as trust and social capital, which further erodes the former, and so forth. And all of this could be occurring while, at the macro level, everything appears in order and trending in the right direction.

Concentration: a cost and cause of cheap

While all of this might sound like an indictment against Walmart what this is really about is *market concentration*. Firms like Walmart would not cost society nearly as much were it not for their scale and sheer market dominance. For example, in comparison to other corporate giants in the food system, Walmart's US$444 billion in sales in 2012 was 12.3 times greater than what was reported by McDonald's (US$36 billion) and 33 times greater than that reported by Monsanto (US$13.5 billion).[41] To give focus to this discussion I will center my gaze on the food system, showing how market concentration, exemplified by Walmart, costs society dearly, even after factoring in for its "always low prices."

Figure 6.1 depicts sales for three sectors – input, food processors and traders, and retail – of the global food system, for the years 2004, 2006, and 2012. The overall size of this "pie" has increased by roughly 50 percent over the eight years outlined. Yet growth has not been symmetrical across the three sectors. The retail sector has been growing at a rate that far and away outpaces the other two. In fact, sales for this sector have doubled from 2004 to 2012. At the same time, sales in the input and processing sectors, while growing in absolute terms, have seen their respective "slice" shrink. And who do you suppose is the world's largest food retailer? That would be Walmart.

Before taking this discussion any further I need to introduce two terms: monopoly and monopsony. Most people are familiar with the former – after all,

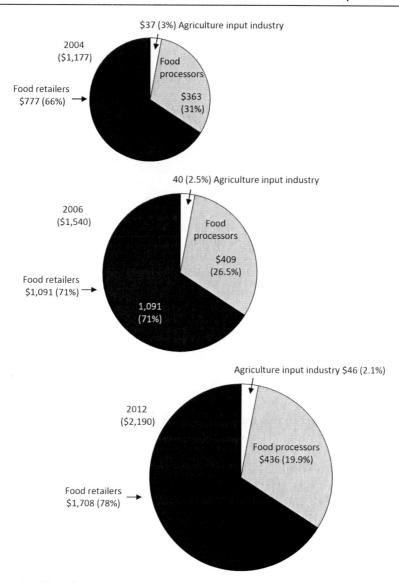

Figure 6.1 Sales of top 10 companies for three sectors of the global food system (in US$ billions)
Source: Carolan (2013)

who hasn't played the popular board game that is its namesake? Monopoly refers to a concentration among sellers to the point at which they, as opposed to the market, set the price of the commodities they are selling. There is tremendous market advantage in having something that others want but which no one else sells, which explains why, in these situations, firms are able to sell their wares at an inflated price. Monopoly, in simplest terms, is a statement of seller power.

There is undoubtedly some of this going on in the retail sector, with, again, Walmart socializing its unfair share of these costs. According to a handful of court cases and media accounts, Walmart's motto ought to read, "Always low prices … until the competition disappears." For example, in 2003, Germany's Supreme Court ruled that Walmart's low cost pricing strategy "undermined competition" and ordered the retail giant to raise their prices.[42] (Walmart has since abandoned the German market.) Or take the account of a shopper in a Nebraska town who bought identical items at two Walmart stores in the same community. As it was reported, there was a 17 percent price difference between these two carts. Turns out, the higher-priced Walmart happened to be in a neighborhood where it had already vanquished the local competition.[43] This story might seem, at its face, hard to believe, after all, wouldn't management at the higher-priced Walmart be concerned about losing customers to the store on the other side of town? Maybe not. We know, for example, that shoppers, for reasons of "convenience," tend to shop at their nearest store, irrespective of its ownership and, to some degree, even price.[44] But I think there is an even simpler explanation. How many people would think to compare prices between two Walmart stores in the same town? I have posed this question to well over 200 students and I can count on two hands the number who said they would.

An even greater litany of costs, however, can be attributed to firms in their capacity as buyers. This brings me to the second term: monopsony – buyer power. This exists when the number of buyers have eroded, allowing them, rather than the market, to set the price for the goods they purchase. Allow me to briefly explain some of these costs and how Walmart, given its size, is responsible for many of them.

Concentration is occurring throughout the food system, in all countries. Figure 6.2 illustrates this concentration for the United States and New Zealand, showing that such a trend is not limited to the former. The power of food processors – the bottleneck in the figure just below "farms" – lies largely in their ability to manipulate prices as buyers of what farmers are selling. Indeed, this buyer power recently caught the attention of the US Department of Agriculture and the US Department of Justice. In 2010, US Attorney General Eric Holder and US Secretary of Agriculture Tom Vilsack hosted five public forums to examine concentration within the US food system. Attending one of the forums and reading transcripts of the others, I can report that the events were full of first-hand accounts of producers being forced to sell at unfair prices due to having only one or two buyers to choose from. But even powerful processors wilt when standing before Walmart, ultimately becoming victims of buyer power too. Fortunately for them, however, they still have, thanks to *their* buyer power over producers, the ability to redistribute these "costs" onto farmers, which, in the end, allows them to remain highly

Retail concentration and rock-bottom prices 123

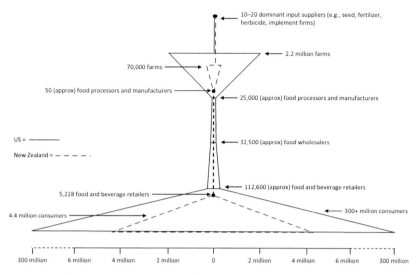

Figure 6.2 Food system concentration in the US and New Zealand
Source: Author

profitable. And in case you are wondering about the farmers: they are not only squeezed as sellers but also as buyers of inputs to firms such as Monsanto, who possess seller power over them.

US-based Smithfield Foods is the world's largest pork producer and processor with annual revenue in excess of US$10 billion. Even so, it would never try to overcharge Walmart for its pork. Even trying to "muscle" the retail giant is out of the question, recognizing that as the largest single global purchaser of pork products Walmart holds considerable buyer power over this otherwise seemingly immovable market force. Food processing giants General Mills and Kraft Foods also know better than to tangle with Walmart. Each generates roughly one-fifth of their total revenue through Walmart retail sales.[45] That translates into approximately US$3 billion and US$11 billion, respectively, in sales annually just through that *one contract*. In light of these figures, who do you think would blink first if Walmart were to demand significant price concessions from these manufactures? The retail sector is further consolidating its power thanks to the establishment and growing popularity of "private labels" – also known as in-store brands – with Walmart's "Great Value" label leading the way. Sales in private labels are growing almost twice as fast as sales of branded products. It is expected that private-label sales will account for 24.1 percent of total grocery sales by 2014.[46]

Supermarkets have been known to provide local growers with an important market for their products.[47] Yet as this sector continues to be shaped by the influences of Walmart – with its unmatched buyer power – these opportunities, I fear, will quickly dry up. Take Walmart's announcement in 2008 to commit to sourcing more "local" produce. Who do you think will supply the retail giant with this food? We already know the answer to that question: a handful of very large farms – not exactly what most people have in mind when they think about "supporting local growers."

The reason for this boils down to, you guessed it, economics – or, more accurately, cheaponomics.

Only large farms can afford – or have access to sufficient credit allowing them to afford – the "minimum" requirements demanded by Walmart. These demands include the purchase of UPC barcode technology, US$2 million in commercial liability insurance, and a financial stability rating (something most farmers neither have or know what it is).[48] Moreover, and as discussed in the previous chapter, large farms are typically capital-intensive, which is another way of saying they are energy-intensive – an intensity that comes with the socialization of a great many costs to society, the environment, and future generations. Given the sheer volume that Walmart deals with, it just makes economic sense – in a world of cheaponomics – for the firm to obtain its products from a handful of (or maybe even one) very large producers rather than from thousands of small-scale farmers. Take beef as an example. Walmart buys over a billion pounds of this product annually just to supply the US market.[49] That translates into more than 2.2 million cows. To meet that demand only through small-scale producers, Walmart would have to enlist an army of feeders and ranchers. The transaction costs involved in coordinating such an effort would be near Herculean. Even if the retail giant did find enough small-scale producers to meet its needs, those feeders and ranchers would certainly not be able to afford the earlier-mentioned technology requirements for managing inventory. These costs, it is worth adding, could be borne by Walmart. It doesn't bear them because it doesn't have to. It has its buyer power to thank for that.

Prosperity is dead, long live "prosperity"!

Prosperity: what do we mean by it? The term is batted around a lot these days; after all, that is the ultimate goal of economic growth – right? The entire premise of having at our disposal – literally – an endless supply of cheap wares is that such an arraignment will enhance what economists call aggregate well-being. Making us *better off*: that's the prize; what we are striving for; something that ought to make us happier and healthier. But wait. Who said anything about happiness and health? And there is the rub: what we really want and what the system (cheaponomics) is oriented toward maximizing are not the same. In fact, all too often, they are polar opposites.

The idea of prosperity is too important to confine to a section of a chapter; too important, even, to confine to a chapter. By now it should be plainly clear that the status quo – cheaponomics – does little to actually enhance well-being for the majority of the world's population. But, then again, what do you expect from a system that socializes costs for the benefit of a few. The subject of prosperity will become increasingly central to my argument from this point on. Having shown the costs of business-as-usual, it is time we start thinking about what an economic system would look like that is interested in creating real *value* as opposed to just cutting *costs*.

On the subject of prosperity, what can we learn from Walmart? Or perhaps more accurately, what can we learn *not to do* from Walmart? There are important lessons to be gleaned from this chapter to inform our discussion of what real prosperity entails. One highlights the dangers that come with over-emphasizing economic growth. What we see clearly thanks to Walmart is that it is painfully hard to increase the "pie" of local and regional markets under cheaponomics. Opening a new Walmart (or Tesco, Target, Home Depot, etc.) has a tendency of *decreasing* disposable incomes in the region by depressing wages and putting people out of work by shuttering other local (and often better-paying) businesses. The data are clear: building a new Supercenter does not generate more wealth but *redistributes* it – and not in a way that enhances overall well-being. Corporate managers know this. Retail development is rarely based on meeting unmet demand and more about "predatory opportunity." The strategy, as described by the president of Boulevard Strategies (a consulting firm that provides economic and retail research and analysis), is to "do it bigger than the other guy and just knock him out of the market. That's where most of the action is these days."[50]

What about growing the "pie" by pulling in retail dollars from neighboring communities? If people come from elsewhere to shop at Walmart the town with the big box wins. Those shoppers, after all, will likely eat and buy gas when in town and perhaps even visit a couple of other shops too. But that is not what is happening. For one thing, stores like Walmart aim to increasingly provide a one-stop shopping experience, which they are able to accomplish by having on site things like restaurants, a bank, gas pumps, an optometrist, accountant services, hair stylists, and an automotive department. Second, to repeat a point made earlier, new big-box stores do not generate new wealth. They merely redistribute it, in a highly inequitable way. So even if – and this is a big *if* – at the community level additional retail dollars are being pulled in from surrounding communities they are only coming in at the expense of surrounding communities. In short: *nothing* in the aggregate is gained or generated. Not wealth. Not well-being. The only thing generating and increased in this scenario is *inequality*, which actually has a downward pull on well-being indicators for the community/region/nation experiencing it – a point I return to in later chapters.

Let us also not forget that few of those "new" dollars being pulled in from elsewhere actually remain within the community. This helps us understand why even among communities that have managed to transform themselves into "successful" regional shopping centers, many end up with *fewer* dollars circulating locally compared to before the big boxes came to town. National chains are now expanding in ways that often cannibalize their own existing store sales, as they seek to fill in gaps between outlets. The shelf life for even the most successful cases therefore appears to be limited as firms look to further saturate markets. This move perhaps makes sense in a macroeconomic world but to those living in the *real* world it translates only into hardship and suffering.

When you are stealing from Peter Humanity to pay Paul Humanity the Humanity household is not any better off. This is especially the case when we think about "wealth" in the broadest of terms, which includes phenomena such as well-being, happiness, health, and ecological sustainability (as the only wealth that really matters to future generations is a livable environment). There is a term for what we are currently pursuing: uneconomic growth – growth that costs more than benefits us.[51] By mistaking redistribution (aka cost shifting) for wealth creation we have created a system that excels at producing uneconomic growth. For example, according to the Millennium Ecosystem Assessment, a report that involved more than 1,300 experts and provides one of the most thorough appraisals of the condition and trends in the world's ecosystems and the services they provide, the total capital stock of the world (most notably natural capital) is degrading faster than wealth created in the formal economy.[52]

It is time to rethink things.

Notes

1 Sinn, Mike (2011) "Government spends more on corporate welfare subsides than social welfare programs," *Think by Numbers*, March, http://thinkbynumbers.org/government-spending/corporate-welfare/corporate-welfare-statistics-vs-social-welfare-statistics/, last accessed January 30, 2013.
2 Cato (2002) "Corporate welfare update," Cato Institute, Washington, DC, May, www.cato.org/sites/cato.org/files/pubs/pdf/tbb-0205-7.pdf, last accessed January 30, 2013.
3 See for example Dube, Arindrajit, and Ken Jacobs (2004) "Hidden costs of Wal-Mart jobs: Use of safety net programs by Wal-Mart workers in California," University of California, Berkeley, Labor Center, University of California, Berkeley, CA, http://laborcenter.berkeley.edu/retail/walmart.pdf, last accessed January 30, 2013.
4 Mattera, Philip, Karla Walter, Julie Blain, and Colleen Ruddick (2007) "Rolling back property tax payments," Good Jobs First, Washington, DC, www.goodjobsfirst.org/sites/default/files/docs/pdf/walmartproptax.pdf, last accessed January 30, 2013.
5 Dube and Jacobs (2004).
6 Freedberg, Sydney and Connie Humburg (2005) "Lured employers now tax Medicaid," *Tampa Bay Times*, March 25, www.sptimes.com/2005/03/25/State/Lured_employers_now_t.shtml, last accessed January 31, 2013.
7 Worden, Amy (2006) "Many Walmart workers use Medicaid: One in six of its employees require the assistance program," *Philadelphia Inquirer*, March 2, http://articles.philly.com/2006-03-02/news/25415171_1_wal-mart-stores-medical-assistance-kelly-hobbs, last accessed January 31, 2013.
8 Good Jobs First (2012) "Hidden taxpayer cost, good jobs first," January 18, Washington, DC, www.goodjobsfirst.org/corporate-subsidy-watch/hidden-taxpayer-costs, last accessed January 31, 2013.

9 Greenhouse, Steven (2005) "Walmart memo suggests ways to cut employee benefit costs," *New York Times*, October 26, www.nytimes.com/2005/10/26/business/26walmart.ready.html?pagewanted=print&_r=0, last accessed January 31, 2013.
10 Bernstein, Jared, Josh Bivens, and Arindrajit Dube (2006) "Wrestling with Walmart, Economic Policy Institute," EPI Working Paper, June 15, www.epi.org/page/-/old/workingpapers/wp276.pdf, last accessed January 31, 2013.
11 As quoted in Moseley, Brandon (2012) "Medicaid: The hidden cost of Walmart's low prices," *Alabama Political Reporter*, September 12, www.alreporter.com/al-politics/political-news/state-news/2741-medicaid-the-hidden-cost-of-wal-marts-low-prices.html, last accessed January 31, 2013.
12 Hines, Alice (2012) "Walmart's new health care policy shifts burden to Medicaid," Obamacare, *Huffington Post*, December 1, www.huffingtonpost.com/2012/12/01/walmart-health-care-policy-medicaid-obamacare_n_2220152.html, last accessed January 31, 2013.
13 Mattera, Philip and Anna Purinton (2004) "Shopping for subsidies: How Walmart uses taxpayer money to finance its never-ending growth," *Good Jobs First,* Washington, DC, www.goodjobsfirst.org/sites/default/files/docs/pdf/wmtstudy.pdf, last accessed January 31, 2012.
14 Mattera *et al.* (2007).
15 For future discussion see Mattera and Purinton (2004).
16 Mattera, Philip and Leigh McIlvaine (2008) "Skimming the sale tax," *Good Jobs First*, Washington, DC, www.goodjobsfirst.org/sites/default/files/docs/pdf/skimming.pdf, last accessed January 31, 2013.
17 Dube, Arindrajit, T. William Lester, and Barry Eidlin (2007) "A downward push: The impact of Walmart stores on retail wages and benefits," UC Berkeley Center for Labor Research and Education, University of California, Berkeley, CA, http://laborcenter.berkeley.edu/retail/walmart_downward_push07.pdf, last accessed February 1, 2013.
18 Goetz, Stephan and Hema Swaminathan (2006) "Walmart and county-wide poverty," *Social Science Quarterly*, 87(2), pp. 211–26.
19 As quoted in Fishman, Charles (2006) *The Wal-Mart Effect* (New York: Penguin), p. 00164.
20 Goetz and Swaminathan (2006).
21 As quoted in Fishman (2006), p. 165.
22 Goetz and Swaminathan (2006), p. 223.
23 Neumark, David, Junfu Zhand, and Stephen Ciccarella (2007) "The effects of Walmart on local labor markets," Institute for the Study of Labor, Discussion Paper Series No. 2545, Bonn, Germany, www.ilsr.org/wp-content/uploads/2011/12/neumark-study.pdf, last accessed February 4, 2013.
24 Jackobs, Ken, Dave Graham-Squire, and Stephanie Luce (2011) "Living wage policies and big-box retail," Center for Labor Research and Education, University of California, Berkeley, CA, http://laborcenter.berkeley.edu/retail/bigbox_livingwage_policies11.pdf, last accessed February 4, 2013.
25 Blodget, Henry (2010) "Walmart employs 1 percent of America," *Business Insider*, September 30, www.businessinsider.com/walmart-employees-pay, last accessed February 5, 2013.
26 Spector, Dina (2012) "16 facts about Walmart that will blow your mind," *Business Insider*, April 23, www.businessinsider.com/crazy-facts-about-walmart-2012-4?op=1, last accessed February 5, 2013.
27 Ibid.
28 Ibid.

29 Seeking Alpha (2012) "Walmart: The perfect indicator for a strong economy," *Seeking Alpha*, August 23, http://seekingalpha.com/article/824501-wal-mart-the-perfect-indicator-for-a-strong-economy, last accessed February 5, 2013.
30 Patel, Amar and Garrett Martin (2011) "Going local: Quantifying the economic impacts of buying from locally owned businesses in Portland, Maine," Maine Center for Economic Policy, Augusta, ME, www.mecep.org/view.asp?news=2003, last accessed February 6, 2013.
31 Ibid.
32 Civic Economics (2012) "Indie impact study series: A national comparative survey with the American Booksellers Association," Summer, Civic Economics, Chicago, IL.
33 Ibid.
34 Urban Conservancy (2009) "Thinking outside the box, urban conservancy in partnership with civic economics," September, Urban Conservancy, New Orleans, Louisiana.
35 Ibid.
36 Ibid.
37 Ibid., p. 7.
38 Brown, David (2009) "Discounting democracy: Wal-Mart, social capital, civic engagement, and voter turnout in the United States," http://ssrn.com/abstract=1398946 or http://dx.doi.org/10.2139/ssrn.1398946, last accessed February 6, 2012.
39 Ibid., p. 4.
40 Goetz, Stephan and Anil Rupasingha (2006) "Walmart and social capital," *American Journal of Agricultural Economics*, 88(5), pp. 1304–10.
41 Carolan, Michael (2013) *Reclaiming Food Security* (New York and London: Earthscan/Routledge).
42 Patel, R. (2009) *Stuffed and Starved: The Hidden Battle for the World Food System* (Brooklyn: Melville House Publishing), p. 235.
43 Mitchell, Stacy (2003) "Germany high court convicts Walmart of predatory pricing," *Independent Business*, February 1, www.ilsr.org/german-high-court-convicts-walmart-predatory-pricing/, last accessed February 7, 2013.
44 Guy, C. (2007) *Planning for Retail Development: A Critical View of the British Empire* (New York: Routledge), p. 178.
45 Bloomberg (2009) "Wal-Mart's store-brand groceries to get new emphasis," February 19, www.bloomberg.com/apps/news?sid=afVJJxZ4oCtY&pid=newsarchive, last accessed February 7, 2013.
46 Toops, D. (2011) "Food processors find public growth for private label," FoodProcessing.com, July 18, www.foodprocessing.com/articles/2011/private-label.html, last accessed February 7, 2013.
47 Reardon, T., C. Timmer, C. Barrett, and J. Berdegue (2003) "The rise of supermarkets in Africa, Asia, and Latin America," *American Journal of Agricultural Economics*, 85(5), pp. 1140–6.
48 Carolan (2013).
49 Food and Water Watch (2012) "Why Walmart can't fix the food system," Washington, DC, http://documents.foodandwaterwatch.org/doc/FoodandWaterWatchReportWalmart022112.pdf, last accessed February 7, 2013.
50 As quoted in Mirchell, Stacy (2006) *Big Box Swindle* (Boston: Beacon Press), p. 37.
51 See, for example, Daly, H. (1999) *Ecological Economics and the Ecology of Economics* (Northampton, MA: Edward Elgar).
52 Millennium Ecosystem Assessment (2005) *Ecosystems and Human Well-Being: Synthesis* (Washington, DC: Island Press).

Chapter 7

Working less for more

This chapter is about labor and leisure ... sort of. Actually, I am taking a lesson from my students. They taught me a while ago that the most relatable way to talk about the inner workings of the economy is through relatable things. We all work. We also all play, hang around with friends, and engage in community-building activities. So why don't I start there. The thing about labor and leisure is that these seemingly separate activities today share the same socioeconomic DNA. As is plainly clear by now, cheaponomics speaks not just of a way of producing (underpriced) goods and (dis-)organizing markets. Its reach extends throughout society, shaping how we think about and act toward the environment and others while underpinning many of our ideals about what "growth" and "prosperity" mean. Work and leisure, as currently practiced, are but expressions of these broader logics. What better topics to use, then, in this quest to unveil cheaponomics and its unsustainable costs.

To kick this conversation off I thought I would let others do some of the "speaking" for me. The following are quotes from interviews conducted in 2010, collected while investigating the ways that work, leisure, and consumption intersect. The three quotes not-too-subtly highlight particular tensions at this point of intersection, which are only amplified by the status quo.

> *Quote #1*: "Since I'm constantly working I'm always thinking about my next vacation. My family and I got a really amazing one planned. It's going cost an arm and a leg, though. So I'm picking up overtime whenever I can get it. Need to work more so we can afford it, which sucks because I hate my job."
>
> *Quote #2*: "Sure; we've thought about having a staycation – for about a second. Why would anyone want to waste their vacation time stuck at home? There's nothing to do there. No one's around. Everyone's working. I've never even met my neighbors!"
>
> *Quote #3*: "We decided about a year back that our household needed the extra income so we're both working full time now. Since then I had to pick up a second job on weekends so we could afford the expense ... The meals away from home, dry cleaning bills, child care, housecleaning

services, a second car, the work-related wardrobe: the expense of it all really adds up in a hurry. But, like I said, we really could use the extra income."

The first quote highlights a familiar paradox: that in the pursuit of leisure many are driven to work more and, in the end, leisure *less*. Quote number two is important in that it gives some context for that which precedes it. Our collective working of long hours, stretched even further by ever-lengthening commute times, makes ghost towns of many neighborhoods. Eviscerated of their social capital stocks, many communities today offer few inducements to encourage people to stick around when they have the time. People instead increasingly feel a "need" to travel to distant lands at every opportunity, as evidenced by the fact that talk of leisure is typically framed in terms of "needing to get away." And so ensues a vicious cycle: more work and "away" leisure risks making communities and neighborhoods even less attractive, which encourages still additional work and "away" leisure, and so on. The story of work, leisure, and consumption, as authored by cheaponomics, could be described as a tragic comedy as it blends aspects of both tragic and comic forms. This dramatic element is exemplified in quote three. I still can't figure out if I should laugh or cry when reading it. In what dystopic world – hinted at in the final quote – could working to have more disposable income produce precisely the opposite effect? Ours, I am afraid.

All of this and more is unpacked in this chapter. Cheaponomics, by nature of its placing profits for the few above prosperity for the many, has created a highly unstable system; though this instability is masked by its willful disregard for cost internalization. But even more worrisome, in its single-minded pursuit of low retail prices we are being robbed of many of the things that give life meaning and, ultimately, worth.

A bipolar economy toward labor

Try squaring this circle.

Earlier I highlighted the centrality of planned obsolescence for spurring economic growth. To repeat a sentence from a book published in 1928 on the subject: "If what had filled the consumer market yesterday could only be made obsolete today, that whole market would be again available tomorrow."[1] The underlying logic that this sentence points to is simple. Cheap goods stimulate demand. And by nature of being "cheap," which means they most certainly are not designed for longevity (nor repair), we can be assured that demand will never be permanently satisfied. It's a brilliant scheme. Or, at least, it is until you play it out to its logical conclusion.

Cheap goods, as I have detailed, are achieved through egregious acts of cost socializing. One population frequently targeted to pay for these costs is workers, who are continually pinched by having their wages lowered (and healthcare and retirement benefits eviscerated) and through the substitution of capital for labor. This in turn creates an incentive to produce even cheaper goods to make up for falling incomes. Yet to do this additional cost-socializing strategies need to be adopted; costs which, again, are borne significantly by workers who then see their purchasing power decrease further, thus creating demand for still cheaper goods, and so on. This is entirely unsustainable. The system acts as though it hates labor, as evidenced by the fact that the market works tirelessly to substitute workers for capital. Yet it also needs labor, for without income earners it all comes grinding to a halt. It is worth noting how cheap credit has helped temporarily alleviate some of these tensions by artificially increasing the purchasing power of consumers, particularly among middle-income earners and below who have seen their incomes, after adjusting for inflation, fall in recent decades. As a "fix," however, cheap credit is temporary and partially the reason for the recent financial crises since 2008. The precipice is within sight. The love–hate relationship expressed by the market toward labor cannot go on forever.

Many economists will tell you that while technology puts people out of work it employs just as many, as someone has to manufacture and maintain this equipment. The previous chapters, however, belie this argument. New technology is manufactured just like the old: with as little human labor as possible. As for "all" the people employed who maintain this equipment, go back to Chapter 2 and re-read about the pathetic job-creating record of data server farms. Capital and energy are cheap and mobile; human labor is far less so. This is a basic economic fact – or, more accurately, a "fiction," as it is due to poor total cost accounting and a tax incentive structure entirely out of whack. And as long as this remains the case, incentives for future innovation will direct firms to over-utilize capital and energy to the detriment of labor.

Economists Robert Ayres and Benjamin Warr argue that "the historic link between output (GDP) growth and employment has been weakened, if not broken."[2] While everyone is entitled to their own opinion they are not entitled to their own facts and the latter do not bode well for future generations hoping to find full employment – at least as the concept is currently understood (involving a 40hr-ish work week). For the last two centuries, job losses in one sector were absorbed in another. This was particularly the case in higher income countries, where, for example, workers displaced out of agriculture could often find employment in a thriving manufacturing sector. The problem, however, is that sectors expected to flourish this century employ very few people – again, think data server farms. Over the last ten years countries in North America, Europe, and Southeast Asia have witnessed a dramatic increase in labor productivity. Yet, unlike in the past, this productivity has yielded few if any additional jobs.[3] The recent recession has only exacerbated this process. The US economy lost almost eight million jobs between 2008 and 2010.[4] During this process of shedding jobs firms have learned to do more with less labor. Most of those jobs lost are therefore not coming back. Where are these people going to go and how are they going to make a living? The solution is in many respects right in front of us. We just need to rethink what we mean by "new" jobs.

Growing jobs by reducing hours

Fairytales can come true …

Once upon a time a large corporation, confronted with global economic upheaval, faced a difficult decision. It needed to shed some 300 workers, out of some 1,500 in total. Or did it? Firms do not have job requirements per se. They have labor requirements, based upon labor costs per unit of production (a calculation which is, again, an artifact of tax and regulatory structures). Job totals are therefore nothing more than an artifact of how those hours are distributed. In recent decades the assumption has been to divide daily labor requirements by eight or nine hours. (According to the American Time Use Survey conducted by the US Department of Labor the average work day for persons aged 25 to 54 with children is 8.8 hours.)[5] This gives firms an approximation of how many people they need to employ. But what if a firm were to use a different denominator? Instead of an eight-hour workday what would happen if we calculated for a six-hour one? The firm would be able to employ more people as hours would need to be spread across more bodies. That is precisely what this company did. It implemented a policy requiring its workforce of 1,500 to go from a traditional eight-hour to a six-hour workday, which saved it from having to make the layoffs. The new arrangement meant everyone had to take a pay cut but because management also initiated production-based bonuses many of those losses were never realized. And because labor hour productivity went up, as it is well-established that workers tend to be more efficient when their eight-hour workday is shortened, the firm remained highly profitable.

This actually occurred.[6] The firm: cereal giant W.K. Kellogg. The year: 1930. The crisis: the Great Depression. The policy was in all estimations a success. Employees used their newly available time to pursue things of their choosing, which often involved activities that built family, community, and citizenship. Surveys at the time indicated that employees were generally happier under this new arrangement, which explains their heightened productivity. For example, the production of boxes of shredded whole-wheat biscuits per hour increased from 83 to 96 once the workday was shortened.[7]

Then the United States entered World War II, eventually resulting in Franklin Roosevelt signing an executive order demanding, among other things, longer workdays so the production needs of a war economy could be met. Moreover, as hundreds of thousands went off to fight, labor went from being abundant to scarce. The labor union initially opposed a policy to return to an eight-hour workday but eventually acquiesced, believing, incorrectly, that there would be a return to a six-hour workday after the war's conclusion.

Workers polled as late as 1946 found that 77 percent of men and 87 percent of women preferred a 30-hour workweek even if it meant lower wages.[8] Curiously, the longer hours and bigger paychecks did little to actually make employees any better off. As one worker would later report:

> Everybody thought they were going to get rich when they got that eight-hour deal and it really didn't make a big difference ... Some went out and bought automobiles right quick and they didn't gain much on that because the car took the extra money they had.[9]

Economist John Maynard Keynes tried his hand back in 1930, in an essay titled "Economic Possibilities for our Grandchildren," to write a predictive paper about life in 2030.[10] His thesis was simple. As steady gains in labor productivity make possible an increase in the output of goods per hour worked, people will not need to work as much to satisfy their needs. As work becomes less necessary "we shall endeavor," writes Keynes, "to spread the bread thin on the butter – to make what work there is still to be done to be as widely shared as possible." According to Keynes' estimates, you and I ought to be working "three-hour shifts or a fifteen-hour week" in roughly 15 years.[11] Nostradamus he was not.

Keynes' most egregious stumble in his attempt at futurism was his inability to distinguish between wants and needs. Keynes grossly underestimated marketers' and advertisers' power of persuasion – what John Kenneth Galbraith would later call the "machinery for consumer-demand creation."[12] In the same essay Keynes writes about status-seeking consumption when noting how human needs fall into two classes:

> Those needs which are absolute in the sense that we feel them whatever the situation of our fellow human being may be, and those which are relative in the sense that we feel them only if their satisfaction lifts us above, making us feel superior to, our fellows.[13]

Yet he then largely ignores this distinction, as the remainder of the article proceeds as though all needs are absolute.[14] Admittedly, Keynes' essay was during a time when disposable incomes were still spent overwhelmingly on basic household expenditures. It would take another couple decades before status-seeking consumption was kicked into overdrive, riding a wave of hyper-consumption helped along by planned obsolescence and glitzy multi-million dollar advertising campaigns. As Ezra Mishan, longtime professor of economics at the London School of Economics, famously noted a half century ago: "Therefore to continue to regard the market, in an affluent and growing economy, as primarily a 'want-satisfying' mechanism is to close one's eyes to the more important fact, that it has become a want-creating mechanism."[15]

For much of the 1920s, shorter work hours were viewed widely as the cure to overproduction and underemployment – a practice that later was called "share-the-work" during the Great Depression.[16] Indeed, hours of work per year began to decline in the United States after roughly 1870, when they averaged about 3,000 a year. By 1929, the total stood at 2,342. By 1973, the total was down still further to 1,077.[17] Yet as Juliet Schor famously details in *The Overworked American*, and more recently in *Plenitude*, this hour-reduction process has since stalled, especially in counties like the United States and Japan.[18] The reasons for this are numerous. Yet rising healthcare costs, which encourage firms to over-work existing full-time employees so as to limit those who qualify for such benefits, and rising inequality, which is reducing middle-class purchasing power and therefore causing millions to think they need to work more hours to make ends meet, are two often-mentioned culprits.[19] This explains, for example, why work hours tend to be longer in countries with greater income inequality.[20]

Free-market advocates would claim that the above trends are an artifact of employees choosing to work longer hours. But this claim has no basis in fact. The data are clear. The labor market is not free. In most cases, the "choice" is between working 40+ hours a week and zero – in other words, losing your job. I remember a student telling me how his boss teased him for days after being informed of the student's decision of choosing to work fewer hours. At least he didn't get fired. It is also disingenuous to say we ought not to regulate labor because we already do so. There are, for example, restrictions on the type of work that children can do (and the hours they can do it) and employers are mandated to give their employees breaks throughout the day. The classic liberal position that claims such regulations make little sense is blind to the asymmetries in power between employers and employees. It argues that if an individual "chooses" to work 80 hours a week for less than the minimum wage in an unsafe and abusive working environment then the government should not be able to tell them they cannot. The choices offered up in cheaponomics, however, are rarely real choices with a full complement of possible scenarios. These are "choices" in name only, presented only after significant choice editing has occurred. Thus, workers "choose" between working 40+ hours a week or getting fired. That is not much of an actual choice when you need to earn an income. So, yes, there may well be workers out there that "choose" to be exploited but that is only because the alternative – thanks to gross asymmetries in bargaining power in the employer–employee relationship – is viewed as even worse.

As for what individuals actually *want*, surveys indicate a mismatch between actual and preferred working hours. Research by Jeremy Reynolds finds that workers in multiple countries would actually choose to work less, if given the (real) choice. In Sweden, 61 percent reported a desire to work fewer hours, while in Japan, Germany, and the United States the figures were 46 percent, 38 percent, and 37 percent, respectively.[21] Elsewhere, research finds a strong positive correlation between a country's GDP per capita and the percent of workers who report wanting to work fewer hours, even if that means earning less money.[22]

As the previous sentence highlights, working less is a double-edged sword. On the one hand, it means more leisure and time to spend with one's friends and loved ones and less stress. Yet on the other hand, working less also means less income and therefore lower household purchasing power. Or does it?

Affording more with less? Yes!

Forget about *ceteris paribus* ("all other things being the same"). Those who wish to dismiss my argument in favor of shorter workdays based on claims that the strategy will reduce household purchasing power and thus overall consumer well-being – an argument I hear often when I take my message on the road – have clearly not read the preceding chapters. If a shorter work week was the *only* change implement then maybe their argument would have a leg to stand on. Yet that is not what I am arguing.

Let me begin by reviewing some of the expenses associated with working more rather than less, beginning with costs to the environment. If the United States had adopted European standards for work hours in 2000 (the latter work 16 percent more hours than their EU-15 counterparts) its CO_2 emissions would have been seven percent lower than in 1990.[23] Why is this? There are two pathways: one quite apparent; the other less so. All else equal, shorter hours of work reduce the scale of the economy compared to what it would be with higher hours – what is known as the scale effect. The second pathway involves the impact of extended work hours on the resource intensity of household consumption patterns – the compositional effect.[24] A recent study looking at 27 high-income OECD countries over the years 1970 to 2007 finds support for the existence of both.[25] The scale effect is to be expected, for the simple reason that environmental impact is tightly coupled to levels of material throughput. A nation's ecological footprint has traditionally been hitched to its GDP per capita. If the latter were to contract due to reductions in work hours then it is a safe bet to expect the same to happen to the former. What is less obvious, and therefore more of a hidden cost to longer hours, is the compositional effect.

As households transfer an increasing share of their time into market activity they are forced to convert a growing portion of their income into gadgets and services that promise to essentially buy them time. To put it plainly, households with less time will "choose," when they can afford it (and often even when they cannot), time-saving activities and products, such as cars over bikes, clothes dryers over air drying, and large rider mowers over push mowers. And, typically, the time-saving option is environmentally-intensive – or energy-*wasting*. A study of French households, for example, concludes that work hours are positively correlated to the consumption of environmentally-intensive (aka processed) foods.[26] The same holds for the time-saving benefits of eating out. A Finnish study concludes that spending an hour at a restaurant consumes 11 kilowatt-hours of energy, whereas an hour spent eating at home – factoring in for travel to purchase food, gas to prepare it, and the like – uses a little more than seven kilowatt-hours of energy.[27] The compositional effect speaks in part to what Juliet Schor has described as a "work and spend cycle." This is said to have occurred when individuals find their market "needs" suddenly expand with an increase in work hours which in turn intensifies the pressure to work even more hours which creates additional "needs" and so on.[28] An example of this can be found in the quotes presented early in this chapter, specifically number three, where an individual describes needing to "pick up a second job on weekends so we could afford to both be working."

This highlights the first wave – though not the most significant – of savings to come from a reduction in work hours as we move toward an affordable (versus cheap) economy. As detailed in the previous paragraph, a great deal of what we think we need we need because we work longer hours. Longer hours are therefore part of the *problem* rather than a solution when it comes to the fulfillment of household needs. Merely by reducing those hours we ought to free ourselves of some of those consumer pressures.

That is, however, just the tip of the savings iceberg. As I said earlier, *ceteris paribus* this is not. In an economy interested in maximizing affordability, individuals will no longer feel the pressure to earn as much while still retaining access to the same outcomes they presently enjoy. Indeed, I would expect access to those outcomes to even improve for a majority of the population due to, among other things, reductions to inequality. You read that right. Once we have done away with cheaponomics – and its expensive "cheap" stuff – and moved toward an economy that places the well-being of all ahead of profits for the few *more* can be had by working and consuming *less*.

How can this be? How could we possibly have more with less? Part of the answer lies in the type of goods we produce; something I have talked at length about in earlier chapters. Manufacturing goods for longevity and that can be easily repaired and ultimately recycled (rather than down-cycled) will likely result in more expensive goods, in the short term. But if that means you are only buying one toaster or one blender or one snow shovel over the course of your life; or if that means owning two or three types of footwear that can be repaired to last the average individual at least ten years; or if that means buying toothbrushes or carpet or digital equipment designed to be 100 percent recyclable and therefore have a zero landfill impact, then any additional upfront retail expenses will more than pay for themselves over the long term. Also, think about all the additional employment opportunities created when we suddenly need people to fix a market full of long-lasting, repairable stuff.

I have a pair of boots that I have owned for over 20 years. I remember getting them in high school (secondary school, for many parts of the world) as a birthday present. They were not cheap, in either the pejorative or retail-price sense. I wore them a lot but unlike my other footwear they seemed to never wear out. They did, of course, eventually, but only after their contemporaries had died and gone to shoe heaven – the local landfill. Yet when this finally happened I didn't have to throw them away because they were designed to be repaired. And that is precisely what I did, over and over again. When new, those shoes probably cost two or three times more than a typical ("cheap") boot. Yet they lasted me over 20 years – or the equivalent of at least ten pairs of cheap boots. That is quite a saving.

Affordable products are also multifunctional. Because the goal has been to maximize throughput (aka growth) by ratcheting up consumption and production, goods today tend to be made to solve one-off "needs." This makes sense. If you are trying to continuously intensify material throughput then solving multiple "needs" with one good works against your objective. Yet once costs are internalized this all changes, as we will begin to take seriously the pursuit of real cost savings. Thus, another low-hanging cost-saving fruit, in addition to focusing on longevity and repairability, would be making goods that can be used in different ways, from multifunctional furniture to single clothing items that double (or triple, quadruple, etc.) as other clothing items and solitary appliances that do the work of what used to require a dozen unique gadgets. Again, this strategy requires considerable upfront design which will inevitably increase the good's retail price. But if this means that fewer goods overall will be "needed" then the long-term savings are clear. Who knows, if this starts us down the path to realizing that we do not require so much overall square foot space in our homes then the costs savings could be great indeed.

There is a still larger low-hanging cost-saving fruit that I have yet to address; one so significant, in fact, that much of the next chapter is devoted to it as well. Perhaps the largest reason why individuals can afford a drop in income in an affordable society, as work hours are spread more evenly across bodies, lies in us rethinking the very notion of "consumption." Aristotle is said to have written that "on the whole, you find wealth much more in use than in ownership."[29] Similarly, Kevin Kelly, founder of the influential magazine *Wired*, has argued passionately that "access is better than ownership."[30] We have become so wrapped up in fighting for our "right to own" that we seemed to have forgotten why we wanted to own in the first place: for access and use. As a result of our economy's reckless behavior we find ourselves awash in second-hand goods. Perhaps this curse could be turned into an opportunity. What if we took steps to expand the second-hand economy and put these unwanted good back to use, rather than landfilling them? What about the overabundance of unused inventory clogging up our closets, basements, and garages? Rentable storage space in the United States increased 740 percent in the last two decades.[31] What if we were to start renting some of those underutilized goods to others who are otherwise contemplating purchasing those goods new – what is known as peer-to-peer renting? If we started consuming access rather than goods per se we would not need to own nearly as much, nor would we need to own the space to store all that stuff. There is enormous unrealized savings in rethinking how we consume, as we move from an individualistic to a more collaborative model of consumption.

Given its importance, I revisit the subject of collaborative consumption in the next chapter. But my point has been made. The savings to be had by moving toward an affordable society are considerable and easily offset any reductions in income that might come from working fewer hours. And I have yet to even mention the enormous *social* benefits attributable to this scheme, which brings me to the next and final section of the chapter.

The truly affluent society

Our long work hours are responsible for the resource-intensive type of leisure that has become so prevalent in high-income countries. After World War II, governments set upon a strategy to make leisure less time-intensive and more goods-intensive – in other words, more commercial.[32] Not that this should be surprising, as it paralleled the broader need that existed at the time – and which continues to this day – to keep consumption growing sufficiently fast to stay abreast of productivity gains.[33] Think also about what happens to our communities and neighborhoods as they become ghost towns between the hours of 8 a.m. and 5 p.m. Long work hours create communities devoid of *community*, becoming spaces deficient of thick social relationships, trust, and mutual respect. Instead, people today are increasingly coming together around connections of affinity, such as sharing a favorite sports team, "liking" something on Facebook, or through a mutual fondness for a television show. (I remember during the first season of the television show *Glee* that many of my Facebook friends posted pictures of their weekly *Glee* parties.) Yet these connections are far weaker, often temporary, and have greater in-and-out movement than those rooted in the hard work that goes into building and maintaining kinship and friendship ties.[34]

Should it be any surprise, then, that leisure today increasingly involves going *to* someplace? At present, helped along in no small part by cheaponomics, many communities are so lowly regarded that they offer few inducements to encourage people to stick around when they have free time. Reducing work hours are an important first step toward remaking communities into places we actually *want* to be. This will not only create an incentive to keep people within those spaces when not working but will further reduce their need for higher incomes as they no longer feel such a desire to take an expensive trip in order to get away. (Recall at the beginning of this chapter the individual quoted who hated to work but needed to take a second job to afford the next family vacation.) The ecological savings alone would be tremendous if communities could be remade to entice residents to stay rather than flee at every opportunity. Estimates, for example, for the overall contribution of travel to tourism's global greenhouse gas emissions is more than 75 percent.[35]

There are solid sociological and economic reasons why we ought to divest some of our time from the energy-intensive, socially destructive professional economy and reinvest it in the more labor-intensive, social-capitalizing amateur economy. Take, for example, the path-breaking research from the 1960s by the economist Gary Becker. In his article from 1965 titled "A Theory of the Allocation of Time" he had the audacity to argue that non-monetized activities yield returns.[36] Prior to Becker economists tended to focus exclusively on the question of time allocation in the context of wages and salaries earned or deferred, such as when individuals go off to school. Yet a world of only dollars and cents this is not.

We all do a lot of work that is immensely valuable but which garners zero wages. Back in 1995 the United Nations estimated that this unpaid work, if monetized, would amount to $16 trillion (or roughly $23 trillion in 2013 dollars), $11 trillion of which was attributed to the invisible non-monetary work undertaken by women.[37] By recognizing the value of this work I am not suggesting we monetize it. Instead I offer this data as evidence that in a society where people work, say, "only" 20 hours a week they are still being highly productive during the week's other 148 hours. Moreover, we cannot limit our understanding of "productivity" to only those services that have an equivalent in the professional economy – like filling out a tax return, caring for one's child, mowing the lawn, or painting your grandmother's house. While these examples are all valuable for household production still additional "work" is needed if we are to produce the livable, attractive communities mentioned earlier that lead to people choosing to forgo long-distance trips for staying nearer to home.

The honorable Richard Posner, currently judge on the United States Court of Appeals for the Seventh Circuit, recently wrote in a review of the book *How Much is Enough* (a book that extols the virtues of the shorter work week), that "most people would quickly get bored without the resources for varied and exciting leisure activities like foreign travel, movies and television, casinos, restaurants, watching sporting events, engaging in challenging athletic activities, playing video games, eating out, dieting, having cosmetic surgery, and improving health and longevity."[38] Posner makes a grave error in his reasoning, however: assuming all other things remain the same in an affordable society. As individuals spend less time at work and more time productively reinvesting in building up the social, human, and political capitals of their communities we should not expect them to become as easily bored. Nor would we turn into brutes, as claimed by Posner: "If they lacked consumer products and services to fill up their time they would brawl, steal, overeat, drink and sleep late."[39] I will grant Posner this much: his prediction could conceivably be realized if the society in question were totally devoid of social capital. The fact he assumes this would occur if people were left with too much free time on their hands bolsters my earlier claim about the status quo having gutted our lives of the important social relationships that give life meaning and worth. But what if we were to bring those relationships back?

Leisure is not just about "letting one's mind wander freely and aimlessly," to again quote Posner.[40] Nor is leisure to be conflated with being lazy and lying around, though, clearly, from a public and personal health perspective these "activities" have their place. Gary Cross writes about this in the context of "democratic leisure."[41] In moving toward fewer work hours the aim is not to turn all additional leisure time into idleness but into democratic leisure: "a balance of work with time free from economic obligations and a form of leisure that provide the widest possible choice, access, and *participation*" (my emphasis).[42]

Cheaponomics undermines community interdependence, which explains why Posner expects a move to shorter work hours to lead us into a twenty-first century version of a Hobbesian state of nature. As Juliet Schor notes, "when people can afford to purchase services, they ask for favors less often," no doubt due in part to the fact that they lack the time to ask and later reciprocate these community-building acts of goodwill.[43] Economic growth, in-and-of-itself, can be incredibly corrosive to community, particularly when it results in each of us looking to the market rather than to each other for love, comfort, help, support, and care.[44] Too often social capital is narrowly attributed to economic growth as an *input*, as trust, mutual respect, and familiarity help grease the wheels of exchange by lowering transaction costs.[45] Yet in modern, cheap economies these greasy social relationships are being replaced by things like contract law, multinational trade agreements, and international governing bodies (e.g., World Trade Organization). These social capital substitutes no doubt reduce uncertainty and therefore the transaction costs of exchange. But at what cost?

As cheap economies become less reliant upon social capital to function they continue to undermine it in other spheres, like the communities in which we live. This led Edward Miguel, Professor of Economics at the University of California, Berkeley, to come to the conclusion back in 2003 that "growth may destroy social capital."[46] My focus thus far has been on how cheaponomics undermines social relationships within affluent nations. Professor Miguel's conclusion, however, is directed specifically toward lower-income nations as they begin the process of being transformed into modern, cheap economies. In his own words:

> Rapidly growing societies periodically experience large technological "shocks" that generate pressure for labor mobility, to take up new factory jobs in growing urban areas, for example. The resulting residential mobility increases labor productivity by matching up workers with particular skills to the employers who need those skills. Yet this mobility also has less

beneficial consequences. Trust and social capital are undermined by extensive labor mobility, as individuals are no longer able to engage in the long-term reciprocal relationships that nurture community cooperation.[47]

A sense of happiness, belonging, and camaraderie are not the only things at stake when talking about social capital. For many, social capital is a matter of survival. Social capital brings with it gains in other capitals – political, human, natural, and so forth – which can be tapped when the situation requires it.[48] More than just the social "glue" that holds societies together (an overused metaphor to describe its function), social capital gives communities Promethean-like qualities. It allows societies to adapt and change, sometimes abruptly, in the face of threats. Social capital, to put it simply, makes societies resilient.[49] Want to take steps to help ensure you are not harmed during the next extreme weather event or natural disaster? Make friends. The literature looking into the question of *who* is most likely to be impacted by adverse events finds social isolation to be, quite literally, a killer.[50]

These bonds do not just happen. Democratic leisure takes time and effort to form. On that point, it is encouraging to know that survey research indicates people would be happier earning less if, in exchange, they could live closer to friends. Roughly 70 percent of the individuals surveyed in a University of Michigan and Cornell study expressed such an opinion.[51] Most of us do not have the resources to pack up our lives and stuff (*all* that stuff!) and move closer to old friends (or to have them move closer to us). But what we do have is the ability to make friends with those already near us, though such friendship-building activities would be considerably easier if everyone was not in such a rush.

Pantzar and Shove offer up the concept of "manufacturing leisure" to remind us of how leisure is a process that involves consumers and producers alike as well as the practical integration of different elements such as ideas, people, technology, and infrastructure.[52] Their point is that it is very difficult for any single group of actors to bring about change. *Collective* action, which admittedly is a lot of work, offers the surest path to success. Fortunately, communities around the world are experimenting with these particular ends in mind.[53] Take, for example, the "20-minute neighborhood," a practical concept that seeks to foster social interdependence while creating deep cuts in energy use and greenhouse gas emissions. The goal is to create a neighborhood where all basic needs and activities – whether for work, play, healthcare, and so forth – can be satisfied within a geographical space accessible by a leisurely bike ride.[54]

What I have tried to highlight in this chapter is the point that the solution to cheaponomics does not lie just in stuff, which is to say, in making things better or with a greater eye toward total cost accounting. The costs being socialized by cheaponomics are not just costs that ought to be internalized. They are costs that should be – and can be – avoided, such as those described in this chapter. Cheaponomics is therefore not just a design, manufacturing, or economic problem – or, in other words, about designing things better, making things more efficiently, or getting the prices right. It is also a sociological problem, in that it is about the altering of social relationships and erosion of community. Additional ways to go about strengthening those relationships are the subject of the next chapter, as I discuss further the concept of collaborative consumption while combating an ideology that refuses to die: productivism.

Notes

1. Mazur, Paul (1928) *American Prosperity: Its Causes and Consequences* (London: Jonathan Cape), p. 99.
2. Ayres, Robert and Benjamin Warr (2009) *The Economic Growth Engine: How Energy and Work Drive Material Prosperity* (Northampton, MA: Edward Elgar), p. xvi.
3. Ibid., p. xvi.
4. Isidore, Chris (2010) "7.9 million jobs lost – many forever," *CNN*, July 2, http://money.cnn.com/2010/07/02/news/economy/jobs_gone_forever/index.htm, last accessed February 27, 2013.
5. United States Department of Labor (n.d.) American Time Use Survey, Bureau of Labor Statistics, Washington, DC, www.bls.gov/tus/charts/, last accessed February 28, 2013.
6. See, for example, Hunnicutt, B. (1996) *Kellogg's Six-Hour Day* (Philadelphia: Temple University Press).
7. Ibid., p. 20.
8. Fitz, D. (2009) "What's wrong with a 30 hour work week," *Z Magazine*, July, www.zcommunications.org/whats-wrong-with-a-30-hour-work-week-bydon-fitz, last accessed February 28, 2013.
9. Botsman, R. and R. Rogers (2010) *What's Mine Is Yours: The Rise of Collaborative Consumption* (New York: Harper), p. 46.
10. Keynes, John Maynard (1963) "Economic possibility for our grandchildren," in *Essays in Persuasion* (New York: W.W. Norton & Co.), pp. 358–73.
11. Ibid., p. 371.
12. Galbraith, John Kenneth (1998) *The Affluent Society*, Fortieth Anniversary Edition (New York: Houghton Mifflin Company), p. 100.
13. Keynes (1963), p. 368.
14. Skidelsky, Robert and Edward Skidelsky (2012) *How Much is Enough? Money and the Good Life* (New York: Other Press), p. 36.
15. Mishan, E. (1967) *The Costs of Economic Growth* (Middlesex, MA: Penguin Books), p. 149.
16. Hunnicutt, Benjamin (1988) *Work Without End: Abandoning Shorter Hours for the Right to Work* (Philadelphia: Temple University Press), p. 67.
17. Schor, Juliet (2010) *True Wealth* (New York: Penguin Books), p. 167.
18. Schor, Juliet (1993) *The Overworked American* (New York: Basic Books); Schor (2010).
19. Schor (2010), pp. 167–8.
20. Bowles, S. and Y. Park (2005) "Emulation, inequality, and work hours: Was Thorsten Veblen right?" *The Economic Journal*, 115, pp. 397–412.
21. Reynolds, J. (2003) "You can't always get the hours you want: Mismatches between actual and preferred work hours in the U.S." *Social Forces*, 81(4), pp. 1171–99; Reynolds, J. (2004) "When too much is not enough: Actual and preferred work hours in the United States and abroad," *Sociological Forum*, 19(1), pp. 89–120.

22 Otterbach, S. (2010) "Mismatches between actual and preferred work time: Empirical evidence of hours constraints in 21 countries," *Journal of Consumer Policy*, 33, pp. 143–61.
23 Rosnick, David and Mark Weisbrot (2006) "Are shorter work hours good for the environment? A comparison of US and European energy consumption," Center for Economic and Policy Research, Washington, DC, www.cepr.net/documents/publications/energy_2006_12.pdf, last accessed March 2, 2013.
24 Knight, Kyle W., Eugene A. Rosa, and Juliet B. Schor (2012) "Could working less reduce pressures on the environment? A cross-national panel analysis of OECD countries, 1970–2007," presented at the Annual Meeting of the American Sociological Association, Denver, CO, August 19.
25 Ibid.
26 Devetter, F. and S. Rousseau (2011) "Working hours and sustainable development," *Review of Social Economy*, 69(3), pp. 333–55.
27 Jalas, M. (2002) "A time use perspective on the materials intensity of consumption," *Ecological Economics*, 41(1), pp. 109–23.
28 Schor (1993).
29 As quoted in Rifkin, J. (2000) *The Age of Access* (New York: Tarcher), p. 76.
30 Kelly, K. (n.d.) "Access is better than ownership," *Exponential Times*, www.exponentialtimes.net /videos /access-better-ownership-0, last accessed March 3, 2013.
31 Botsman and Rogers (2010), p. 13.
32 Hunnicutt (1988), p. 312.
33 Hunnicutt (1988), p. 42; see also Cross, G. (1993) *Time and Money: The Making of Consumer Culture* (London and New York: Routledge).
34 Schor (2010), p. 141.
35 Scott, D., P. Peeters and S. Gössling (2010) "Can tourism deliver its 'aspirational' greenhouse gas emission reduction targets?" *Journal of Sustainable Tourism*, 18(3), pp. 393–408.
36 Becker, Gary (1965) "A theory of the allocation of time," *The Economic Journal*, 75 (299), pp. 495–517.
37 United Nations (1995) "Valuing women's work, United Nations," Human Development Report, p. 97, Washington DC, http://hdr.undp.org/en/media/hdr_1995_en_chap4.pdf, last accessed November 11, 2013.
38 Posner, Richard (2012) "'Working 9 to 12: How much is enough' by Robert Skidelsky and Edward Skodelsky," *New York Times*, August 17, www.nytimes.com/2012/08/19/books/review/how-much-is-enough-by-robert-skidelsky-and-edward-skidelsky.html?pagewanted=all, last accessed March 4, 2013.
39 Ibid.
40 Ibid.
41 Cross (1993).
42 Ibid., p. 3.
43 Schor (2010), p. 140.
44 See, for example, Bauman, Zygmunt (2011) *Culture in a Liquid Modern World* (Cambridge: Polity).
45 See, for example, Halpern, David (2005) *Social Capital* (Cambridge: Polity), p. 71.
46 Miguel, E. (2003) "Comment on: Social capital and growth," *Journal of Monetary Economics*, 50, p. 196.
47 Ibid., pp. 195–6.
48 See, for example, Emery, M. and C. Flora (2006) "Spiraling-up: mapping community transformation with community capitals framework," *Community Development*, 37(1), pp. 19–35.
49 Zakour, Michael John, and David F. Gillespie (2013) *Community Disaster Vulnerability* (New York: Springer), pp. 62–5.

50 Brauch, Hans Gunter (2011) "Concepts of security threats, challenges, vulnerability and risks," in *Coping with Global Environmental Change, Disasters and Security*, edited by H.G. Brauch, Ú. Oswald Spring, C. Mesjasz, J. Grin, P. Kameri-Mbote, B. Chourou, P. Dunay, and J. Birkmann (New York: Springer), pp. 61–106, p. 69.
51 Benjamin, Daniel, Ori Heffetz, Miles S. Kimball, and Alex Rees-Jones (2010) "Do people seek to maximize happiness? Evidence from new surveys," National Bureau of Economic Research, Cambridge, MA, Working Paper 16489, www.nber.org/papers/w16489.pdf?new_window=1, last accessed March 7, 2013.
52 Pantzar, M. and E. Shove (2005) "Manufacturing leisure: Innovations in happiness, well-being and fun" (Helsinki: National Consumer Research Centre), www.ncrc.fi/files/4717/2005_01_publications_manufacturingleisure.pdf, last accessed March 5, 2013.
53 See, for example, Costanza, R., G. Alperovitz, H. Daly, J. Farley, C. Franco, T. Jackson, I. Kubiszewski, J.B. Schor, and P. Victor (2012) "Building a sustainable and desirable: Economy-in-Society-in-Nature," New York, United Nations, http://sustainabledevelopment.un.org/content/documents/Building_a_Sustainable_and_Desirable_Economy-in-Society-in-Nature.pdf, last accessed March 5, 2013.
54 McNeil, N. (2010) "A twenty minute neighbourhood for bicycles?" http://nathanmcneil.files.wordpress.com/2010/05/mcneil20minuteposter2.pdf, last accessed March 5, 2013.

Part III

Transitioning toward affordability

Chapter 8

Comforting the productivist zombie

H&M, Old Navy, Target, Zara, Fashion 21, Gap, and Hollister: no longer does one risk being labeled cheap when seeking out cheap clothes. Cheap is the new normal. Indeed, it is cool to be cheap. You could even say it is hard to be cool by not being cheap. Fast fashion – that is what it is called.[1] And that is what fashion has become – fast – because it has become so damn cheap. The consumer price index in the United States for apparel that stood at 139 in 1993 dropped to 115 by 2010.[2] No wonder Americans went from buying an average of 34 new pieces of clothes a year in 1991 to 67 in 2007 – or a new piece of clothing every 5.4 days.[3] Decades ago, fashion seasons followed the annual cycle of spring, summer, autumn, and winter. Today, fast fashion cycles are compressed into far shorter periods. Companies like Zara, for example, have shrunk these cycles to two weeks, which is the time between when store inventories are "refreshed."[4] The level of waste generated by this industry is appalling. Everyone, both within and outside of it, agrees that something needs to be done. But what?

Enter the Sustainable Apparel Coalition. Member companies (including brands, retailers, and manufacturers), which are estimated to be responsible for more than one-third of the apparel and footwear produced globally, have pledged to lead the apparel industry toward developing improved sustainability strategies.[5] Its goal: to produce more efficient, energy-saving supply chains that cut retail and manufacturing costs while also lessening the toll of cheap clothes on human and environmental health. Sounds great. Too bad, as a solution to the ills of cheaponomics, it is without a heartbeat or soul.

What is the point, in terms of real cost savings, of producing goods more efficiently in an industry committed to a business model that involves marketing and manufacturing items "obsolete" after two weeks? I know someone with a mock Sierra Club sticker on their hunting rifle explaining that "No animals were harmed in the making of this product." As labels are rolled out by the Sustainable Apparel Coalition, touting the lighter eco-impact of some of its member companies' fast fashion, I will be sure to remember that ironic sticker on my friend's gun. One label is clearly a joke; the other attempting, through satire, to make a statement about the efficacy of green and ethical labels.

The holy alter of efficiency. We have been worshipping before it on bended knee for decades. Hard not to; it is so apolitical, nonthreatening, and safe. It is the equivalent of a tender pat on the back and a whisper in the ear: "No need for real change; consumers stay the course; all that is needed are a couple tweaks at the production end." Efficiency points an accusatory finger at our (inefficient) implementation, thereby shielding the system itself from any critical scrutiny.

What, then, is efficiency hiding? As explained repeatedly over the last seven chapters, the real problem with cheaponomics is not its inefficient use of resources. It is with cheaponomics *itself*. I have no problem with efficiency. In fact, I will be among the first to kneel down before it once it is moved from the church of cheap to a site of worship more interested in affording individuals real improvements in well-being. This chapter begins by highlighting some of the downsides of efficiency. From here discussion turns to the subject of what will need to be changed so that we can exploit efficiency gains without the costs that presently make such gains unsustainable.

Leaving rebounds on the basketball court

I have total faith in the Sustainable Apparel Coalition. The bringing together of all those bright minds, determined personalities, and deep pockets will undoubtedly reduce the amount of resources consumed by the apparel industry *per unit produced*. And that will likely, as they advertise, also reduce costs along the supply chain, which means even cheaper products for consumers.[6] Win-win situation, right? You can put the balloons and confetti away. This is not something we ought to be celebrating. Why? What happens to rates of consumption when something becomes cheaper, like when resources are saved through efficiency gains? They go *up*. Economics 101: want to sell more of something, sell it for less – especially when talking about goods with elastic demand (such as fast fashion), where a drop in price is met with a proportionally equal increase in demand. It is a truly wicked paradox: that in our rush to save the environment and natural resources through efficiency gains we may be unintentionally *hastening their demise*.

We have known about this for 150 years. In his 1865 book, *The Coal Question* (in the chapter titled "Of the Economy of Fuel"), William Stanley Jevons highlighted the paradox of how the rising efficiency of coal used in production was associated with rising coal consumption. Specifically, Jevons showed that improvements to iron production that reduced the amount of coal wasted by two-thirds led to a *tenfold* increase in total consumption in Scotland between 1830 and 1863. There are actually two terms that are relevant to this discussion. The first is the rebound effect. This is said to occur when gains in efficiency fail to lead to proportional reductions in consumption, such as, for example, when a 20 percent gain in efficiency leads to a reduction in consumption or waste of only 10 percent. When a rebound effect is more than 100 percent of the efficiency gain it is called a Jevons paradox – after William Stanley Jevons. What Jevons details in *The Coal Question* is a Jevons paradox, where a 66 percent gain in coal efficiency in iron production led to a 1,000 percent increase in total coal consumption. The latter increases in consumption more than offset the conservation benefits of improved efficiency.

Let me give you an example that hits closer to home, literally. A few years back my wife and I switched out the incandescent bulbs in our house for compact fluorescents (CFL). CFL bulbs are the poster child for proponents of efficiency. And why shouldn't they be: the average CFL lasts between 8 and 15 times longer than an incandescent. CFL bulbs also consume 20 to 33 percent of the electricity of the older (by roughly 200 years!) technology. Only 10 percent of the energy used by incandescents generates light. The rest is lost as heat. In other words, we essentially wasted 90 percent of all the electricity used last century for lighting. (You can also thank cheap electricity for that.) All of these statistics touting the marvelous savings of CFL bulbs are absolutely true, as long as all other things remain the same. When humans are in the equation, however, you can be sure that this condition is rarely met. Thanks to humans, all others things are rarely equal. Change one condition and chances are good that others will change too, as evidenced by the rebound effect and Jevons paradox. I am speaking from experience. My wife and I changed our behaviors after installing CFL bulbs throughout the house. Before the changeover we hated leaving lights on in unused rooms and never left them on for security purposes. No nightlights for the kids. No front porch lights. No light above the kitchen sink when away on extended trips. Nothing. Not anymore. The difference, you might say, is night and day. Nightlights: on. Security lights: on. The light above the kitchen sink when away: on (and a few others too). I have CFL bulbs to thank for this change of heart and behavior.

I cannot be certain whether this example represents a Jevons paradox or a rebound effect. I am guessing it is the latter, that the overall efficacy gained by switching over to CFL bulbs *still* outweighs our increased household bulb use. If true, can we then say that the CFL conversion translates into a net ecological savings? Not necessarily. Again we have to ask, beyond the above-mentioned change in behavior, does everything else remain the same? Some additional unpacking of the rebound effect is now required. There are three generally recognized categories of rebound effects.

- Direct rebound effects: efficiency gains that decrease the effective price of the resource in question and therefore lead to an increase in its consumption.
- Indirect rebound effects: with a decrease in per unit price more income is available to spend on other products and services which in the end result in the consumption of more resources and/or energy.

- Economy wide rebound effects: long-term changes in the economy caused by technological innovation which changes consumer preferences, social institutions, and norms (e.g., around "convenience" and "comfort") and locks society into a trajectory of ever-increasing material throughput.

The fact that my wife and I now keep more lights on more often, because CFLs make it cheaper for us to do so, is a direct rebound effect. The rebound effects beyond this, however, are much more difficult to track. What if we took those savings and used the money to buy airfare to some faraway place? This refers to an indirect rebound effect. So much for the ecological savings of CFL bulbs. Money saved is money inevitably spent on something else. Personal saving rates in the United States hit a paltry one percent in 2005, down from more than 14 percent in 1975. And while rates rose slightly in the years following the tanking of the global economy in 2008 they are trending downward yet again.[7] If you are like the average person in the United States, whatever is saved by buying energy-efficient windows, hybrid cars, or by growing your own food is used to get something else – a vacation to some tropical destination, the newest iPhone, more fast fashion, or perhaps a second home. It is hard to see how *any* resources are being saved in the end through efficiency. Even when you end up sticking that money away in a bank account or in the stock market what do you think happens to it? It gets reinvested back into the economy *to buy more stuff*. And I have not even addressed economy wide rebound effects yet.

Oil price spikes in the 1970s stimulated tremendous research and development in the area of automobile fuel economy. When oil prices fell in the 1980s the efficiency gains made in the prior decade were translated into making vehicles more powerful and better equipped (heavier) while possessing the same fuel costs per mile as earlier models. Enter sports utility vehicles – aka SUVs. Efficiency gains in the 1970s, therefore, did not reduce energy consumption so much as raise consumer expectations around issues relating to the experience of transportation and the comfort therein implied – an example of an economy wide rebound effect. These expectations have since transformed the entire transportation market and represent a yardstick of sorts against which all forms of mobility are now measured. Even public transportation, to some degree, has to live up to these energy-intensive expectations as individuals have grown accustomed to a certain level of comfort.[8]

Let us not forget how a reduction in cost of outputs from one sector will likely lower the cost of inputs to another sector and thereby increase both production and consumption throughout the entire economy.[9] So, for instance, energy efficiency gains in steel production could very well translate into a reduction in the price of steel, which could equally mean cheaper automobiles, a greater demand for these commodities, and, in the end, a spike in the global demand for gasoline. Economy wide rebound effects are notoriously difficult to track. But the logic in support of their existence is clear.

New products and services, under the status quo, will always be created to exploit markets opened up by lower costs thus creating an overall increase in energy and resource consumption. That is how markets work. And it is also why cheaponomics is so problematic, because the price signals, which ought to be discouraging us from exploiting scarce, non-renewable resources, are directing the economy over a cliff.

Take how the range of uses for electric lighting expanded greatly as it became progressively cheaper. Per capita lighting consumption in the UK increased dramatically from 1800 to 2000. This was largely due to the falling cost of lighting services (lighting efficiency improved during the period by a factor of 1,000) but also because of a steadily growing GDP per capita, which, itself, was made possible thanks to cheap electricity.[10] A study by Roger Fouquet and Peter Pearson, researchers at Imperial College London, trace the evolution of demand for lighting in the UK as technology of lighting progressed from medieval candles to eighteenth-century oil lamps, nineteenth-century gas lights, and, finally, twenty-century electric incandescent bulbs. Every time a more efficient lighting technology has been introduced our consumption of lighting increased dramatically. Incandescent bulbs, inefficient as they are relative to CFL technology, are 700 times more efficient than nineteenth-century oil lamps, whereas our consumption, measured in lumen-hours per capita, is over 6,500 times greater than in the 1800s. More recently, incandescent bulbs have seen their efficiency double from 1950 to 2000 while per capita lighting during that period has quadrupled.[11] As electricity became cheaper new markets were also created, such as around the idea of illuminating unattended spaces (security lighting) as well as those outside the home (outdoor lighting). Utility companies have been happy to translate efficiency gains into lower utility prices, believing it to be more profitable to sell a lot of electricity at low margins than a little at high margins. Doing this has effectively hooked much of the economy on cheap electricity, which explains why, for instance, so many turn a blind eye to such egregiously expensive things like cheap coal. With so much of the world now dependent upon cloud computing, social media, online streaming, and the like (see Chapter 2) we have all become cheap electricity addicts.

The amount of energy, for example, required to produce each unit of the world's economic output – what is known as "energy intensity" – has fallen steadily over the past half century. Global energy intensity is now more than 33 percent lower than it was in 1970.[12] Energy intensity in both the United States and the UK is approximately 40 percent lower today than in 1980.[13] Global carbon intensity – the amount of CO_2 emitted for each unit of economic output produced – declined by some 25 percent between 1980 and 2006. Every dollar spent in the United States in 1980 translated into one kilogram of CO_2 emitted, whereas in 2006 it equaled 770 grams.[14] Hooray for efficiency! Now for the bad news.

While we may be producing each unit – from lumen-hours to cheap jeans, food, mobile phones, and the like – more efficiently we are also producing more units; so many more, in fact, that we have more than offset any gains in efficiency. Thus, even with those aforementioned reductions in carbon and energy intensities, global CO_2 emissions have *increased* 105 percent (or 2 percent annually) since 1971 and are projected to rise by another 39 percent (or 1.4 percent annually) by 2030.[15] Research by sociologist Richard York examines trends in total CO_2 emissions and the carbon intensity for the world's top-five CO_2-emitting nations: China, the United States, Russia, India, and Japan. In 2006, these countries accounted for 55 percent of total world emissions, 52 percent of world GDP, and 46 percent of world population. York found that although each economy is steadily becoming more efficient in terms of CO_2 emissions (per unit of GDP) their overall CO_2 footprints are trending in precisely the opposite direction. In the case of the United States, while CO_2 emissions per inflation adjusted unit of GDP have decreased by roughly 45 percent between 1980 and 2005 total CO_2 emissions have increased by more than 70 percent.[16]

Decoupling is talked about a lot these days. In case you are not familiar with the term, in the eco-economic arena it refers to the ability of an economy to grow without corresponding increases in environmental pressure – a break, in other words, in the link between environmental bads and socioeconomic goods.[17] Sounds great, right? With decoupling, production processes are radically transformed and goods and services thoroughly redesigned until economic output becomes independent of material throughput. Think "paperless office" at a grand scale. At the moment, economic output and material throughput are tightly coupled.

Tim Jackson, in *Prosperity Without Growth*, stresses the importance of differentiating between "relative" and "absolute" decoupling when using the term.[18] Relative decoupling refers to a decline in the ecological intensity per unit of economic output. In this situation, resource impacts decline relative to the GDP which could still be rising. Absolute decoupling refers to a situation in which resource impacts decline in absolute terms, regardless of what the GDP is doing. Resource efficiencies must increase at least as fast as economic output does and must continue to improve as the economy grows for absolute decoupling to be occurring. Jackson points out that an economy can correctly claim that it has relatively decoupled its economy in terms of energy inputs per unit of GDP. However, in this situation, *total* environmental impacts would still be increasing, albeit at a slower pace of growth than in GDP. Jackson suggests this distinction ought to temper claims by technology-optimists who use the term "decoupling" as an "escape route from the dilemma of growth."[19] For as he and others point out, while there is considerable evidence to support the existence of relative decoupling in global economies evidence for absolute decoupling just isn't there.[20]

Decoupling is viewed as our Get Out of Jail Free card; the way in which we will be able to have our cake (and eat as much as we want) and so will future generations too. There is just one small catch. There is nothing to indicate – particularly in light of the aforementioned rebound effect – that decoupling is even possible. (Think "paperless office" and how the digital revolution ended up having just the opposite effect.)[21] As described earlier, we presently cannot even achieve efficiency gains fast enough to offset total global CO_2 emissions, even though CO_2 is widely considered one of the easiest decoupling challenges for the simple reason that we know how to generate energy without emitting greenhouse gases. Not that I think total decoupling is essential either. It is only a necessity if our hope is to square the circle and save over-consumption and planned obsolesce from an otherwise certain demise as we do away with cheaponomics. Once we realize we do not need to have it all, while continually striving to replace what we have with the next "best thing," than it becomes easier to see that sustainability could still be achieved absent of total decoupling.

To get to that point we need to have a frank conversation about ownership. Is there a way to still achieve the ends we desire and not over-consume? That question is the focus of the next section.

From consumer to citizen choice

The so-called modern municipal waste stream shuttles our trash away. In fact, it does this too well, at least according to some, by making it too easy to forget about all the costs that go along with living in a disposable society – what some scholars have called the distancing of waste.[22] Out of sight out of mind. This is certainly true, to an extent. The garbage collectors that ferry the waste generated by my household away could just as well be fairies in the eyes of my two kids. They come once a week by the cover of night, for just a few seconds, riding a loud beast that spews smoke, beeps (at least when backing up), and is covered in flashing lights. And then they are gone along with our trash. Magic! Or so it would seem.

We all still rely upon these near-magical qualities of the municipal waste stream, though arguably not as much as we did 10 or 20 years ago. Increasingly individuals are opting to handle their trash themselves, by living with it. In November 2004 a survey of more than 1,600 respondents was administered by the Australia Institute commissioned to understand the nature and extent of waste in Australia.[23] The research discovered that surveyed households spent, on average, AU$1,226 every year on items that were never used. That means Australians as a whole essentially waste more than AU$10.5 billion a year on goods that, for all intents and purposes, should have never been bought. If the same holds true for, say, US households, then Americans spend roughly US $150 billion annually on goods they never use. *That's* the trash we are living with: the clothes, exercise equipment, power tools, electronic gadgets, and knickknacks that we choose not to set out for the garbage fairies but which still live out their lives forgotten and untouched.

No wonder our homes have grown so much over the last 60 years. In 1950, the average home in the United States was 983 square feet.[24] By 2007, it had grown to 2,521 square feet.[25] With the global recession in 2008 the figure actually shrank by some 100 square feet, at least for a year or two. The downward trend ultimately proved temporary. Average home sizes are increasing again.[26] All of this has also occurred while the average number of people per household has *shrank*, from roughly 3.7 in 1950 to a little more than 2.6 today.[27] Something else not reflected in those statistics: more than half of all homes built in 1950 did not have a garage; today, that figure is closer to 8 percent (and many of those built today are large enough for two or more cars).[28] Yet apparently our homes and garages are not growing fast enough. We increasingly feel the need to rent additional space for all that stuff we never (or rarely) use. According to the Self-Storage Association (SSA), there are more than 53,000 personal storage facilities in the United States alone. The total self-storage rentable space in the United States totals some 2.3 billion square feet. That is more than 78 square miles of self-enclosed space (or more than three times the size of Manhattan Island in New York).[29] Want to talk about some of the costs of over-consumption? Even when just focusing on those directly incurred by consumers – as *consumers* – the numbers are rather remarkable. On top of the roughly $150 billion a year Americans waste on goods they will never use they are also spending, as all this unused stuff has to be put somewhere, an additional $22 billion in storage fees (a figure that reflects the annual revenue generated by the self-storage industry in the United States).[30]

I could use this information to prosthelytize to those who buy things they never use. But then, who hasn't done this? Perhaps it's my Catholic upbringing but I find this holier-than-thou finger wagging entirely disingenuous, after all, let she or he who is without sin cast the first stone. Rather than being wrenched by guilt I prefer taking a more optimistic slant to the above statistics (recognizing also that we still need to change our ways). All that unused stuff has already extracted a significant toll on the environment. Why not, then, put it to use so more stuff does not meet a similar fate, of consuming still more resources only to be born and lie idle in some rented storage space for years? All those unused goods represent an enormous idling capacity.[31] The fact is, while owners might not use that stuff others could. So let's get it into the hands of those who would.

Just about every semester I survey my class (titled Global Environmental Issues) of 100 undergraduate students and ask them about the things they own but never or rarely use. Recently I had a class that reported owning collectively 88 power drills – 88! Granted, four students reported owning more than one. But still, for something that was on average said to be used once a year, that is a tremendous amount of hole-making idling capacity. Even the cars the students owned spent more time parked than in use – a lot more. They reported being in their cars, on average, about ten minutes a day. That leaves 1,430 minutes where the car was just sitting, yet still racking up costs in terms of depreciation, tax, title, license, insurance, and (in most cases) parking.

This leads discussion into territory broached briefly in the last chapter when the seemingly radical suggestion was made of teasing apart access from ownership and valuing the former over the latter; though, as was also noted, there is nothing particularly new here as valuing use over ownership dates back to at least Aristotle.[32] To put it simply: what we really want is the opened can and not the can opener. Enter what has become known as collaborative consumption.[33]

This is not, however, your grandmother's sharing economy; not entirely at least. Rachel Botsman and Roo Rogers, in their path-breaking book on collaborative consumption, *What's Mine is Yours*, tell the story about how Airbnb was founded. Airbnb matches travelers looking for rooms with locals who possess extra space they are looking to rent. (Given the earlier statistics about how the average home size is on the rise while the average household size is shrinking there is plenty idling space capacity to go around.) The company provides accommodations in 192 countries and has booked, since being founded in 2008, more than ten million nights worldwide.[34] When one of the company's founders, Brian Chesky, first told his grandfather about Airbnb's business model, "It seemed totally normal to him. My parents had a different reaction." It later dawned on Chesky that Airbnb is "not the modern invention, hotels are."[35] When his grandparents were younger they stayed with friends and friends of friends when traveling. That was the norm. Today, the norm is hotels. But who is to say that is the way is has to be?

Airbnb is just one firm in a multibillion dollar a year sharing economy commonly referred to as peer-to-peer renting (aka P2P renting): the process of one private individual renting an underused item (or space) to another. The web is bristling with P2P sites, like irent2you.com, rentmineonline.com, and iletyou.com. These sites enable individuals to make use of those aforementioned unused goods by renting them to others. The former are able to draw some income from this process – the sharing economy is estimated to be a US $10 billion-plus market – while keeping the latter from having to purchase a brand new good which they would likely only use sparingly.[36] As long as you get the can opened do you really care if you own the can opener? From an environmental standpoint alone, it is far better if we could accomplish the ends we value without always owning the means to achieve them. It has been estimated that if the United States shifted a mere fifth of its household spending from purchasing to renting the country would cut CO_2 emissions by roughly two percent (or 13 million tons) annually.[37]

Another example of providing access rather than ownership is Zipcar, the world's largest car-sharing company. Car sharing is a short-term car rental model where cars are scattered throughout a community to improve access rather than all being centrally housed at one location, as is the case with traditional car rentals. Zipcar allows members to reserve a car for as little as one hour. Reservations can be made in a few seconds online through a mobile phone app. As of November 2012, Zipcar had 767,000 members – up from 650,000 just 12 months earlier – and offered 11,000 vehicles through North America and Europe.[38] As of December 2012, an estimated 1.7 million people – roughly 800,000 located in the United States – were car-sharing members in 27 countries.[39]

According to *The Economist*, one car-sharing rental can replace up to 15 owned vehicles.[40] But it is not just about replacing car ownership with car rental. Car sharing has shown to be successful at replacing *cars*, period. In July 2009, Zipcar started its "Low-Car Diet Challenge," involving 250 persons – some that were self-admittedly heavily reliant on their cars – from 13 cities. All participants agreed to give up their personal vehicle for one month and use Zipcar (they were given a free membership in exchange for participating in the challenge). Once the challenge was over all participants were surveyed. The results, particularly in light of what was said in previous chapters about the costs of the automobile, are encouraging. Participants reported reducing their vehicle miles traveled by 66 percent while increasing the miles they walked and biked by 93 and 132 percent, respectively. Close to half of the participants also reported losing weight. And perhaps most important of all: 61 percent said they planned to continue their new transportation habits even after the challenge has concluded.[41]

German car manufacturer Daimler views the transaction costs of using Zipcar as still too high. Its Car2Go service is similar to Zipcar's, except it requires no reservation or a two-way trip. A mobile app allows you to locate the company's nearest Smart car in any of the 17 cities worldwide where the service is presently available and access the car immediately with a windshield card reader. You are even able to see online beforehand the car's fuel gauge (for gasoline-powered vehicles) or its battery's state of charge (for electric-powered vehicles). Once in, you can take it anywhere within the city and leave it at your destination for the next person. Car2Go has more than 275,000 customers as of January 2013.[42]

Daimler is also working on Car2Gether.[43] This project, which is still in its pilot stage, involves a mobile app that matches local drivers with people in the neighborhood looking for a ride. Riders submit a request to a driver and both profiles are linked to their Facebook pages and Twitter feeds; sites that use actual identities rather than pseudonyms and therefore give viewers a more complete picture of the person than something like averagejoe555 as found on eBay. Once the ride is over both participants then have the opportunity to rate each other; a score that immediately becomes part of their social media reputation. This creates real incentives, beyond the obvious economic ones, to not be a jerk (or worse).

The money directly saved alone in a sharing economy ought to get people's attention. As mentioned in the previous chapter, these savings point to still further evidence that there are ways to restructure things so that the same ends can be accomplished working and earning far less than we currently do. Though, for example, the average New Yorker renting a room through Airbnb is supplementing their income to the tune of an additional $1,600 per month.[44] So perhaps in an affordable society income streams could be more diversified than they are at the moment, where presently one's job represents their sole source of income (save for the one percent that make most of their money through investments). Or take Zipcar. The average member saves an estimated US$600 a month after switching to this service.[45] That adds up to US$7,200 every year. Double that if a household were to trade-in both of their cars and vote for access over ownership. In an affordable society, access becomes the privilege, ownership the burden.

Something else remarkable happens once we begin to value access over ownership. In a sharing economy things begin being made with an eye toward longevity. Products need to be made, in other words, so they can be shared and rented. "The Mesh" is a term coined by Lisa Ganskey, in a book under the same name, to describe network-enabled sharing.[46] In a Mesh-based economy, the goal moves from selling as many cheap things as possible, over and over again as they break down and/or become obsolete, to selling the same service multiple times through a single product. Beyond having a longer use life, better designed products are, by definition, safer to use because they are less likely to fail or break in-use. Businesses interested in participating in the sharing economy have an incentive to purchase longer-lasting products that can be serviced and repaired. This would not only be for liability reasons but also for purposes of maintaining customers' trust, namely, that the company in question can be trusted to rent access to safe and well-maintained products. In short, in a sharing economy better designed products are actually at a competitive advantage, even those costing more than the cheaply made alternatives.

Sticks, carrots, and collaborative action

Michael Spence, a 2001 Nobel laureate for economics and a senior fellow at Stanford's Hoover Institution – a conservative think-tank not known for housing economic rabble-rousers – wrote an article in *Forbes* a couple of years back titled "Markets Aren't Everything."[47] In this piece, Spence celebrates the work of scholars like Elinor Ostrom, who had just been awarded the Nobel Prize in Economic Sciences (along with Oliver E. Williamson), whose research highlights that resources can be effectively managed and distributed without the aid of formal markets. As Ostrom and others have detailed, common-property resources (such as forests) have been effectively managed, in some cases for centuries, thanks to things like informal social norms, trust, and social capital.[48] Yet what if, in this age of social media, something like a traditional commons is forming for citizen consumers? Just a few years ago the thought of the non-market coordination of large groups of people from around the world for purposes of resource allocation seemed impossibly complex and exceedingly expensive. The transaction costs, to use conventional economic parlance, were just too great to create a sharing economy. If you had something and wanted to trade, rent, or just give it away your options were limited. You could put an ad in your local newspaper's classified section or spend an afternoon placing fliers up around town and on community bulletin boards. Then you crossed your fingers and waited. Even if someone did get back to you the chance of a successful transaction remained a longshot. With a classified ad you are limited to just a couple of lines of text. More often than not, a quick phone call revealed something about the product that was not to the caller's liking – perhaps they wanted a different color or model. Social media and the internet more generally have changed all of that.

I remember as a child my dad once using the classified section of local newspapers to find a used van for his business. (He was a high school science teacher during the school year and residential and farm painter over the summer – so he could afford to teach, as he would tell people.) We scoured most of northeastern Iowa that summer looking at more than a dozen vans. The short ads, which at most gave the vehicle's color, year, model, and mileage, always left us guessing until we saw the vans first-hand. The whole experience was a terrible waste of time and gas. Fast forward to today: when dad buys a vehicle (he still paints, though he's retired from teaching) that guesswork is removed. He now can get pictures of the vehicle and video of it running and even assess ahead of time the seller's reputation (if buying from a site like eBay). At least when it comes to used vans in northeastern Iowa, markets cannot compete with social media for efficient allocation of this resource. Or perhaps there really *is* something more generalizable going on.

But I am getting ahead of myself. Let's take a step back, to the year 1968.

"Picture a pasture open to all."[49] So begins a story that will be retold more times than can be counted in an essay arguably more often cited (more than 20,000 times according to Google Scholar) than any other written since. The essay is Garret Hardin's classic, "The Tragedy of the Commons."[50] The story continues:

> It is to be expected that each herdsman will try to keep as many cattle as possible on the commons. Such an arrangement may work reasonably satisfactorily for centuries because tribal wars, poaching, and disease keep the numbers of both man and beast well below the carrying capacity of the land. Finally, however, comes the day of reckoning, that is, the day when the long-desired goal of social stability becomes a reality. At this point, the inherent logic of the commons remorselessly generates tragedy.[51]

Assuming that each herdsperson wishes to maximize their gain, they begin to ponder the consequences of adding one more animal to their herd. They soon realize that the costs and benefits of such an action are unevenly distributed. The herdsperson receives all the proceeds from the sale of the additional animal whereas the effects of overgrazing are shared by all – in other words, the costs of this action are socialized. It is therefore perfectly rational for, and therefore expected that, herdspersons in this situation will continually add animals to their herd – *all* herdspersons. Therein lays the tragedy: everyone acting in their own self-interest, when resources are shared and limited, will have catastrophic ends. This led Hardin to conclude, famously, and bleakly, "Freedom in a commons brings ruin to all."[52]

Hardin's essay, and the logic upon which its argument rests, while provocative, makes a fatal omission: namely, that people, especially when within the same community, tend to *talk to one another*. Communication kicks the knees out from under *homo economicus* (economic human), as a purely rational, selfish person who single-mindedly strives to maximize profit. Scenarios like the Prisoner's Dilemma, where individuals are intentionally separated from each other and not allowed to talk, might show how prisoners behave under highly controlled situations. But we are not prisoners and society is not a prison. Decades of social science research document how repeated face-to-face interaction builds social capital and trust over time and reins in the type of selfish behavior assumed in Hardin's essay.[53] When individuals are placed in a situation where they cannot communicate with others they are indeed more likely to act selfishly with regard to the use of shared resources. The moment they are allowed to communicate, however, they begin to think more in terms of what is best for the collective and less in terms of their individual interest.[54]

Circling back to the subject of collaborative consumption: this highlights tremendous potential *social* returns to be gained as we invest in a sharing economy. When you consume collaboratively, you build social networks, nurture trust, and generate social capital.[55] Yet how do we know that these social relationships are sufficient to coordinate the distribution of resources that previously required markets? This brings us to a second critique of Hardin's seemingly self-evident argument that freedom in a commons brings ruin to all: namely, that the pasture Hardin describes so eloquently is not even a commons but an open-access regime.

Open-access resources are those with no limits to who can access and use them – think of the open sea and the atmosphere. Common-property regimes, conversely, might appear from the "outside" unregulated but from within the community governing the resource in question there are very clear local customs, trust, and informal social norms guiding behaviors in ways that are highly efficient and effective. Paul Samuelson, in a classic essay that was first published in 1954, effectively split the world's resources up into two types: private goods, which are excludable (you can be excluded from consuming them unless you paid for them) and rivalrous (whatever you consume no one else can), and public goods, which are non-excludable (you can consume them regardless of if you paid for them) and non-rivalrous (whatever you consume others can too).[56] This basic division is consistent with the way the world is divided up under cheaponomics – a world where there are only private property exchanges in a market setting and government-owned property organized by the state. Coupled with this is an equally narrow view of the individual. They are either a consumer or a voter.[57] The work of Elinor Ostrom, whom I introduced earlier, helped show the narrowness of this worldview. There is, it turns out, a third way, which cannot be neatly placed in either box marked "market" or "state." This third way also shows how we are so much more than just *individual* consumers and *individual* voters.

A big barrier to getting to a sharing economy – from me-based cheaponomics to we-based affordability – is trust. It is one thing to rent a power drill from a neighbor; quite another to let a total stranger sleep in your house. At the moment, most sharing platforms build trust into the exchange by building a self-policing community, where users are required to have profiles and there is a community rating system. The next step looks to be developing a community rating system that travels with you from website to website – a second life reputation that may one day grow to be just as important, from an exchange standpoint, as your first life reputation (such as your credit score). An example of this is TrustCloud, which creates the equivalent of a sharing economy credit rating only for trust. Using proprietary algorithms, TrustCloud aims to measure individuals' trustworthiness by analyzing transactions on the web while also drawing upon information from sites like Facebook, LinkedIn, Twitter, and Google+. This trail of online data exhaust, it is believed, can be a reliable predictor of our consistency, responsiveness, and overall trustworthiness. And while " there's always the argument that anyone can be an ax murderer," admits TrustCloud cofounder Xin Chung, "you get a lot more indicators in data exhaust than you do in walking up to somebody in khakis and a crisp white shirt on the street. I'd pick the data exhaust any day."[58]

Sites like Yelp, TripAdvisor, and eBay use pseudonyms that may reveal very little about the user's actual identity. Even so, they have created systems that are surprisingly effective and efficient at eliciting desired behaviors. Research indicates that sellers receive positive feedback on eBay 99 percent of the time and buyers 98 percent.[59] Users realize their behavior today is not one-off and will greatly impact their ability to engage in future transactions. Consequently, they strive – sometimes going to great lengths – to achieve that positive feedback, knowing, for example, that highly reputable sellers receive on average an 8 percent premium over identical items offered by sellers with lower/few ratings.[60] A bad review on eBay, however, stays on eBay and does not follow you around. Another way around this self-policing system is simply to create another "personality" on eBay by generating another nameless and faceless pseudonym. There is no "reset" button with things like TrustCloud; no chance, in other words, to declare trust bankruptcy and start anew.

All of this sharing also has the potential to be tremendously transformative in terms of its wider impacts upon the economy. As Umair Haque, author of *The New Capitalist Manifesto* and contributor at the *Harvard Business Review*, explains, while sharing platforms will not bankrupt a company like a Home Depot or Best Buy they will likely cut into their bottom line. "If the people formerly known as consumers begin consuming 10 percent less and peering 10 percent more, the effect on margins of traditional corporations is going to be disproportionately greater," notes Haque, "which means certain industries have to rewire themselves, or prepare to sink into the quicksand of the past."[61]

Not even the banking industry is safe from the transformative potential of community, we-based, economies. The global recession and the too-big-to-fail banking system have undermined trust toward this industry, opening the door to peer-to-peer lending sites like Lending Club and Zopa. Generally, interest rates in peer-to-peer loans are set either by lenders who compete for the lowest rate on the reverse auction model or are fixed by a third party on the basis of their analysis of the borrower's credit. Lenders mitigate their risks – as loans are not backed by government guarantees – by being able to choose who they lend to and by diversifying their investments among different borrowers. As opposed to too-big-to-fail, peer-to-peer banking offers a different model: too-resilient-to-fail. As Danielle Sacks, the award-winning writer at *Fast Company* magazine, reminds us, the promise of the new sharing economy lies in the fact that distributed systems are highly resilient.[62] This resiliency was on display in the late 1970s during the Irish banking crisis. During this time bankers actually went on strike and warned that the nation's economy would collapse without a banking system. Rather than bringing the country to its knees the crisis created an opening for a peer-to-peer banking system, which essentially emerged out of nowhere with local pubs transforming almost overnight into local banks. As Haque astutely points out, "If you think about it, who is a better judge of character in Ireland than the bartender?"[63]

There is an old saying that could have been written precisely for this more collaborative style of consumption: there is power in numbers. One of the largest barriers to participating in sharing systems is the perceived risk of scarcity.[64] It is hard to get people to give up ownership when access is in question. For commodities that can be mailed this is less of an issue. But peer-to-peer car-sharing cannot be accomplished using FedEx any more than idle rooms can be shipped to travelers in need of a place to sleep. The good news is that those numbers are growing, which means the question of access is becoming less of one in many cities around the world.

Social media used to reduce the transaction costs associated with collaborative consumption are also being used to transform old-style consumption. The transformational pivot point, again, centers on taking something that has traditionally been me-based and transforming it in something more we-based. Enter, for example, the carrotmob (aka buycott).

Rather than focusing on punishing stores and firms for their environmental and social atrocities, why not reward those for listening to and acting on behalf of our collective concerns? "Traditional activism revolves around conflict," explains Schulkin.[65] Brent Schulkin is at the center of a movement that employs a reverse boycott – what is known as a carrotmob. The carrotmob, simply defined, is a type of activism based on the idea of using carrots (or incentives) to reward businesses who wish to act more socially and/or environmentally responsible but cannot for fear of being put at a competitive disadvantage. (The Sophie's choice of cheaponomics for firms: exploit the planet and your workers but remain in business or better internalize costs by taking care of your employees, the surrounding community, and the environment and kill your chances of remaining in business.) Instead of creating enemies, a carrotmob focuses on positive cooperation. In his first attempt at this, Schulkin solicited bids from 23 stores in the San Francisco area to find which business would promise to spend the highest percentage of the carrotmob's profits on more, among other things, energy-efficient lighting. In return, Schulkin promised to deliver, with the help of social media, a rambunctious horde of concerned individuals who pledged to buy stuff from the highest bidder. It is worth noting that the goal of this horde was to buy things that would have been purchased anyway, like household goods (e.g., toilet paper) and food items, so as not to encourage over-consumption. The boycott, as it is called, occurred on March 29, 2008, when hundreds lined up to get into K&D Market, the local convenience store that pledged to spend the highest percent of its profits (22 percent) on efficiency improvements. The carrotmob spent more than $9,200 that day – almost five times more than was sold on an average day in that store. Since then, carrotmobs have spread to ten other US cities, Finland, and France.[66]

As Schulkin points out, using the example of toothbrushes to make his point:

> Do I really care if I get Oral-B, Colgate, Crest, Aquafresh. No one cares. What if we got a million people and we went to these toothbrush companies and say: "Look, here is what we want – recyclable toothbrushes, compostable toothbrushes, solar powered toothbrush factories, organic, fair trade toothbrushes, cage-free toothbrushes."[67]

His toothbrush example is particularly apt as it reminds us of some of the limitations of a sharing economy. There are just some items that just cannot, indeed nor should they, be shared. Yet even in those cases there remain ways to transform the economy. In either case, the mechanism of transformation remains the same: us acting collectively.

Real choice

In the end, it is about creating a system predicated on choice. *Real* choice. Not that Coke or Pepsi model thrust upon us by cheaponomics, where the "choice" left to make is between two equally sugary, equally caffeinated, equally global cola beverages. This begs the question: what do we mean by choice? In cheaponomics, choice means having a multitude of market options; of having, well, choice *as a consumer*. Yet when you look at this choice more closely it begins looking less like what we ought to be desiring and more like something to be avoided. All that glitters is not gold, and the same can be said of consumer choice.

Barry Schwartz, in his book *The Paradox of Choice*, highlights how too much choice can be, in his words, debilitating, even tyrannical:

> As the number of available choices increases, as it has in our consumer culture, the autonomy, control, and liberation this variety brings are powerful and positive. But as the number of choices keeps growing, negative aspects of having a multitude of options begins to appear. As the number of choices grows further, the negatives escalate until we become overloaded.[68]

Using even stronger language, Schwartz concludes by explaining how, "at this point, choice no longer liberates, but debilities. It might even be said to tyrannize." Tyrannize: strong word. Too strong, perhaps, if it were not for the considerable data he uses to back up his claims.

To take just one study: college students were asked to evaluate an array of specialty chocolates. One group of students were given a selection of six chocolates to taste; another, 30 chocolates. The students with less (consumer) choice overwhelmingly rated their satisfaction with the chocolates higher than those faced with having to choose between 30 chocolates. In another room, students were given the option of receiving a small box of chocolates, from those they tasted, instead of a cash payment. Those in the group that tasted six chocolates were four times more likely to select the box of chocolate over cash.[69] Schwartz admits that there are a number of variables at play. Yet his research points to one in particular that repeatedly rears its head: "a large array of options may diminish the attractiveness of what people *actually* choose, the reason being that thinking about the attractions of some of the unchosen options detracts from the pleasure derived from the chosen one."[70] To put it simply: consumers have a tendency to dwell on what they could have chosen but did not, which inevitably undermines the pleasure received from whatever it is they did buy. We continually ask ourselves, to put it more simply still, "what if?" And we are worse off because of it; recognizing too that the more consumer choice there is the more "what ifs" we have to contemplate.

One strategy – a cheaponomics strategy – is to combat this with overconsumption, where some of those choices are purchased with the intent of reducing the number of "what ifs" left to fret over. Yet there is another option: reducing our choices as consumers in order to increase our choices as *citizens*. Think of it as prioritizing citizen choice over consumer choice.[71] Thus, rather than fetishizing consumer choice we view it as but a means to broader ends, like freedom, civic participation, self-actualization, and social, emotional, and psychological nourishment. Sometimes consumer choice helps afford these ends, *but not always*. In fact, there is evidence to indicate it can have just the opposite effect, as indicated in any of the previous chapters. At the moment, we are continually confronted by what economist Alfred Kahn called the "tyranny of small decisions" – e.g., Coke or Pepsi? – when we could otherwise be using that time to build strong, vibrant, and just communities and households.[72]

It is my hope that this tyranny will lesson as we become more interested in opened cans and holes rather than can openers and power drills – as we move, in other words, toward a more collaborative model of consumption. Granted, it is not the type of "democracy" that people like Milton Friedman envision, where freedom is exemplified by such acts as each person being able to "vote, as it were, for the color of tie he [or she] wants."[73] But this is a pithy understanding of democracy, especially in light of how it has the real potential to *detract* from civic and community engagement and therefore reduce citizen choice. Remember also, voting alone does not a democracy make. Voting involves selecting between already chosen candidates. But what if you do not like the candidates you are forced to choose between; or, worse still, what if they are all equally unhealthy for you and/or the environment? How do you vote, in other words, for a color of tie not provided by the market? Or, as opposed to a tie, let me bring back the toothbrush example. I want – I really do – to be able to buy fully compostable toothbrushes. How do I signal to the market – "vote" – to express my preference as a consumer when no such candidate exists? I can't. That is one of the problems with consumer choice as a mechanism for social change. The change it produces must first be initiated by the very system we are looking to radically modify. The only chance for real change lies within us as *citizens*.

And what better way to start thinking more like citizens and less like consumers than by starting to share.

Notes

1 Cline, Elizabeth (2012) *Overdressed: The Shockingly High Cost of Cheap Fashion* (New York: Portfolio).
2 Federal Reserve Bank (n.d.) "Consumer price index for all urban consumers: apparel, economic research," Federal Reserve Bank of St. Louis, http://research.stlouisfed.org/fred2/graph/?s[1][id]=CPIAPPNS, last accessed March 8, 2012.
3 Schor, Juliet (2011) *True Wealth* (New York: Penguin), p. 29.

4 Lamson-Hall, Patrick (2013) "Fast fashion winners and losers," *The Business of Fashion*, March 4, www.businessoffashion.com/2013/03/op-ed-fast-fashion-winners-losers.html, last accessed March 8, 2013.
5 Kester, Corinna and Dana Ledyard (2012) "The sustainable apparel coalition: A case study of a successful industry collaboration," Center for Responsible Business, Haas School of Business, University of California, Berkeley, http://responsiblebusiness.haas.berkeley.edu/CRB_SustainableApparelCaseStudy_FINAL.pdf, last accessed March 8, 2013.
6 Kaye, Leon (2011) "Clothing industry giant launch sustainable apparel coalition," *Guardian*, March 1, www.guardian.co.uk/sustainable-business/clothing-industry-supply-chain-coalition, last accessed March 11, 2013.
7 Federal Reserve Bank (n.d.) "Personal savings rate," Federal Reserve Bank of St. Louis, Economic Research, http://research.stlouisfed.org/fred2/graph/?id=PSAVERT, last accessed March 12, 2013.
8 See, for example, Redman, Lauren, Margareta Friman, Tommy Garling, and Terry Hartig (2013) "Quality attributes of public transport that attract car users: A research review," *Transport Policy*, 25, pp. 119–27.
9 Herring, Horace and Rubin Roy (2007) "Technological innovation, energy efficient design and the rebound effect," *Technovation*, 27(4), pp. 194–203.
10 Fouquet, R. and P. Pearson (2006) "Seven centuries of energy services: The price and use of light in the United Kingdom (1300–1700)," *The Energy Journal*, 27(1), pp. 139–77.
11 Ibid.
12 World Bank (2008) "World development indicators" (Washington, DC: World Bank); World Coal Association (n.d.) "Coal" (London: World Coal Association), www.worldcoal.org/coal/, last accessed March 13, 2013.
13 Jackson, T. (2011) "'Peak stuff' message is cold comfort," *Guardian*, November 1, www.guardian.co.uk/environment/2011/nov/01/peak-stuff-message-greenktechnology?intcmp=239, last accessed March 13, 2013.
14 Ibid.
15 OECD (2010) *OECD Factbook 2010: Economic, Environmental, and Social Statistics* (Paris: Organization for Economic Cooperation and Development).
16 York, Richard (2010) "The paradox at the heart of modernity: The carbon efficiency of the global economy," *International Journal of Sociology*, 40(2), pp. 6–22.
17 See for example OECD (n.d.) "Indicators to measure decoupling of environmental pressure from economic growth," Organisation for Economic Co-operation and Development, Paris, France, www.oecd.org/environment/indicators-modelling-outlooks/1933638.pdf, last accessed July 24, 2013.
18 Jackson, Tim (2009) *Prosperity without Growth* (New York and London: Earthscan).
19 Ibid., p. 85.
20 See also, for example, Alcott, Blake, Mario Giampietro, and Kozo Mayumi (2008) *The Jevons Paradox and the Myth of Resource Efficiency Improvements* (London: Earthscan); York (2010).
21 York, Richard (2006) "Ecological paradoxes: William Stanley Jevons and the paperless office," *Human Ecology Review*, 13(2), pp. 143–7.
22 Clapp, Jennifer (2002) "The distancing of waste: Overconsumption in the global economy," in *Confronting Consumption*, edited by Thomas Princen, Michael Maniates, and Ken Conca (Cambridge, MA: MIT Press), pp. 155–76.
23 Hamilton, Clive, Richard Denniss, and David Baker (2005) "Wasteful consumption in Australia," Discussion paper 77, The Australian Institute, pp. 5–6, www.tai.org.au/documents/dp_fulltext/DP77.pdf, last accessed March 16, 2013.
24 Botsman, R. and R. Rogers (2010) *What's Mine is Yours: The Rise of Collaborative Consumption* (New York: Harper), p. 14.

25 Kavoussi, Bonnie (2012) "Average home rise rose 4 percent in 2011," *Huffington Post*, June 7, www.huffingtonpost.com/2012/06/06/average-home-size-2011_n_1575617.html, last accessed March 17, 2013.
26 Ibid.
27 Nasser, Haya El and Paul Overberg (2011) "After 50 years of decline, household size is growing," *USA Today*, May 5, http://usatoday30.usatoday.com/news/nation/census/2011-05-04-Census-Households-Demographics_n.htm, last accessed March 17, 2013.
28 Botsman and Rogers (2010), pp. 14–15.
29 SSA (n.d.) Fact Sheet, as of 6/30/2012, Self Storage Association, www.selfstorage.org/ssa/Content/NavigationMenu/AboutSSA/FactSheet/default.htm, last accessed March 17, 2013.
30 Ibid.
31 Botsman and Rogers (2010), p. 83.
32 Rifkin, J. (2000) *The Age of Access* (New York: Tarcher), p. 76.
33 See Botsman and Rogers (2010).
34 See www.airbnb.com.
35 Botsman and Rogers (2010), p. xiii.
36 Sacks, Danielle (2011) "The sharing economy," *Fast Company*, April 18, www.fastcompany.com/1747551/sharing-economy, last accessed March 18, 2013.
37 Botsman and Rogers (2010), p. 107.
38 Zipcar (2012) "Zipcar reports 2012 third quarter results," November 8, http://ir.zipcar.com/releasedetail.cfm?ReleaseID=719904, last accessed March 18, 2013.
39 Goggans, Louis (2013) "Community car," *Memphis Flyer*, February 21, www.memphisflyer.com/memphis/community-car/Content?oid=3352492, last accessed March 18, 2013.
40 *The Economist* (2012) "Seeing the back of the car," *The Economist*, September 22, www.economist.com/node/21563280?frsc=dg%7Ca, last accessed March 18, 2013.
41 Botsman and Rogers (2010), p. 74.
42 Steinberg, Stephanie (2013) "Car sharing services grow and expand options," *New York Times*, January 25, www.nytimes.com/2013/01/26/business/car-sharing-services-grow-and-expand-options.html?ref=technology&_r=0, last accessed March 18, 2013.
43 Daimler (n.d.) "Car2gether – ride sharing 2.0," www.daimler.com/technology-and-innovation/mobility-concepts/car2gether, last accessed March 18, 2013.
44 Botsman and Rogers (2010), p. xviii.
45 Keegan, P. (2009) "Zipcar: The best new idea in business," CNNMoney, August 27, http://money.cnn.com/2009/08/26/news/companies/zipcar car rentals.fortune/, last accessed March 18, 2013.
46 Ganskey, Lisa (2010) *The Mesh: Why the Future of Business is Sharing* (New York: Penguin).
47 Spence, M. (2009) "Markets aren't everything," *Forbes*, October 12. www.forbes.com/2009/10/12/economics-nobel-elinor-ostrom-oliver-williamsonopinions-contributors-michael-spence.html, last accessed March 18, 2013.
48 See, for example, Ostrom, E. (1999) *Governing the Commons: The Evolution of Institutions for Collective Action* (New York: Cambridge University Press); Ostrom, E., J. Burger, C. Field, R. Norgaard, and D. Policansky (1999) "Revisiting the commons: Local lessons, global challenges," *Science*, 284(5412), pp. 278–82.
49 Hardin, G. (1968) "The tragedy of the commons," *Science*, 162, pp. 1243–8, p. 1243.
50 Ibid.
51 Ibid., p. 1244.
52 Ibid., p. 1248.

53 See, for example, Pretty, J. and H. Ward (2001) "Social capital and the environment," *World Development*, 29(2), pp. 209–27; Putnam, R. (2001) *Bowling Alone* (New York: Simon & Schuster).
54 See, for example, Orbell, J., A. van de Kragt, and R. Dawes (1988) "Explaining discussion-induced cooperation in social dilemmas," *Journal of Personality and Social Psychology*, 54, pp. 811–19.
55 Drogen, L. (2011) "Social capital and collaborative consumption," *Surview Capital*, January 13, www.leighdrogen.com/social-capital-and-collaborativeconsumption/, last accessed March 18, 2013.
56 Samuelson, Paul A. (1954) "The pure theory of public expenditure," *Review of Economics and Statistics*, 36(4), pp. 387–9.
57 Ostrom, Elinor (2010) "Beyond markets and states: Polycentric governance of complex economic systems," *American Economic Review*, 100, pp. 1–33, p. 2.
58 Sacks (2011).
59 Botsman and Rogers (2010), p. 140.
60 Ibid., p. 140.
61 As quoted in Sacks (2011).
62 Sacks (2011).
63 As quoted in Sacks (2011).
64 Lamberton, Cait and Randall Rose (2012) "When is ours better than mine? A framework for understanding and altering participation in commercial sharing systems," *Journal of Marketing*, 76, pp. 109–25, p. 109.
65 As quoted in Caplan, J. (2009) "Shoppers, unite! Carrot mobs are cooler than boycotts," *Time*, May 15, www.time.com/time/magazine/article/0,9171,1901467,00.html, last accessed March 25, 2013.
66 Smith, C. (2008) "Ready, set, shop!" *San Francisco Magazine*, May 12, www.modernluxury.com/san-francisco/story/ready-set-shop-0, last accessed March 25, 2013.
67 Interview from http://vimeo.com/925729, at 7:43 minutes.
68 Schwartz, Barry (2004) *The Paradox of Choice: Why More is Less* (New York: Imprint), p. 2.
69 Ibid., p. 20.
70 Ibid., p. 20, emphasis in original.
71 See, for example, Carolan, Michael (2013, forthcoming) "Future food 'needs': From consumer to citizen choice," *Sociologia Ruralis*.
72 Kahn, Alfred (1966) "The tyranny of small decisions: Market failures, imperfections, and the limits of economics," *Kyklos*, 19, pp. 23–47; the concept originally refers to a situation where a number of decisions, individually and small in size, cumulatively result in an outcome which is neither optimal nor desired.
73 Friedman, Milton (2009) *Capitalism and Freedom: 40th Anniversary Edition* (Chicago: University of Chicago Press), p. 15.

Chapter 9

Real prosperity is priceless

Hooray, the Great Recession is over! Or so you might have believed if you happened to catch some of the headlines to sprinkle news webpages in March and April of 2013: CNN, "Dow, S&P close at new highs";[1] CBS, "Markets keep rising after Dow hits record high";[2] and Forbes, "Dow closes at record 14,254 as rally keeps rolling."[3] And then you went back to searching Monster.com for a job.

Those singing the praises are the few that truly benefit from cost-socializing socialism: "It's good to be one of the one percent!" As a percentage of (US) national income, corporate profits stood at 14.2 percent in the third quarter of 2012. That represents a larger share than at any time since 1950. As for the portion of income that went to employees, that presently stands (April 2013) at 61.7 percent – the lowest percentage in almost 50 years![4] Corporate earnings have outpaced household disposable income, from the end of 2008 to early 2013, by a ratio of almost 20 to one.[5] Recall in Chapter 7 when I wrote, quoting Robert Ayres and Benhanmin Warr, that "the historic link between output (GDP) growth and employment has been weakened, if not broken."[6] More of the same equals less for more (and even more for the one percent). The Dow has recovered all of its losses from the Great Recession, gaining more than 120 percent from its low in March of 2009 – the third-strongest bull market for the Dow since World War II. And yet: the US job market has recovered only 5.5 million of the 8.7 million jobs lost because of the financial crisis – the worst labor-market recovery since World War II.[7] Take United Technologies, a company located in Hartford, Connecticut, that develops such high-tech products as fuel cells, aircraft engines, and heating, ventilation, and air conditioning (HVAC) systems. With its 218,300 employees, United Technologies' workforce remains largely identical to what it was in 2005, even though its annual revenue has increased US$15 billion since that time (to US$57.7 billion in 2012). Just days after the company's shares surpassed the US$90 mark (reaching record levels), in February 2013, the firm announced it would eliminate 3,000 workers, that is on top of the 4,000 let go in 2012.[8] This helps explain why inflation-adjusted average income in

2013 is eight percent lower than in 2007, when the Dow hit its previous high, and why almost *all* – 93 percent to be exact – of pre-tax incomes gains of the current economic "recovery" have thus far gone to the top one percent.[9]

The problem, as is plainly (and painfully) clear from previous chapters, cannot be resolved with any magic bullet. Greener technology, alone, cannot help us, nor will, again in-and-of-itself, better cost internalization practices, additional government regulation, or more sustainable consumption practices. But even when taken collectively, we ought to be generally skeptical of any complement of solutions based entirely on the rhetoric of "more" and "less." Yes: real cost reduction is going to require that we consume and waste less and intervene in the market more. But we are also going to have to start doing things differently: consuming and wasting less by consuming and wasting in another way. This reveals a way forward that does not rest entirely on the discourse of *sacrifice*, where we are told we must give up both ownership and access. Instead, I propose shifting the debate to being about the *freedom* that comes from unburdening ourselves from the former. Think of this as a third way; a path away from the stale and unimaginative politics, played out time and time again, in the "market vs. government" debate and toward something more collaborative and (all) people-centered.

Getting there is not going to be easy. This is why I have avoided following the standard formula of leaving "solutions" exclusively for the last chapters. The previous chapters lay out, in their own ways, steps for delivering us from a system organized around cheapness to one concerned about affordability. I do not claim to be saving a bombshell for this or the following chapter, where all loose ends are tied and the ingredients for a perfectly affordable society proposed. The good news is that I do not think we need to be looking for bombshells any more than magic bullets. Everything we need for an affordable society already exists. We just need to roll up our collective sleeves and get to work.

In growth we trust

I once knew a guy years back (when I knew guys that regularly wore cologne) who insisted on wearing a particularly repulsive pheromone spray. I still (regretfully) recollect the smell of it, like a sweaty gym sock. But he was insistent as to its effectiveness at attracting the opposite sex. "It might smell bad," I remember him saying, "but that just means it's working." The only thing it attracted was snide looks but he persisted, believing the problem lay in the level of application. Ignoring the evidence, which was telling him that his beliefs about the spray were demonstrably false, he stood firm and wore even more.

Twenty years later and I still remember this guy. The facts were so clear. Yet he willfully decided to ignore them; an omission that came at the cost of his reputation, about US$50 a bottle (the stuff was expensive), and probably a few dates too. I used to think, "How could anyone be so daft?" Now I am not so sure his actions were all that odd.

It seems like, as a society, we are equally insistent about the efficacy of economic growth, as a harbinger of happiness and individual and societal well-being and health – a one-way ticket, one might say, to the good life. And this insistence does not seem to be dashed in the least by the facts, which tell us that our beliefs about economic growth are demonstrably false, especially after a certain level of affluence is reached. Instead, we respond not much differently from my pheromone-wearing mate. "It might smell bad," I can image proponents of growth saying, "but that just means it's working." Try as I might, I cannot find the evidence to back up this claim. The more I look at the data the more I cannot help thinking: it smells because it *stinks*, especially after a modest level of per capita wealth is reached.

Economic growth, after about US$15,000 GDP (gross domestic product) per capita, has zero correlation to longer life expectancies (see Figure 9.1). In fact, as discussed in Chapter 4, we are starting to see the life expectancies in a growing number of counties in the United States slide *backwards*.[10] Nor does it appear to generate any additional returns to subjective well-being, as the relationship between average per capita income and percent of population reporting happiness and satisfaction with life as a whole flattens out as countries transition into middle-income status.[11]

What about the effects of free markets? What are its links to well-being? The answer should already be perfectly clear, based on all that has been said in earlier chapters. Free markets work best in allowing those benefiting from the status quo to socialize the costs to the rest of the world. As far as generative mechanisms of (present and future) human and environmental welfare are concerned, there are far more effective things than free markets we ought to be trying.

Figure 9.2 plots the Index of Economic Freedom with Happy Life Years data. For those unfamiliar with the former, it is generated by the US-based think-tank the Heritage Center and the *Wall Street Journal* and is composed of ten economic measurements grouped into four broad categories: 1) rule of law (property rights, freedom from corruption); 2) limited government (fiscal freedom, government spending); 3) regulatory efficiency (business freedom, labor freedom, monetary freedom); and 4) open markets (trade freedom, investment freedom, financial freedom). Countries that score 80 to 100 are considered "free," 79.9 to 70 "mostly free," 69.9 to 60 "moderately free," 59.9 to 50 "mostly un-free," and 49.9 to 40 "repressed." The Happy Life Years measure combines life expectancy at birth and self-reported satisfaction surveys. Proponents of this index argue that doing this – combining these two measures – helps overcome some of their individual limitations. One could imagine, for example, a society where people live long lives but are perfectly miserable, such as in cases where medical technologies stretch life out well after quality of life begins to diminish. Similarly, one could imagine a scenario where people live contently in a country but not for long, perhaps due to overindulgence. It is common to measure the health of nations by the average

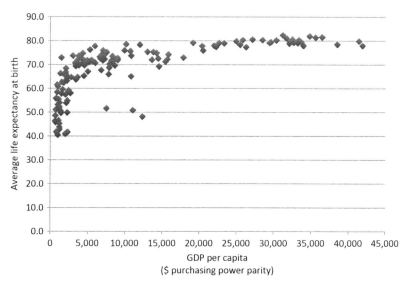

Figure 9.1 Relationship between life expectancy and GDP ($ purchasing power parity)
Source: Data obtained from FAO

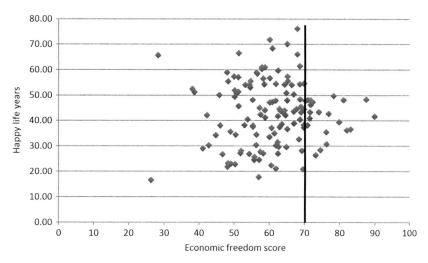

Figure 9.2 Relationship between economic freedom score and happy life years
Source: Data obtained from The Heritage Center and New Economics Foundation

number of years people live free from chronic illness. This is often expressed in the Disability Adjusted Life Years (DALYs) index. Happy Life Years (HLYs) are calculated to be analogous to the DALYs. HLYs therefore equal life expectancy at birth multiplied by the country's happiness score (on a scale of 0 to 1). Let us say, for illustrative purposes, that the life expectancy in

Country X is 60 years. If everybody were perfectly happy (happiness score of 1), the average HLYs for this country would be 60. If the country's average happiness score was 0.5, the per capita HLYs lived would be 30.

There are two rather striking features about the relationship between these two variables. The first is the noticeable lack of any overall correlation; a particularly significant finding given that free-market disciples do not even question if economic freedom is positively correlated with longer, happier lives – they just assume it to be, at a statistically significant level. Economic freedom, in other words, appears to have very little impact on a country's HLYs. More striking still, however, is where the two variables do seem to have some relationship with each other. At the high end of the economic freedom score the correlation between variables is *negative*. To put it plainly, "mostly free" (70 to 79.9) and "free" (80 to 100) nations perform generally *less well* in terms of their ability to generate happy long lives compared to countries with less economic freedoms. Not a single country with an economic freedom score of 70 or greater averages 50 HLYs or more. Perhaps an explanation of this, to evoke language from the previous chapter, lies in how countries with lower levels of economic freedom, when properly organized, allow for greater *citizen choice* and all the enhancements to quality of life that can spring from this enriched democratic way of being.

This all points to two limits we ought to be talking about: the limits associated with measuring economic growth using GDP per capita and the limits of economic growth itself (regardless of the measure). GDP measures the rate at which money flows through an economy, regardless of the reason for the exchange. So, for example, the *trillions* of dollars spent annually on obesity-related diseases and disabilities, as detailed previously in Chapter 4, have been a boon for the world's GDP. And this figure does not even include the additional billions spent every year on such medical procedures as liposuction, tummy tucks, stomach stapling, and gastric banding. Do you see why there is such resistance to abandoning the GDP as the gold standard measure of "progress"? Cheaponomics, in re/producing an economy that is so damn expensive – but where the costs are socialized to obfuscate the truth – is able to turn to the GDP to bolster its own reputation. Indeed, according to this measure the greater the expenses thrust upon society the better!

Enron, the infamous American energy company (with claimed revenues of over US$100 billion in 2000), which *Fortune Magazine* named "America's Most Innovative Company" for six consecutive years in the late 1990s, did essentially the exact same thing that our economy is praised for doing. The company's nearly Herculean revenues were generated largely through creative accounting practices, like by buying and selling products and services to themselves. This allowed them to simultaneously report (tax deductible) losses from the purchase, profits from the sale, and trading revenues by brokering the transaction. Enron went bankrupt in 2001 and the top architects behind this criminal scheme were imprisoned.[12] Meanwhile, the status quo (aka cheaponomics) is allowed to continue, even after allowing banks to pollute the global economy with trillions of dollars of toxic mortgages, bringing it to the brink of ruin while imposing enormous additional costs upon workers and homeowners around the world.[13]

This also points to why economic growth is a terrible proxy for real prosperity, in the sense of making people truly better off. Fresh water supplies around the world are becoming more and more polluted, forcing people to turn increasingly to bottled water. While a great development as far as economic growth is concerned (global sales in 2010 hit US$86 billion), it is an abysmal turn of events from the perspective of human and environmental well-being.[14] Climate change? Some sectors of the economy and pockets of the global community will suffer horribly in the not too distant future due to extreme weather events and rising sea levels. But think of the trillions of dollars that will be injected in the economy, as those with the financial means engage in defensive consumption and attempt to shop their way to safety.[15] Conversely, the presence of those most likely to suffer the most from polluted water and climate change – namely, the poor in low-income countries (a deadly double-whammy) – do not even register in the eyes of GDP. Their suffering will not even constitute a blip in this truly gross measure of prosperity.

Not surprisingly, then, alternative measures of prosperity arrive at completely different rankings. This is particularly the case for those focusing on the ends that ought to matter, like human and environmental welfare, instead of economic growth, which is neither a means (at least after a modest level is achieved) nor an end. Take, for example, the Happy Planet Index (HPI). The premise behind the HPI is that real prosperity is not just about enhancing the well-being of humankind but doing so not at the Earth's expense, so future generations also have natural capital stores to be enriched from.[16] HPI scores range from 0 to 100. High scores reflect a society with high life expectancy, high life satisfaction, and a low ecological footprint. This measure turns convention on its head. For example, the United States ranks an unflattering 114th place, while Costa Rica comes out on top. Costa Ricans live slightly longer than Americans, report having much higher levels of life satisfaction, and do all this with an ecological footprint that is less than a quarter the size of the average US citizen. The average Costs Rican also has *one-fourth* of the wealth (in terms of GDP per capita) as the average American. The HPI supports the argument that it is not environmental throughput (aka economic growth), as least after a certain modest level is reached, that makes for happy and healthy societies. For example, Vietnam and Cameroon have the same ecological footprints (1.3 hectares). Yet whereas the average resident of Cameroon does not live past 50 years and reports low life satisfaction, the average Vietnamese lives as long as most Europeans (73.7 years) and reports being happier than the average South Korean.[17]

Economic growth is to some degree protected by some powerful self-serving voodoo. This explains why the vast majority of people are sick and tired of the status quo – a 22-nation global poll for the BBC World Service, for instance, shows that majorities in 17 of those countries think today's economic system is unfair.[18] Even so, we remain unable to channel that angst and collectively bring about meaningful change. Growth seems to leave the door for a better life open, even if just a crack – though the door may well be chained and therefore will never open any further. As the late Henry Wallich (former governor of the US Federal Reserve) famously put it, "Growth is a substitute for equality of income. So long as there is growth there is hope, and that makes large income differential tolerable."[19] James Speth put it this way: "Growth has often been America's 'out' – the way, many believed, that the nation could somehow square the circle and reconcile its love of liberty with its egalitarian pretensions."[20] One time US vice-presidential candidate Paul Ryan seems to have bought into this line of thinking, as he, and others with similar economic proclivities, chide those who question the inherent goodness of macroeconomic growth. They see the rising tide – like, for example, the Dow's record performance detailed at the beginning of this chapter – and assume that it will, or will eventually, raise all boats, not bothering to take a closer look to see if, say, those vessels are chained to the bottom or if they are taking on water and sinking. As Ryan told a crowd in Virginia during the 2012 election, "Mitt Romney and I are not running to redistribute the wealth; Mitt Romney and I are running to help Americans create wealth."[21]

Growth is nothing more than a tool to achieve particular ends. And like any tool, if not used properly, it can be destructive to life and limb. It is neither a master nor religion, even though individuals like Ryan would like us to believe so. While *some* economic growth seems necessary – there is nothing romantic about living in abject poverty – the mechanism for generating additional well-being returns changes once a country reaches a certain level of affluence. After that point, what a country does with affluence matters more than simply generating more growth for the sake of growth itself. This brings us to the issue of inequality and the tremendous costs borne by societies plagued by gross levels of it.

The cost of inequality

It is amazing how there continue to be reasonable people that can look at today's economic landscape and still not cringe at the levels of inequality that exist within and between nations. Allow me to provide just a couple of examples to set the scene.

- Two-hundred years ago, affluent (or what at the time were self-described as "civilized") countries had three times more wealth than so-called poor countries. By the end of colonialism, in the 1960s, the former were 35 times richer. Today, they are roughly 80 times richer.[22] The 250 richest people on earth, with a combined wealth of US$2.7 trillion, have more than the poorest *3.5 billion*, with a monetized combined worth of US$2.2 trillion.[23] The former represent a body count smaller than classes I have taught, while the latter equal more people than found in the world's six most populous nations, China (1.354 billion), India (1.21 billion), the United States (316 million), Indonesia (237 million), Brazil (194 million), and Pakistan (183 million).

- The last time we saw levels of inequality like those seen currently in countries like the United States was just prior to the Great Depression. Yet those levels were ephemeral compared to today, as the Great Depression (and the tax policies to emerge as a result) proved a great equalizing force. After World War II, the American economic pie grew equally and steadily for all income segments; indeed, incomes at the bottom grew faster than those at the top.[24] The last 30 years have come with dramatic increases in inequality. The share of national income going to the top one percent has more than doubled in the United States since 1980, increasing from 10 to over 20 percent (while for the top 0.01 percent their share of income has more than quadrupled).[25] Table 9.1 details what incomes would have been in 2005 had they grown at the same rates as in the decades immediately following World War II. As it were, incomes since the late 1970s have grown at a frantic pace for the wealthiest of Americans, whereas for the middle class and below they either stagnated or dropped.[26]
- Inequality in the UK is approaching levels not seen since the reign of Queen Victoria; a bleak time, famously depicted by Charles Dickens, when gross levels of inequality made life brutal and short for millions of Britons.[27]
- South Africa is one of the most unequal countries in the world. Its levels of inequality have gotten worse since the end of apartheid. The country's Gini coefficient, which measures inequality on a scale of 0 to 1 (the lower

Table 9.1 Where the one percent fit in the hierarchy of income

Income group	Total loss/gain in annual income★	Average loss/gain per household per year★	Current average household income after-taxes
Top 1%	**$673 billion more**	**$597,241 more**	Top 0.01% = $31 million 99.0% to 99.9% = $1.35 million
96–99%	**$140 billion more**	**$29,895 more**	91% to 98.9% = $167,000
91–95%	**$29 billion more**	**$4,912 more**	
81–90%	$43 billion less	$3,733 less	20% to 90.9% = $42,000
61–80%	$194 billion less	$8,598 less	
41–60%	$224 billion less	$10,100 less	
21–40%	$189 billion less	$8,582 less	
Bottom 20%	$136 billion less	$5,623 less	Bottom 19.9% = $17,800

Notes: ★ Compared to what incomes would have been had all income groups grown at the same rate in 1979–2005 as they did in prior decades.
Source: Hacker and Pierson (2010); *New York Times* (2011).

the less inequality), was 0.7 in 2008. (For some comparison: the Gini coefficient for the United States, which is also considered to be plagued egregiously with levels of inequality, is 0.486.) The top 10 percent in South Africa in 2008 took home 58 percent of the income. South Africa now has a rival: China. Recent data show a startling trend. The top ten percent of Chinese households took home 57 percent of the income in 2010. That same year, the country's Gini coefficient was calculated to be 0.61 – far greater than in prior years when it hovered between 0.41 and 0.48.[28]

In light of the overwhelming data pointing to the growing inequalities associated with business as usual, powerful evidence of benefits being concentrated, there remain those who continue to choose to conflate opinions for facts. I recently came across one such example of cheaponomics denial by Rob Bluey, a journalist and blogger for the Heritage Foundation. He posted, back in early 2012, a chart with the title, "The Top 10 percent of Earners Paid 70 Percent of Federal Income Taxes."[29] The title is meant to evoke a sense of sympathy, *for the rich*. And judging by the comments posted below the chart: mission accomplished. But once you understand the ridiculous level of inequality that underlies those figures Bluey's title actually makes *my* point. If the top one percent of earners in the United States takes home more than 20 percent of all income then of course the top 10 percent are going to pay more – *way more* – than 10 percent of all federal income taxes. Bluey also mentions, with obvious indignation, that the bottom 50 percent of earners in the United States hardly pay any federal income tax – still further evidence, he contends, that the system is unfairly stacked against the wealthy. But let's think for just a second about why that is. The average income for the bottom 90 percent in the United States is US$36,000 – the bottom *90 percent*.[30] The poverty threshold in the United States for a family of four is US$23,550; for a family of seven, US$35,610. That's right: the average income for 90 percent of all income earners in the United States is barely enough to adequately feed a family of seven. So, in short, the bottom 50 percent of earners hardly pay anything in federal income taxes because they don't make anything.

Proponents of the status quo – of markets that are free to socialize as many costs as possible – are quick to chide policies that result in any redistribution of wealth, preferring instead to use the narrative of "needing to focus on upward mobility."[31] The problem is: the deck is stacked so wildly against the bottom 90 percent that the only way to focus on upward mobility is with at least some redistribution. The fact that the top one percent captured 21 percent more than the average income gains during the economic recovery's first years (between 2009 and 2011) makes it painfully clear that the system is simply incapable, as currently structured, of raising all boats.[32] (In other words, wealth concentration among the top one percent has grown faster than income gains between 2009 and 2011.) It has been calculated that for every US$100 worth of growth in the world's income per person, just 60 cents finds its ways to reducing poverty below the US$1-a-day poverty threshold. This therefore means that in order to get everyone in the world to a very modest US$3-a-day income would require such a level of economic growth that we would need to find 14 more planets like Earth to achieve it![33]

Let's leave to the side ethical questions about inequality. From a purely practical standpoint – and the data are perfectly clear on this point – highly unequal societies are terribly inefficient at generating well-being.[34] This ought to be obvious. In more equal societies the next potential Steve Jobs, Ravi Shankar, Wolfgang Amadeus Mozart, Michelangelo, Shakespeare, or Albert Einstein has a much better chance of reaching their full potential than if they were trapped on the wrong side in a highly unequal society. Inequality does not just harm those who happen to be part of the bottom 90 percent. It is injurious to all as it keeps societies from fully prospering upon the capabilities of its people.

Julian Simon famously wrote in 1981 of people being "the ultimate resource," in a book under the same title.[35] Simon was pro-population growth. The greater the collective brainpower, he reasoned, the faster we will find answers to all the ills that currently trouble us. Each birth increases our chances of yielding another, say, Aldo Leopold (though I doubt Simon would take much comfort in that) or Einstein. Yet this reasoning is completely divorced from the socioeconomic conditions on the ground. Had Einstein been born to a poor family in, say, Calcutta (the capital of India during the British Raj until 1911) or an African American family in the deep south (during a time of racial segregation and lynching), I doubt we would be speaking of him today. My point is that the world is already full of these underutilized "ultimate resources"; otherwise invisible capabilities that, if just given a chance, could do great things. Let's focus first on taking care of those already-present ultimate resources.

I recently watched a video clip of Milton Friedman, the famous economist and Nobel laureate first mentioned at the end of Chapter 1, praising greed for its ability to maximize the human condition:

> the greed of producers, who wanted to produce something that they can make a dollar on; the greed of consumers who wanted to buy things as cheaply as they could. Did government play a role in this? Very little; only by keeping the road clear for human greed and self-interest to promote the welfare of the consumer.[36]

There will therefore be those who claim that the type of society I am envisioning will be one of reduced innovation, creativity, and happiness. Too bad for them; the previous paragraphs prove this argument to be self-evidently false. As we move to reduce the concentration of benefits and the socialization of costs we will simultaneously be unleashing human potential, to a degree unknown under the status quo.

Before we put this topic behind us I would like to address one more point: the argument that inequality motivates. This is where the defenders of the status quo confuse equality for equity. The goal is not to make everyone the same; a point I will return to shortly when discussing the writings of Amartya Sen. Most recognize the importance of differential reward to channel those human potentials in directions that enhance human welfare. Yet knowing precisely when inequality levels become "too much" – that's a tricky question. That being said, there is nothing tricky about knowing whether current levels are too high. The evidence is clear: they most definitely are.

Herman Daly offers the following instructive observation to help us think through this thorny subject.[37] He proposes a factor of ten as an inequality ceiling. In doing this he notes that the military and universities have managed to keep their ratios close to (or even below) this level while maintaining tremendous drive among individuals within these organizations. In the US military, for instance, the highest-paid generals make roughly ten times the wages of a private. In a university, the prized rank of Distinguished Professor brings with it a salary that is roughly six to eight times that of a full time non-tenure track instructor. Compare this to the corporate world. Take Walmart: in 2012 its CEO, Mike Duke, made US$20,700,000 – that's roughly 950 times more than the company's average full-time workers.[38] The CEO of Walmart also makes roughly 110 times more than a top-ranking US general and distinguished professor. Is that an efficient and effective distribution of resources? Is the CEO of Walmart 110 times more motivated than the top brass in the US military? Do we honestly believe he is delivering 150 times more value to society than, say, a Nobel Prize-winning professor? Many countries are comfortable talking about and actually taking steps to implement a "minimum wage." What about, then, setting a national "maximum wage"? If you support the former why not also support the latter? Citizens of Switzerland voted in March 2013 to set restrictions to curb executives' pay, such as by outlawing the transfer of large bonuses, known as "golden parachutes," to top officers when their company has been acquired by another. It is a long way from setting a maximum wage but definitely a step in the right direction.

Forget about GDP per capita. Want to know how well-off a country's populous is? Look at its inequality indicators. Whereas absolute wealth is a terrible indicator of a country's level of prosperity – especially after its population have achieved a modest per capita income – inequality proves to be a strong indicator, as it is negatively correlated to a whole host of prosperity and well-being metrics. The data on this subject are compelling. More equal societies have fewer health and social problems (see Figure 9.3),[39] treat women and children better,[40] have a greater sense of collective responsibility to those in other countries (see Figure 9.4),[41] possess lower rates of mental illnesses, are more willing to cooperate with international environmental agreements,[42] and have higher levels of food security.[43] Innovation also appears to be enhanced by equality, to further support a point made earlier (about

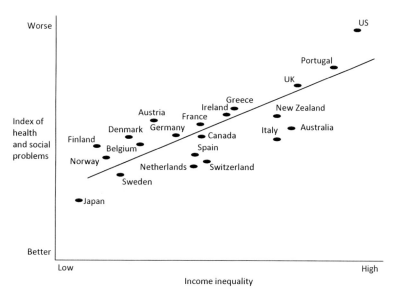

Figure 9.3 Relationship between health and social problems and inequality among selection of high-income countries
Source: Adapted from Wilkinson and Pickett (2009)

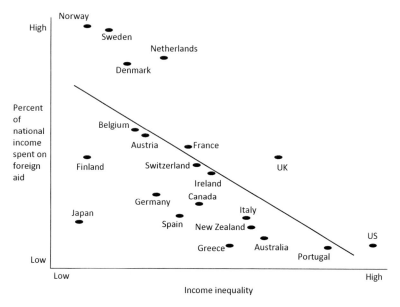

Figure 9.4 Relationship between spending on foreign aid and inequality among selection of high-income countries
Source: Adapted from Wilkinson and Pickett (2009)

utilizing *all* of our ultimate resources), as more equal societies have higher levels of patents granted per capita.[44]

Second-best economics

Too-big-to-fail firms and over-compensated CEOs are to cheaponomics as malnutrition is to poverty. And these qualities, market concentration and gross levels of wealth concentration, tell us that the market is not working and that it needs help. Milton Friedman liked to talk about how greed is good.[45] The problem with that stance is that greed can only really exist in a market ravaged by distortions. In truly competitive markets, profits above the normal rate of return simply cannot be sustained. Massive profits, the nutrients that fertilize the germination of greed if left unrestrained, inevitably attract market entry and thus competition. Eventually those competitors capture some of those returns until profits (above a normal rate of return of capital) are driven to zero. If competitor firms are not doing this, there are barriers to competition (and/or barriers to entry).[46]

And are there ever barriers and distortions, which is why we might want to start viewing "market failures" as simply "markets behaving as markets do." The former assumes an idealized condition where prices convey accurate, complete information, in the sense that *all* costs are internalized (including an accurate monetization of those things for which there are no markets), while also allowing for a "normal" rate of return for the marginal unit of each good or service traded. But that is not how markets *actually* work.

This is an immensely important point, as the entire Hayekian house of cards has zero foundation unless the premise of price signals holds. (Friedrich Hayek is a famous twentieth-century economist who championed classic liberalism and free-market principles.) Accurate pricing signals are what give markets their celebrated self-organizing properties; what allows them to effectively utilize massive amounts of information in a way that enhances individual freedom and liberty without any (or minimal) "outside" intervention. Getting close doesn't cut it. Either the costs are all perfectly internalized or they are not.

This brings me to what is known as the "general theory of second best." This concept was first introduced almost 60 years ago in *The Review of Economic Studies*, in a paper under the same title.[47] The authors asked the question: what would happen if the price of just one commodity did not equal its marginal cost of production? Or, to put it in a way free of standard economic parlance: what if the market didn't get the price right for one good or service? What would this second-best scenario do to the market's self-organizing properties and to the type of first-best (idealized) conditions described in so many of today's economic textbooks? The authors conclude that there is no simple rule for setting prices in a second-best world, which, it is important to note, is precisely the world we live in. The first-best world, it turns out, is an all-or-nothing proposition, as Peter Victor, an ecological economist, has pointed out.[48]

If prices are not fully and accurately informative a very different picture of a "market economy" emerges from that supposed by conventional economics: one that gives space for extra-market forces, such as government intervention to the types of collaborative governance discussed in previous chapters.

So we can stop with this obsession over marketization; of trying to place a price tag on everything as though, if by doing this, we will somehow create a system of allocation that is efficient, sustainable, and just. You can put a price on everything and still know the value of nothing, as Raj Patel reminds us in *The Value of Nothing*.[49] Michael Sandel, Professor of Government at Harvard University, explains to us what happens to societies that seek to place everything up for sale.[50] In the aptly titled *What Money Can't Buy: The Moral Limits of Markets*, Sandel notes how commodification has a tendency to corrupt that which it touches:

> We don't allow children to be bought and sold on the market. Even if buyers did not mistreat the children they purchased, a market in children would express and promote the wrong way of valuing them. ... Or consider the rights and obligations of citizenship. If you are called to jury duty, you may not hire a substitute to take your place. Nor do we allow citizens to sell their votes, even though others might be eager to buy them.[51]

Couple this with the issue of inequality. In the world dreamed up by first-best economists, wealth is not just about the ability to buy bigger homes, more cars, or faster boats. As money comes to buy increasingly more – more access, ownership, influence, and privilege – one's location in the socioeconomic hierarchy (e.g., the bottom 90 percent versus the top 10 percent) matters tremendously in the type of life one will be able to live. Marketization corrodes community – something singled out repeatedly in earlier chapters as being of considerable importance in an affordable society. As money comes to buy more things, the fewer opportunities there are for people of different backgrounds and classes to interact with each other – just the opposite direction we ought to be going in a world already paralyzed by xenophobia, fear of "the other," and gated ways of living. The more we let markets dominate our lives, especially in a world plagued by rising inequality, the more we move in the direction of a market-based apartheid society. In light of the alternative, I would take second best any day.

Why rights presuppose responsibilities

This is not about being against markets themselves. As Amartya Sen once wrote, "to be generically against markets is like being generically against conversation."[52] But we need to realize that markets can take many different forms, like those existing outside the formal market economy (as found in a sharing economy). There is also, as Michael Sandel points out, an enormous difference between having a market economy and being a market society.[53] Markets can be vibrant, just, communal, and collaborative, bonding people and places together in novel and interesting ways. Yet they can also be faceless, placeless, and destructive; the macroeconomic equivalent of the drone pilot who is tens of thousands of miles away from the damage inflicted to those "on the ground." An affordable society, among other things, embraces individual rights but sees them as conditional upon acting responsibly, versus cheaponomics, where rights are to be elevated above (and mostly irrespective of) responsibilities.

The status quo has a remarkably narrow understanding of the individual's relationship to society. A core premise, for example, of classical liberalism is that people will act responsibly by doing something with nature in a way that ultimately benefits all of humankind. To quote Lysander Spooner, a nineteenth-century political philosopher and libertarian: "the only way, in which [the wealth of nature] can be made useful to mankind [or womankind], is by their taking possession of it individually, and thus making it private property."[54] I wonder what Spooner, or John Locke before him, would think of land speculating, derivative trading, and all the other practices, many of them outlined in previous chapters, that involve taking while giving very little in return to humankind. It seems we have forgotten that individual rights presuppose responsibilities to society at large.

It was not always like this. Take the law of stray animals, a centuries old legal principle that has since been turned on its head. British common law long ago established that while an individual can own a bull that ownership comes with responsibilities, such as making sure fences are not in disrepair and that gates are closed and locked. If you did not live up to these responsibilities and your bull got loose and wreaked havoc on your neighbor's property, trampling their garden, destroying clotheslines, and impregnating a cow, then it was your responsibly to make your neighbor whole, such as by paying to have everything repaired or by lending a hand to make things right.[55]

Today, other peoples' bulls are spoiling our air and water, polluting our financial markets, eroding communities, and trampling the well-being of billions. Why? Because we are told property rights are sacred, having seemingly forgotten that rights only work to enhance societal welfare when complemented with a sense of responsibility for our actions. Let's not forget those cases where the two remain tightly bundled. Americans, for example, have a fundamental right to free speech. But they also have a responsibility to not yell "fire" in a movie theater or "bomb" on an airplane – indeed, to do so is a criminal offense.

Amartya Sen's theory of justice helps us think through this relationship between rights and responsibilities.[56] What makes Sen's approach to justice so interesting is his focus on capabilities – versus, say, John Rawls' focus on primary goods – as being necessary for people to function fully in the lives they choose. Sen contends that justice should not be about the distribution of goods and services but rather about how individuals are able to utilize those goods and services so they can flourish. In Sen's words, the "focus has to be, in this analysis, on the freedoms generated by commodities, rather than on the commodities seen on their own."[57] In this sentence he is directly criticizing the efficacy of consumerism as a means of enhancing individual and societal welfare. Yet if one were to substitute "commodities" for "primary goods" the criticism could just as easily apply to Rawls' theory of justice. For Rawls, justice and ultimately prosperity are tied to the availability of what he called primary goods, such as civic and political liberties, income and wealth, access to public office, and "the social basis of self-respect."[58] Sen is critical of Rawls in how his fixation upon primary goods causes him to overlook the fact that people are not able, for a host of structural reasons, to translate available primary goods into actual welfare-enhancing opportunities. We see this happening all around the world, where billions technically have access to civic and political liberties, income and wealth, public office, and self-respect. Yet for the great majority that just isn't enough. Our current focus on economic growth and individual rights cares nothing about what those individual commodities and liberties *actually do* for people, in terms of if they in reality make us better off; all that matters is that commodities are produced and sold and that individual rights are protected – no matter the cost.

Thus for Sen prosperity – *true* prosperity – requires positive rights, like the right to utilize goods and services in ways that allow people to flourish. But it also, and equally, requires negative rights, such as the right to live in an environment where that process is not interrupted by, say, toxic waste, environmental racism, patriarchy, or runaway inequality. This is another way of saying people have to realize that their rights extend only so far. And when that threshold is crossed they have a *responsibility* to restore the positive rights they infringed upon. To put it more simply still: we have to realize that freedom ultimately requires restraint. Until we realize this, we are left living in a world where freedom for the pike is death for the minnow. While this might be an acceptable arrangement in the lakes of Minnesota I frequented as a child (where the large pike freely roams) it is an unacceptable social condition, particularly in light of the fact that most socioeconomic "minnows" (the bottom 90 percent in the US and bottom 99.9 percent worldwide) exist in this state through no fault of their own.

The twentieth-century historian E.P. Thompson reminds us that Britain had, in the sixteenth and seventeenth centuries, an "old moral economy" of provision that emphasized the common well-being of society and placed limits on the market.[59] In this economy, millers, bakers, and other merchants involved in the British food system were "considered as servants of the community, working not for a profit but for fair allowance."[60] This is a far cry from the world we live in today, where excessive profits, too-big-to-fail firms, and stifling market concentration have become the norm. Cheaponomics was in part made possible thanks to the "breakthrough of the new political economy of the free market ... [and] the breakdown of the old moral economy of provision."[61] But this breakthrough has come at a great cost. The old moral economy was predicated upon care first and economics second. It was a society with markets, as opposed to being a market society.

Eat the low-hanging fruit first

Growing up we had a neighbor with a large old apple tree that bore a lot of fruit. I remember the tree's owner telling my sister and me that she always ate the lowest hanging fruit first, ideally before other kids in the neighborhood got them (and who, unlike us, did not have permission to pick the fruit). Like that tree, there are a lot of very practical fruit that we could pick from when setting out to create an affordable alternative to cheaponomics. Some are lower than others; not all are as equally ripe or as sweet; and some might even have a worm or two in them. Much like the apple pie my mother would make from our "harvest," there are a number of ways to move in the direction of an economy, in the broadest sense (*oikonomia*), which places societal well-being ahead of excessive profits for the few. To conclude this chapter I elaborate a bit more on what some of these lower hanging fruits are as they pertain to the subjects of governance and government. (The following chapter elaborates on more fruits, even those requiring a little more work to incorporate into our affordable pie.) And like my neighbor's apples from childhood, we really cannot afford to wait for these fruits to fall on the ground. By then it might be too late. We best pick them now and start baking.

Governance: more democracy, participation, and collective action

I have already elaborated on the importance of getting people together – of talking, sharing, and collaborating – so this should come as no surprise. Sen would also support this recommendation, as he believes more participatory methods are preferable for deciding what it is people value and the type of life they wish to live. In making his argument, he sticks a thumb in the eye of political theorists who presume to know better than the people themselves in terms of what they need and want. The problem, in his words, is:

> with insisting on one pre-determined canonical list of capabilities, chosen by theorists without any general social discussion or public reasoning. To have such a fixed list, emanating entirely from pure theory, is to deny the possibility of fruitful public participation on what should be included and why.[62]

The practice of participatory budgeting certainly does this. Participatory budgeting is a process of democratic deliberation and decision-making where residents collectively decide how to allocate part of a municipal budget. It originated in the 1980s in Brazil but has since spread to more than 1,000 cities.⁶³ The practice has even reached the United States. Chicago was the first city to utilize the practice in 2010, when a ward allowed its residents to decide how to spend US$1.3 million of its discretionary funds. More recently, four city districts in New York handed the authority to residents to determine the fate of almost US$6 million.⁶⁴ There were plenty who were initially skeptical about the process, thinking everyone would just focus on their personal needs. But, as we have already learned, when you get people *talking* me-based thinking quickly flips to we-based. One participant from Chicago noted that at earlier "community meetings everyone was complaining about their block ... But now every single committee has taken stewardship of the whole ward as their mission."⁶⁵

A market society creates barriers to collective action. It does this not so much by reducing opportunities as by increasing the transaction costs of getting together. The market plays an increasing role in shaping who we interact with and the aims of that interaction. For example, the aims of consumers are different from, say, sharing neighbors, collaborating community members, or participants of a participatory budgeting scheme. It seems like we have to work harder today to interact as citizens because increasingly interactions are centered on consumption and work. Economist Albert Hirschman, in his brilliant treatise *Exit, Voice, and Loyalty*, argues that people generally have two classes of responses at their disposal when they are unhappy.⁶⁶ They can either *exit* the situation or they can protest and give *voice* to their troubles. In the marketplace – and in a market society – exit becomes the primary (sometimes only) available response to displeasure. If you do not like a particular brand of popcorn you stop buying it. If a brand of socks irritates your skin you buy from a competitor. If an ice cream parlor repeatedly shorts you on scoops you stop going. The marketplace makes exit easy, but at the expense of voice. Ever try giving voice to your displeasure over a consumer item? I tried recently. It was my mobile phone service provider. I was on hold for 30 minutes. Never did get to give voice to my concerns (I eventually had to hang up because my son was crying in the next room). In social relationships, exit is the response of last resort. And for good reason: it is a highly inefficient and ineffective way to communicate displeasure in the hope that things will be made better. When someone exits in the marketplace it could be for any number of reasons, such as death, unemployment, a change in diet for reasons that have nothing to do with dissatisfaction (e.g., religious obligations), or divorce (I know someone who changed ketchup brands after separating from their partner as it reminded them of a time they were actively trying to forget). Even when exit is the result of genuine displeasure, without voice there is no way to figure out why one exited. Whatever change does happen is usually woefully incomplete because the market has no way to know what we *really* want. And if we are looking for something that it cannot provide, like a world that places greater constraints on the market rather than one constrained by it ... well, you can forget about it.

Government: not more but different

The government must also play a role in this, namely, by working *for* rather than against us (or at least 90 percent of us). And, importantly, I am not talking about more government but different government. Indeed, the whole argument about whether there ought to be more or less government is based either in religion or ideology because it has no grounding in fact. For example, you will often hear so-called champions of free enterprise argue for minimal government intervention to allow for the seamless integration of global markets (aka globalization).[67] But this argument belies the reality of globalization.[68] As Dani Rodrik, Professor of International Political Economy at Harvard University, explains in a highly cited paper on the subject, even after controlling for a host of variables "there is a positive correlation between an economy's exposure to international trade and the size of its government."[69] International trade is incredibly risky. Governments must therefore grow to mitigate some of the risks that accompany it. In short, without government intervention there could be no globalization. So even though they say otherwise – and perhaps without even knowing it – the world envisioned by free marketeers is quite literally dependent upon government. In the end, it is a matter of kind rather than of degree.

A fundamental principle of economists is that it is better to tax bad things rather than things viewed as having societal value.[70] A practical first step in altering what the government does could involve a shift in taxes away from labor and toward pollution.[71] The strategy of taxing pollution has been around a while and is generally known as "Pigovian taxes." English economist Arthur Cecil Pigou argued over a century ago that the existence of externalities justifies government action.[72] He advocated for pollution-avoidance charges and welfare-damage costs – in other words, taxes – which would be applied to any and all offending firms and activities. Such taxes would discourage particularly egregious behaviors, internalize some of the costs not fully accounted for, and generate revenue to pay for the cleanup of past socialized costs as well as the expenses associated with the administration and monitoring of firms. Admittedly, the question of what the tax rate ought to be is open-ended, particularly once we recognize that such taxes are often not just about internalizing *existing* costs but paying for (or at least some of the) costs *already* socialized.

We also need to be aware of how such taxes disproportionately affect poorer households, which, as earlier described, there are plenty of. That is because, by nature of trying to internalize costs that were previously socialized, such taxes often result in more expensive goods, services, and energy. And since the poor spend a greater percentage of their income on consumption than the wealthy, anything that makes goods more expensive will be regressive – though much of this price increase will likely be temporary as society restructures itself to account for more expensive inputs and energy.[73] Yet one of the advantages of ecological taxes over, say, conventional governmental regulation is that the former provide a mechanism for generating revenue to offset pricing spikes for the lowest-income groups. There are ways to make ecological taxes progressive. For example, a tax-free minimal level of energy or water per person per week could be established. This might actually make certain things *less* expensive for the poor than they are presently; an outcome that I entirely support. (The 1.1 billion living on a dollar a day or less in the world need to consume *more*, not less.)[74] From there, the tax rate could increase with levels of consumption. As discussed in Chapter 2, instead of making electricity progressively cheaper, to the point of being *free*, for companies like Google and Facebook (to power their "server farms"), price would go in the opposite direction so those firms pay more of the actual costs of their business model.

Cost minimization – for *them*, not society – is a core task for any firm. This practice takes many forms. Under a business-as-usual scenario, it is often most efficiently achieved through externalization, as I have detailed. Cost socialization is encouraged by current tax and regulatory policies. For roughly the last hundred years, material costs have been dropping faster than wages, especially when compared to wages in fully developed economies.[75] Why? Many countries have very generous tax codes that provide tax deductions on equipment depreciation. A particularly egregious example of this is what is known in the United States as accelerated depreciation, which allows companies to write off their capital investments considerably faster than the assets actually wear out. Technically speaking, accelerated depreciation is a tax deferral but so long as a firm continues to invest in capital the tax deferral can be indefinite. In early 2008, in an attempt to stimulate investment, the US Congress and President George W. Bush dramatically expanded these depreciation tax breaks by creating a "bonus depreciation" provision that allows companies to immediately write off up to 75 percent of the cost of their investments in new equipment.[76] Meanwhile, labor continues to be heavily taxed in countries like the United States. Add to all this cheap energy and it should become obvious why firms choose to invest in labor-saving technologies, especially when talking about workers in high-income countries that cannot as easily have costs socialized onto them as in low-income countries (thanks to certain laws, regulations, and something called democracy). A labor-intensive economy does *not* have to be more expensive than a capital-intensive economy. It is, at the moment, but only because we allow so many costs associated with the latter model to be socialized. If we were to internalize those costs, while also reflecting upon what it is we really value, I have no doubt that the incentives would point us in a different direction. In this scenario, at least for many sectors of the economy, we would be looking for ways to increase our reliance upon labor.

Another form of pollution we should consider taxing is advertising, especially that directed at children. Think "pollution" is too strong a word? I will let an advertising insider (a *very* insider) make the case for me. The following admission comes from Rory Sutherland, Vice Chairman of the marketing firm Ogilvy UK and (at the time of the quote) President of the Institute of Practitioners in Advertising:

> The truth is that marketing raises enormous ethical questions every day – at least it does if you're doing it right. If this were not the case, the only possible explanations are either that you believe marketers are too ineffectual to make any difference, or you believe that marketing activities only affect people at the level of conscious argument. Neither of these possibilities appeals to me. *I would rather be thought of as evil than useless.*[77]

There is a considerable body of research that examines the links between "intrinsic" and "extrinsic" values and consumption.[78] Intrinsic values refer to aspects of life that we find inherently rewarding, whereas the reward of extrinsic values lies in the validation given to us by others. When an individual places greater importance on extrinsic values, they are more likely to express prejudice toward others, be less concerned about the environment and human rights, and express lower levels of personal well-being and happiness.[79] Research looking specifically at adolescents and their environmental behaviors indicates those that strongly endorse intrinsic values are likely to turn off lights in unused rooms, recycle, and engage in other pro-environmental behaviors.[80] Elsewhere we find indication of a strong positive correlation between the ecological footprints of adults and their possession of extrinsic values.[81] You get one guess on which values advertisers target.

Answer: extrinsic values.

What, then, does it mean to be subtly inculcated, over the course of decades, into becoming envious, status-seeking hyper-consumers? Clearly, the effects are subtle and the result of years of exposure – a type of bioaccumulation of the mind and spirit – as we tend not to rush to purchase everything we see advertised. This gives us at least a partial explanation for the phenomena mentioned earlier this chapter, about how residents in very affluent countries (e.g., the United States), where advertisements are practically as ubiquitous as air, report being less happy than residents in countries with considerably less wealth (e.g., Costa Rica). A study examined the impact of the use of Channel One – a daily ten-minute news bulletin with two minutes of advertisements – in US schools and how exposure to it influenced attachment to extrinsic values.[82] Two neighboring schools were looked at with very similar student and parent demographics: one had Channel One; the other did not. Teenagers enrolled at the school with Channel One had much higher levels of extrinsic values than the control group. This corroborates more recent research pointing to links between hours of watching television and a lack of concern about environmental problems and an increased prevalence of extrinsic values.[83]

We could create advertising-free zones. Most places of religious worship are advertisement free. Why not do the same with schools and other public places where children are frequently present? We could even create an outright ban on advertising in public spaces, as is presently in place in São Paulo, Brazil. And why not limit specific types of advertisement that are clearly meant for children? In Greece, television advertisements for toys are banned from 7 a.m. to 9 p.m. In Norway and Sweden, it is illegal to target through advertisements children under the age of 12. Finally, and bringing the subject back to taxes, advertisements in countries like the United States are actually a tax-deductible expense, which creates clear incentives for firms to engage in more of this "polluting" behavior. In light of everything just covered in the last couple of paragraphs, there is considerable justification for taxing this "bad" instead of encouraging it by allowing firms to claim it as a tax-deductible expense.

The last point I will mention directs us back to material covered in prior chapters. We need to create/rewrite laws and regulations to encourage, rather than discourage, a sharing economy. Many of our laws developed over the last century were designed to manage increasingly polarized or exploitative economic relationships: employer/employee; landlord/tenant; developer/homebuyer; business/investor; and producer/consumer. These legal categories, however, do not accurately capture the collaborative nature of relationships in a sharing economy. Collaboration lacks many of the same power dynamics of the old economy. Indeed, it is often very difficult to determine whether certain labor, real estate, securities, commercial, and other regulations even apply to activities in the sharing economy.[84] To quote from a faux advertisement posted in an article in the *Journal of Environmental Law and Litigation*:

> SEEKING 500,000 SHARING LAWYERS
> Every community in the U.S. will soon need "sharing lawyers," "grassroots transactional lawyers" or whatever you may prefer to call these new legal specialists. By our estimation, with around 30,000 incorporated towns and cities in the U.S., we will soon need at least 100,000 sharing lawyers. As the sharing economy becomes the predominant economic force in our society, all transactional lawyers in the U.S. (approximately 500,000) should consider transforming the focus of their practices to smooth the way toward a more sustainable economy.[85]

Perhaps if more in the profession followed this call it would not be the butt of so many jokes.

Reclaiming value

As ought to be clear, the solution to cheaponomics involves more than just internalizing costs. The futurist Alvin Toffler famously asked a room full of CEOs what it would cost their respective firms if all new recruits had not been toilet trained and they had to pay for the training of this skill. How would – how *could* – you internalize into the market economy this cost? We therefore also need to reclaim those values that the market has either taken from us or rendered invisible. An example of a value rendered invisible is all the immensely valuable work done within the home, thanks to which CEOs do not have to worry about, among other things, their employees soiling themselves at work. But the market also *takes*, by, for instance, reducing democracy to consumer choice, we-orientations (e.g., intrinsic values) to me-orientations (e.g., extrinsic values), and communicating communities (*à la* Elinor Ostrom) to isolated prisoners (Garrett Hardin, the Prisoner's Dilemma, etc.).[86]

It is time we reclaimed some of that value by pushing back against the market. An affordable society is priceless, literally, in that it is premised on the placing of limits on the market. In doing this, it seeks to afford individuals, communities, and nations the capabilities to develop and enhance their overall well-being in directions of their own choosing – *that's* real choice. Cheaponomics, conversely, for the vast majority of the world's population, has just the opposite effect: it disables. Which world do you want to live in?

Notes

1. Pepitone, Julianne (2013) "Dow, S&P close at new highs on health are rally," *CNN.com*, April 2, http://money.cnn.com/2013/04/02/investing/stocks-markets/index.html, last accessed April 9, 2013.
2. CBS News (2013) "Markets keep rising after Dow hits record high," *CBSnews.com*, March 6, www.cbsnews.com/8301-505123_162-57572766/markets-keep-rising-after-dow-hits-record-high/, last accessed April 9, 2013.
3. Schaefer, Steve (2013) "Dow closes at record 14,254 as rally keeps rolling," *Forbes*, March 5, www.forbes.com/sites/steveschaefer/2013/03/05/dow-hits-record-high-as-rally-keeps-rolling/, last accessed April 9, 2013.
4. Schwartz, Nelcom (2013) "Recovery in US is lifting profits, but not adding jobs," *New York Times*, March 3, www.nytimes.com/2013/03/04/business/economy/corporate-profits-soar-as-worker-income-limps.html?_r=0, last accessed April 9, 2013.
5. Ibid.
6. Ayres, Robert and Benjamin Warr (2009) *The Economic Growth Engine: How Energy and Work Drive Material Prosperity* (Northampton, MA: Edward Elgar), p. xvi.
7. Gongloff, Mark (2013) "Dow hits record high: Here's why it doesn't matter," *Huffington Post*, March 5, www.huffingtonpost.com/2013/03/05/dow-record-high_n_2783096.html?view=screen, last accessed April 9, 2013.
8. Ibid.
9. Noah, Timothy (2013) "The one percent gobbled up the recovery, too," *New Republic*, February 12, www.newrepublic.com/article/112397/one-percent-gobbles-economic-recovery#, last accessed April 10, 2013.
10. See Kulkarni, S., A. Levin-Rector, M. Ezzati, and C. Murray (2011) "Falling behind: Life expectancy in US counties from 2000 to 2007 in an international context," *Population Health Metrics*, 9(1), pp. 1–12.
11. See, for example, Jackson, Tim T. (2009) *Prosperity Without Growth* (London: Earthscan); Wilkinson, R. and K. Pickett (2009) *The Spirit Level: Why More Equal Societies Are Almost Always Better* (New York: Penguin Books).

12 Though found guilty on ten counts Kenneth Lay, the company's CEO, died of a heart attack before he could be sentenced.
13 Stiglitz, Joseph (2012) *The Price of Inequality* (New York: W.W. Norton), p. 173.
14 Rani, Bina, Raaz Maheshwari, Ankita Garg, and Magan Prasad (2012) "Bottled water – a global market overview," *Bulletin of Environment, Pharmacology and Life Sciences*, 1(6), pp. 1–4.
15 Szasz, A. (2007) *Shopping Our Way to Safety: How We Changed from Protecting the Environment to Protecting Ourselves* (Minneapolis: University of Minnesota Press).
16 New Economics Foundation (2009) "The un-happy planet index 2.0" (London: New Economics Foundation), www.happyplanetindex.org/publicdata/files/happy-planet-index-2-0.pdf, last accessed April 14, 2013.
17 Ibid.
18 BBC (2012) "Economic system seen as unfair: Global poll," *BBC World Service*, April 25, www.globescan.com/images/images/pressreleases/bbc2012_economics/BBC12_Economics.pdf, last accessed April 15, 2013.
19 Wallich, H. (1972) "Zero growth," *Newsweek*, January 24, p. 62.
20 Speth, James (2009) *The Bridge at the Edge of the World* (New Haven: Yale University Press), p. 122.
21 Sink, Justin (2012) "Ryan chides Obama over 'redistribution' comment at Va. rally," *The Hill*, September 9, http://thehill.com/blogs/blog-briefing-room/news/250343-ryan-chides-obama-over-redistribution-comment-at-va-rally, last accessed April 15, 2013.
22 The Rules (2013) "Global wealth inequality: What you never knew you never knew," *TheRules*, April 3, www.youtube.com/watch?v=uWSxzjyMNpU&feature=share, last accessed April 22, 2013.
23 Hickel, Jason (2013) "The truth about extreme global inequality," *Aljazeera*, April 14, www.aljazeera.com/indepth/opinion/2013/04/201349124135226392.html, last accessed April 22, 2013.
24 Stiglitz (2012), p. 4.
25 Oxfam (2013) "The cost of inequality: How wealth and income extremes hurt us all," *Oxfam*, January 18, www.oxfam.org/sites/www.oxfam.org/files/cost-of-inequality-oxfam-mb180113.pdf, last accessed April 22, 2013.
26 Hacker, J. and P. Pierson (2010) *Winner Take All Politics* (New York: Simon & Schuster); *New York Times* (2011) "Where the 1 percent fit in the hierarchy of income," *New York Times*, October 28, www.nytimes.com/interactive/2011/10/30/nyregion/where-the-one-percent-fit-in-the-hierarchy-of-income.html?_r=0, last accessed April 22, 2013.
27 Oxfam (2012) "The perfect storm: Economic stagnation, the rising cost of living, public spending cuts, and the impact on UK poverty," *Oxfam* Oxfam Briefing Paper, June, http://policy-practice.oxfam.org.uk/publications/the-perfect-storm-economic-stagnation-the-rising-cost-of-living-public-spending-228591, last accessed April 22, 2013.
28 *The Economist* (2012) "To each, not according to his needs," *The Economist*, December 15, 21568423-new-survey-illuminates-extent-chinese-income-inequality-each-not, last accessed April 22, 2013.
29 Bluey, Rob (2012) "Top 10 percent of earners paid 70 percent of federal income taxes," *The Foundry*, The Heritage Network, The Heritage Foundation, January 29, http://blog.heritage.org/2012/01/29/chart-of-the-week-top-1-percent-paid-38-percent-of-taxes/, last accessed April 22, 2013.
30 *New York Times* (2011).
31 See, for example, comments by Paul Ryan quoted in Chait, Jonathan (2011) "The ideological fantasies of inequality deniers," *New York Magazine*, October 12, http://

nymag.com/daily/intelligencer/2011/10/the_ideological_fantasies_of_i.html, last accessed April 22, 2013.
32 Saez, Emmanuel (2013) "Striking it richer: The evolution of top incomes in the United States," University of California, Berkeley, Department of Economics, Working Paper, January 23, http://elsa.berkeley.edu/~saez/saez-UStopincomes-2011.pdf, last accessed April 22, 2013.
33 Boyle, David and Andrew Simms (2009) *The New Economics: A Bigger Picture* (London: Earthscan), p. 40.
34 See, for example, Dietz, T., E. Rosa, and R. York. (2012) "Environmentally efficient well-being: Is there a Kuznets curve?" *Environmental Geography*, 32, pp. 21–8; Knight, K. and E. Rosa (2011) "The environmental efficiency of well-being: A cross-national analysis," *Social Science Research*, 40, pp. 931–49.
35 Simon, J. (1981) *The Ultimate Resource* (Princeton: Princeton University Press).
36 Milton Friedman on how regulation stifles innovation and raises prices, www.youtube.com/watch?v=g-6_xEfY3pM, last accessed April 23, 2013.
37 Daly, H. (1996) *Beyond Growth: The Economics of Sustainable Development* (Boston: Beacon Press).
38 Rupp, Lindsey and Renee Dudley (2013) "Walmart's CEO Duke's pay rises to $20.7 million last year," *Bloomberg*, April 23, www.bloomberg.com/news/2013-04-22/walmart-ceo-compensation-rises-to-20-7-million-in-2013.html, last accessed April 23, 2013.
39 Wilkinson, R. and K. Pickett (2009) *The Spirit Level: Why More Equal Societies Are Almost Always Better* (New York: Penguin Books).
40 Ibid.
41 Ibid.
42 Wilkinson, R., K. Pickett, and R. De Vogli (2010) "Equality, sustainability, and quality of life," *BMJ*, 341, pp. 1138–40.
43 Carolan, Michael (2013) *Reclaiming Food Security* (New York and London: Earthscan/Routledge).
44 Wilkinson *et al.* (2010).
45 Milton Friedman on how regulation stifles innovation and raises prices, www.youtube.com/watch?v=g-6_xEfY3pM, last accessed April 23, 2013.
46 Stiglitz (2012), p. 35.
47 Lipsey, R.G. and Kelvin Lancaster (1956/7) "The general theory of second best," *The Review of Economic Studies*, 23(1), pp. 11–32.
48 Victor, Peter (2008) *Managing without Growth: Slower by Design, not Disaster* (Cheltenham: Edward Elgar), p. 42; Victor is an economist by training and a self-described ecological economist: see www.pvictor.com/Site/Brief_Bio.html, last accessed November 11, 2013.
49 Patel, Raj (2009) *The Value of Nothing: How to Reshape Market Society and Redefine Democracy* (New York: Picador).
50 Sandel, Michael (2012) *What Money Can't Buy: The Moral Limits of Markets* (New York: Farrar, Straus, and Giroux).
51 Ibid., p. 10.
52 Sen, Amartya (1999) *Development as Freedom* (New York: Alfred A. Knopf), p. 6.
53 Sandel (2012), p. 10.
54 Spooner, Lysander (1855) *The Law of Intellectual Property* (Boston, MA: Bela Marsh), http://lysanderspooner.org/node/10, last accessed April 25, 2013.
55 Carolan, Michael (2010) *Decentering Biotechnology: Assemblages Built and Assemblages Masked* (Farnham, UK: Ashgate), p. 50.
56 Sen (1999).
57 Ibid., p. 74.

58 Rawls, John (1999 [1971]) *A Theory of Justice* (Cambridge, MA: Harvard University Press), p. 54.
59 Thompson, E.P. (1971) "The moral economy of the English crowd in the eighteenth century," *Past and Present*, 50, pp. 76–136.
60 Ibid., p. 83.
61 Ibid., p. 136.
62 Sen, Amartya (2005) "Human rights and capabilities," *Journal of Human Development*, 6 (2), pp. 151–66, p. 158.
63 Choi, Serin (2012) "Expanding participatory budgeting in New York City," *Looking Ahead*, 3, pp. 32–4, p. 32.
64 Lerner, Josh and Donata Secondo (2012) "By the people, for the people: Participatory budgeting from the bottom up in North America," *Journal of Public Deliberation*, 8(2), www.publicdeliberation.net/jpd/vol8/iss2/art2, last accessed April 25, 2013.
65 Lerner, Josh and Megan Wage Antieau (2010) "Chicago's $1.3 million experiment in democracy," *Yes!* April 20, www.yesmagazine.org/people-power/chicagos-1.3-million-experiment-in-democracy, last accessed April 25, 2013.
66 Hirschman, Albert (1970) *Exit, Voice and Loyalty* (Cambridge, MA: Harvard University Press).
67 See, for example, Republican National Committee (2012) "We believe in American: Republican platform 2012," www.gop.com/wp-content/uploads/2012/08/2012GOPPlatform.pdf, last accessed April 26, 2013, p. 1.
68 See, for example, Cameron, David (1978) "The expansion of the public economy: A comparative analysis," *The American Political Science Review*, 72(4), pp. 1243–61; Rodrik, Dani (1998) "Why do more open economies have bigger governments," *Journal of Political Economy*, 106(5), pp. 997–1032.
69 Rodrik (1998), p. 997.
70 Stiglitz (2012), p. 213.
71 Stiglitz (2012), p. 213; Hawken, Paul, Amory Lovins, and L. Hunter Lovins (1999) *Natural Capitalism* (New York: Little, Brown and Company), p. 164.
72 Pigou, A. (1912) *Wealth and Welfare* (London: Macmillan).
73 Weizsacker, Ernst von, Karlson Hargroves, Michael Smith, Cheryl Desha, and Peter Stasinopoulos (2009) *Factor of Five* (London: Earthscan), p. 321.
74 OCED (2005) *Development Co-operation Report 2004* (Paris: OECD), p. 1.
75 Jackson (2009), pp. 92–3.
76 ITEP (2011) "Corporate taxpayers and corporate tax dodgers, tax justice and the Institute on Taxation and Economic Policy," Washington, DC, www.ctj.org/corporatetaxdodgers/CorporateTaxDodgersReport.pdf, last accessed April 27, 2013, p. 11.
77 Sutherland, R. (2010) "We can't run away from the ethical debates in marketing," *Market Leader*, January, www.marketing-society.org.uk/SiteCollectionDocuments/knowledge-zone/market-leader/january-2010.pdf, last accessed April 27, 2013, p. 59.
78 Carolan, Michael (2013) *Society and the Environment: Pragmatic Solutions to Ecological Issues* (Boulder: Westview Press), p. 260.
79 See, for example, Alexander, J., T. Crompton, and G. Shrubsole (2011) "Think of me as evil: Opening the ethical debates in advertising," Public Interest Research Centre (PIRC) and WWF-UK,http://assets.wwf.org.uk/downloads/think of me as evil.pdf, last accessed April 27, 2013; Roccas, S., and L. Sagiv (2010) "Personal values and behaviour: Taking the cultural context into account," *Social and Personality Psychology Compass*, 4, pp. 30–41.
80 Kasser, T. (2005) "Frugality, generosity, and materialism in children and adolescents," in *What Do Children Need to Flourish? Conceptualizing and Measuring Indicators of Positive Development*, edited by K. Moore and L. Lippman (New York: Springer Science), pp. 357–73.

81 Brown, K. and T. Kasser (2005) "Are psychological and ecological well-being compatible? The role of values, mindfulness, and lifestyle," *Social Indicators Research*, 74, pp. 349–68.
82 Greenberg, Bradley and Jeffrey Brand (1993) "Television news and advertising in schools: The 'Channel One' controversy," *Journal of Communication*, 43(1), pp. 143–51.
83 See, for example, Good, J. (2007) "Shop 'til we drop? Television, materialism, and attitudes about the natural environment," *Mass Communication and Society*, 10, pp. 365–83; Schor, J. (2005) *Born to Buy* (New York: Scribner).
84 Kassan, Jenny and Janelle Orsi (2012) "The legal landscape of the sharing economy," *Journal of Environmental Law and Litigation*, 27, pp. 1–20.
85 Ibid., p. 2.
86 See, for example, Patel (2009); Sandel (2012).

Chapter 10

Ten recommendations for the good, affordable, and affording

I recently had another go at *The General Theory of Employment, Interest, and Money* (1936) by John Maynard Keynes, one of the greatest economists of all time (who, coincidentally, was neither formally trained in economics nor in possession of a degree above a BA, which was in mathematics). Easily one of the most influential books in economic theory ever written, it is widely credited with creating the terminology and shape of contemporary macroeconomics.[1] It is also incredibly dense and at times difficult to comprehend. Yet the ideas it expresses and futures it seeks to spawn are, by Keynes' own estimation, deceptively simple. The problem, however, lies in the entrenched nature of the status quo, to the point of it having become self-evident and seemingly beyond any meaningful reproach. As Keynes confessed in the final paragraph of the English Preface:

> The composition of this book has been for the author a long struggle of escape, and so must the reading of it be for the readers if the author's assault upon them is to be successful – a struggle of escape from habitual modes of thought and expression. The ideas which are here expressed so laboriously are extremely simple and should be obvious. The difficulty lies, not in the new ideas, but in escaping from the old ones, which ramify, for those brought up as most of us have been, into every corner of our minds.[2]

Beyond the multitude of brilliant points made in this masterpiece, this one in particular stood out for me, which is not terribly surprising as I was simultaneously pondering cheaponomics and its firm grip upon our lives. The problem with cheaponomics and the value of the alternatives expressed in previous chapters *are* extremely simple and *should* be obvious. Yet we continue to cling onto the same tired ways of thinking that got us into this mess. Like a child's unquestioning belief in Santa Claus, we wait patiently for the fairies of decoupling, infinite substitutability, and economic growth. At least Santa delivers.

Time lecturing on this subject has taught me the importance of clarity, as, to again return to Keynes' point, the status quo has a way of clouding perceptions of alternatives. Before offering up suggestions on how we can make society more enabling for everyone, concluding the book on a hopeful note, I want to reiterate a couple of points about what I *am* and *am not* arguing.

It is possible to be dismissive of (infinite) economic growth while allowing for the existence of economic activity. One could no more be generically against markets as they could be generally against conversation.[3] Both can be linked to tremendous hardship. Yet it seems a grave overreaction to stop talking or exchanging with one's neighbor out of concern of something negative happening as a result. Indeed, I would be more worried of grave consequences occurring were we *not* to do either.

To be critical of market societies not a call for more government. Cheaponomics lives off of false choices – such as market versus government – as they keep us sufficiently distracted by helping cloud understandings of alternatives. According to the cheaponomics worldview there are only private property exchanges in a market setting and government-owned property organized by the state. Coupled with this is an equally narrow view of people: as either individual consumers or voters. An affordable society isn't about more or less government any more than it is about us being more or less an individual. It *is* about doing government and markets differently and living lives that enhance our sociality.

To be for extra-market planning is not a call for Communism or Socialism. The truth of the matter is that markets, even so-called "free" ones, are heavily reliant upon planning – look at the US Federal Reserve System and its chairman who sits at its helm and tries to steer this economic goliath. Recall also what was said about globalization in Chapter 9, where its positive relationship to the size of government is highlighted. Frankly, I would be happy if we did away with those capitalized "-isms" entirely. Capitalism versus Socialism/Communism: another example of a false choice perpetuated by cheaponomics.

Finally: forget about ceteris paribus ("all other things being the same"). Do not fall for the trap set by cheaponomics apologists, when they point to a solution outlined previously (or below) in *isolation* and criticize its feasibility. Advocates of the status quo, for example, have at times tried to cast my argument as being only about the production of more expensive goods. "Quite a privileged position to take," I recall one person once telling me. Potentially a fair critique, *if nothing else changes* – that is to say, if the goal were only to internalize costs currently socialized. Yet that solution only takes us further down the rabbit hole as it implies not only that we could put a price on everything but that we should. Think about the problems of this position; of what it implies. For one thing, it tacitly embraces the idea that putting a price on stuff somehow makes it OK to continue inflicting harm – as long as, again, consumers pay more for goods that have been made on the backs of exploited workers, the environment, and/or future generations. Real affordability does not come from stuff, even better priced stuff. It arises out of a whole new pattern of social organization: of working less; sharing, which includes peer-to-peer renting; repairing, and when necessary recycling (versus down-cycling); building community; and of prioritizing access over ownership. Cheaponomics is a systemic problem. To talk about real alternatives, then, is to assume that very little stays the same.

Ten recommendations to start a dialogue

Social scientists are generally close-lipped about prescribing solutions, knowing full well that nothing can substitute for talk and collective action. We may study instances of activism or the dynamics of a social movement but as a general practice leave it up to the people themselves to decide what's best for them. I have also seen this through my own research, the importance of organic, bottom-up social change.[4] *That* change tends to be the most lasting, just, and sustainable.

My time in the classroom and on the lecture stage, however, has taught me a somewhat different lesson: an appreciation of the difficulties that come from focusing exclusively on what's wrong with the world.[5] Perhaps most concerning, from a social change standpoint, is the near debilitating effect it can have on the very audience one hopes to galvanize into action. Too much talk about problems without attention to solutions can convey a sense of hopelessness. Yet, the truth is, we have every reason to be hopeful.

To help get this conservation going, and to conclude things, I offer ten recommendations. These suggestions are directed at making things more affordable and society more affording. They were selected with an eye toward some of the more egregious cases of cost-socializing socialism highlighted in previous chapters. Not all cases, by any means. But it's a start.

1 Reform political processes by increasing transparency and enhancing democracy

At a basic level, it is much harder to get away with cost socialism in countries with a robust civil society, which is why firms often opt to take their business (and costs) overseas to nations that offer their citizens fewer rights and privileges. But beyond that, democracy continues to be wildly distorted even in countries considered to be highly "democratic." For example, the *Citizens United* ruling (where the US Supreme Court held that the Constitution prohibits the government from restricting political independent expenditures by corporations, associations, or labor unions) gave firms and the one percent an oversized bullhorn through which to engage in political speech, as they can now, as witnessed during the last US presidential election, contribute hundreds of millions of dollars to individual campaigns. Meanwhile, the rest of us are confined to political speech equivalent of a whisper as we cast our one vote.

At the very least, if corporations are to contribute millions to a campaign the shareholders ought to vote to do so, rather than leaving it up to the firms' executive officers.

As ought to be clear by now, cheaponomics is centrally a *social* and *political* problem, which means we should not expect markets (or economists) to get us out of the fix we are in. This might seem obvious. Yet problems related to the economy are often cast in surprisingly apolitical and asocial terms.[6] The following comes from a 2006 story in *The Economist*:

> Thanks to a jump in productivity growth after 1995, America's economy has outpaced other rich countries' for a decade. Its workers now produce over 30% more each hour they work than ten years ago. In the late 1990s everybody shared in this boom. Though incomes were rising fastest at the top, all workers' wages far outpaced inflation. But after 2000 something changed. The pace of productivity growth has been rising again, but now it seems to be lifting fewer boats.[7]

We are told in this report that "something changed" after 2000. But what? It is not entirely clear, though later it is explained that "the consensus is that the main cause was technology, which increased the demand for skilled workers relative to their supply, with freer trade reinforcing the effect."[8] Explanations given for such market failures, when things are not allocated fairly and well-being not generated evenly, are often cast in technocratic – read apolitical – jargon: technology; supply; demand … . It is what science and technology studies (STS) scholars refer to as an example of boundary work. By framing a problem a particular way you can control who can and cannot work to solve it. If a problem can be fully explained by, and captured in, a marginal cost curve, we let economists have a go at it. Then there is the problem of cheaponomics.

Finally, we need to improve the transparency and accountability of institutions. Some, like the World Bank and International Monetary Fund (IMF), operate completely outside the reach of civil society. Even firms are moving in this direction, as executives take an ever-larger slice of the corporate pie and where calls for corporate governance – where shareholders call the shots and not managers – go unanswered. Enhancing participation and transparency in influential institutions certainly will not guarantee that they behave in ways that enhance the well-being of all stakeholders, rather than just the one percent. Yet it seems reasonable to assume that the more organizations can be made accountable to the 99 percent the more the latters' livelihoods will matter in boardrooms when decisions get made.

2 Enhance (and enforce existing) antitrust laws

More than 120 countries around the world have adopted or are in the process of adopting antitrust legislation. Laws designed to protect and enhance competition exist in every country of the Organization for Economic Cooperation and Development (OECD). While such legislation dates back two millennia, to Ancient Rome, "modern" antitrust legislation has been around more than 100 years. The Canadian antitrust law of 1889 (rooted in the Act for the Prevention and Suppression of Combinations formed in restraint of Trade) and the Sherman Act of 1890 in the United States were the first national laws prohibiting agreements between firms that unduly restrict competition. The latter was named after Senator John Sherman who argued that the Act "does not announce a new principle of law, but applies old and well recognised principles of common law."[9] The 1980s saw the adoption of similar laws in many middle-income countries, most notably Central and Eastern European nations and former Soviet republics as they transitioned into market economies. China adopted a comprehensive competition law on August 30, 2007, which took effect on August 1, 2008.

But I would not go around patting ourselves on the back just yet. It is one thing to *have* antitrust laws on the books; another entirely to talk about their effective *enforcement*.

I have talked to legal scholars about this; about the apparent lack of enforcement of antitrust legislation around the world. At least as the question applies to the United States, I was told – on more than one occasion and by more than one lawyer – that the bar has moved considerably in the last 100 years. Antitrust laws are still being enforced, they tell me, just not at a threshold that seems to make any sense. Indeed, as detailed particularly in Chapter 6, most markets today are anything but "free." The sheer profitability of today's firms is evidence of that fact. When markets are truly competitive firms cannot extract exorbitant profits; not for very long at least, as such earnings attract further market entry and thus additional competition.

Lastly, vigorously enforced antitrust laws are good for *democracy*. This ought to be obvious from the perspective of media consolidation, where progressively fewer individuals and organizations control increasing shares of the mass media. A robust civil society is premised on an equally robust press and media to inform the citizenry. We have a real problem when those sources of information can be easily controlled, such as when ownership of news outlets falls almost entirely in the hands of the one percent. But beyond that, think about how oversized firms, by nature of being oversized, have more of a say in *anything* than the rest of us. The beauty of the "one person one vote" principle is that it doesn't play favorites. Cheaponomics, sadly, does.

3 Reform bankruptcy laws at international and intranational levels

While cast as a relationship between equals, there are gross asymmetries between borrowers and lenders – to the benefit of the latter – in terms of access to information, knowledge of the market, and bargaining power. Consequently, it is profoundly unfair that borrowers suffer nearly all of the consequences that come with bad debt.[10] Placing the onus and risk on the shoulders of lenders creates an incentive for them to be more responsible about lending. It is also worth remembering that a sharing economy, one where access is privileged over ownership, does not need to float on credit bubbles. So the very *need* for credit, in an affordable society, is lessened.

We have long recognized that human rights ought to take precedent over the rights of creditors, which is why bankruptcy law was developed and why we no longer imprison individuals over unpaid debts. Why not adopt the same principle when debt applies to nations? At present, lower-income countries are required by international lending bodies, like the IMF and World Bank, to prioritize payment of debt to creditors over spending on services that matter to their citizens, like on healthcare, clean water, and agriculture subsidies to small-scale farmers.[11] Lower-income countries are collectively US$4 trillion in debt.[12] Much of what they pay to creditors – what is known as "debt service" – is interest, leaving the principal largely untouched. Thus, like friends of mine neck deep in credit card debt making monthly minimum payments, some countries have paid their loan off many times yet the amount owed continues to rise thanks to accumulating interest.

4 Reform tax codes

Tax codes need to be more progressive. I could point to studies indicating that a top tax rate greater than 70 percent would not negatively impact investment and innovation within a country.[13] (The super-rich in the United States, for example, pay income taxes at a rate of 15 percent on most of their earnings, though it could be less depending on the investment.) For some guidance on the subject I could point to such captains of industry as Warren Buffet, who wrote the following in an Op-Ed for the *New York Times* in 2011:

> I have worked with investors for 60 years and I have yet to see anyone – not even when capital gains rates were 39.9 percent in 1976–77 – shy away from a sensible investment because of the tax rate on the potential gain. People invest to make money, and potential taxes have never scared them off. And to those who argue that higher rates hurt job creation, I would note that a net of nearly 40 million jobs were added between 1980 and 2000. You know what's happened since then: lower tax rates and far lower job creation.[14]

Yet taxes, at least in the United States, are a sacred cow of sorts, having become far too politicized of a topic for me to expect any reasonable discussion to be had on the subject. That's OK. Cooler heads in other countries can take up this discussion. Show those of us in the United States that the debate should not be about whether there ought to be more or less taxes. Instead, let's talk about how we might do taxes differently. And continue to demonstrate – for we already have empirical evidence of this coming out of

Scandinavia – that a well thought out and, most importantly of all, *fair* tax code makes *everyone* better off.

5 Improve access to education and healthcare

As Elizabeth Warren (now US Senator Warren) and Amelia Warren Tyagi document in *The Two Income Trap*, families in the United States are going broke on the basis of housing, health insurance, healthcare, and education.[15] Over the last 30 years, tuition costs in this country have increased 1,120 percent. For some points of comparison, the "skyrocketing" cost of healthcare rose during this period "only" 600 percent, while housing costs grew 375 percent.[16] The share of the average US household budget devoted to education grew 22 percent between 1999 and 2010; for healthcare, the increase was almost 17 percent.[17] Not that the United States is entirely alone with this experience. While still more affordable than that available in the United States, higher education is becoming increasingly expensive throughout Europe. For example, fees at Irish universities that cover the cost of registration, exams, and student services rose from the equivalent of US$240 per student in the mid 1990s to US$2,000 today.[18]

No wonder we're working such long hours. We have to work more so we can afford to send our kids to school and to pay for those pesky doctor's visits. And yet: looking at mortality statistics, many in the United States are still coming up short. The life expectancy in some counties in the United States, for instance, is *lower* than what's found in countries like Algeria and Bangladesh, which is in the mid-sixties for men and low-seventies for women.[19]

The United States spent nearly US$8,000 per person in 2009 on healthcare services, while other countries spent between one-third (Japan and New Zealand) and two-thirds (Norway and Switzerland) as much with equal or better outcomes.[20] Not a hard statistic to believe when you understand how cheaponomics operates and the actions it incentivizes. By encouraging the socialization of costs cheaponomics produces ends that are often wildly expensive. An example of this is the defensive healthcare model. The aim of this practice, popular particularly in the United States, is to treat sickness rather than incurring the upfront costs that come with producing an overall healthier environment that ultimately leads to less sickness and lower overall costs. A healthier environment that produces healthier and happier people does not have to be more expensive. In fact, if other countries are any guide, its price tag is considerably lower.

6 Encourage full employment that creates full, just, and sustainable communities

This recommendation ought to speak for itself. But just in case it does not, or you did not read Chapter 7, here's a brief refresher.

A shorter work week, say, 20 hours, could go a long way to helping alleviate a number of urgent, interlinked problems: overwork, unemployment, over-consumption, climate change, empty communities (especially between the hours of 9 a.m. and 5 p.m.), low levels of well-being, gross levels of inequality, unsustainable lifestyles, and the like. Something as simple as moving toward a shorter work week could radically change the pace of our lives, reshape habits and conventions, enrich social relationship and communal spaces, and profoundly alter consumerist cultures. Arguments for something like a 20-hour work week can generally be placed into one of three categories.[21]

- *Living within our (and future generations') natural capital means.* Jumping off the work–spend treadmill helps break us from the habit of living to work and working to consume. In its place, we still find ways to achieve many of the same ends (e.g., peer-to-peer renting) while having more time to build relationships and community.
- *Social justice and greater well-being for all.* Shorter work weeks will distribute paid work more evenly across the population. This act will have near immediate positive impacts on well-being by eliminating unemployment and long working hours while simultaneously enriching family and community relationships. It will also reduce levels of inequality, as everyone, while not in the exact same boat (as explained in Chapter 9, this is not about making everyone the same), is at least in a similar category of floating vessel. In short, divesting time from the energy-intensive, socially destructive professional economy and reinvesting it in the more labor-intensive, social-capitalizing amateur economy is better for *everyone*: the planet, our families and communities, and future generations.
- *Real prosperity.* Shorter working hours give us a better chance at adapting the economy to the needs of society and the environment, rather than subjugating our lives and the environment to the needs of the economy.

7 Strengthen policies that protect people

It is far too easy to socialize costs. We need to enact policies that make this practice more difficult. Before getting worked up over the "r" word – regulation – let's remember that markets work only *because of* regulation. Business could not exist without contracts, which are made possible by a web of government-enforced rules and regulations. Regulation even helps businesses function *better* by laying out clear rules about what they can and cannot do. As Harvard business professor Michael Porter argues, stricter environmental regulations are actually in the best interests of many firms and countries as they provide these actors an important competitive advantage – what is known in the business community as the Porter Hypothesis.[22] The Porter Hypothesis reminds us that, among other things, regulation spurs innovation, as it creates incentives for firms to adjust to social and environmental realities – like diminishing natural resources. Those nations and regions slow to commit to stricter environmental regulations are doing so at their own peril. They will eventually pay dearly for their short-sightedness after "peak" turns to "scarce" charging headlong toward "exhausted," as their firms struggle to compete against those ready to operate in a world with a different complement of natural capital stocks.

We currently assume the worst of people and the best of the technologies that are created at the hands of these (if we are to believe economists) self-centered, selfish people. When it comes to assessing the potential threats of novel technologies and setting up environmental, health, and safety regulations, the tendency, in many parts of the world, is to take the position of "innocent until proven guilty." This represents, at its most basic level, the traditional risk assessment. Risk assessment, in effect, places the onus on regulatory agencies and the general public to prove that a given technology or industrial activity is not safe. Or, to put it another way, we have to falsify the statement "It's safe." An alternative to the traditional risk assessment is the precautionary principle. The precautionary principle is generally recognized as having emerged in the 1970s, though its ethos dates back to the Hippocratic Oath, which states "First do no harm."[23] Its first international application came in 1984, at the First International Conference on Protection of the North Sea. From there, it has been integrated into numerous conventions and agreements, including, for example, the Maastricht Treaty on the European Union, the Barcelona Convention, the Global Climate Change Convention, and Principle 15 of the Rio Declaration. One popular definition of the precautionary principle comes from the 1998 Wingspread Statement on the Precautionary Principle:

> When an activity raises threats of harm to human health or the environment, precautionary measures should be taken even if some cause and effect relationships are not established scientifically. In this context the proponent of the activity, rather than the public, should bear the burden of proof.[24]

As already discussed in Chapter 3, we need to rethink how we regulate the things we unleash onto the world. Whether that involves adopting a more precautionary stance or substituting the cost–benefit analysis, and practices like discounting, for something that treats people less like a statistic I must leave for future discussions (though I vote for doing both). I also caution against focusing too much on just regulation. Regulation is something we do at the "back end" of the production process, after a product has been made. At that point, after millions of dollars have often already been spent researching and developing the item, we find it much harder to put the toothpaste back into the tube. Why not then start the conversation at the "front end" of the production process, before a technology has been developed and mass-produced?

As sociologist of science Brian Wynne points out, attempts to improve public participation in risk assessments, while admirable, have served to reinforce attention on only back-end science questions about consequences or risks instead of looking at why such widespread public dissatisfaction exists toward certain technologies in the first place.[25] In short, a democratic regulatory politics should not kick in only after something has been developed, recognizing too that at this point managers often start feeling real pressure to show a return on the investment. Instead, the *entire* production process should become democratized, from conceptual cradle to material grave. This will encourage the production of technologies that are not only more just and less risky but which also likely have greater societal – and not just stockholder – value.

8 Encourage labor-intensity/-mobility and international equity

Capital is currently far too mobile; labor, not mobile enough. As a result, we find a race-to-the-bottom scenario playing out as firms move around the world looking for places to cost pollute. The highly mobile nature of capital has helped keep wages low, as the threat of moving to another country is used quite successfully to hold worker demands in check. To emphasize how capital mobility affects the bargaining power of workers, Joseph Stiglitz, a Nobel Prize-winning economist at Columbia University, asks us to "imagine, for a moment, what the world would be like if there was free mobility of labor, but no mobility of capital."[26] He continues this thought experiment noting that:

> countries would compete to attract workers. They would promise good schools and a good environment, as well as low taxes on workers. This could be financed by high taxes on capital. But that's not the world we live in, and that's partly because the 1 percent doesn't want it to be that way.[27]

Capital is not inherently more mobile than labor. Indeed, centuries ago I image just the reverse was the case. I think it would have been considerably more difficult for, say, a blacksmith or miller to relocate their entire business to some faraway land than it would have been for their apprentice to assume a new apprenticeship elsewhere. If energy wasn't so "cheap", for example, I can easily image a world where labor is, once again, more mobile than capital.

Beyond adopting policies that more accurately price oil, there are other suggestions out there that aim to increase labor mobility while enhancing international equity. One that is particularly intriguing comes from Dani Rodrik (from the last chapter). As Rodrik explains, "If the leaders of the advanced nations were serious about boosting incomes around the world and in doing so equitably, they would focus single-mindedly on reforming the rules that govern international labor mobility."[28] This is, in fairly specific terms, what he has in mind:

> Rich nations would commit to a *temporary* work visa scheme that would expand their total labor force by no more than 3 percent. Under the scheme, a mix of skilled and unskilled workers from poor nations would be allowed to fill jobs in the rich countries for a period of up to five years. To ensure that the workers return home at the end of their contracts, the programs would be supported by a range of carrots and sticks applied by both home and host countries. As the original migrants return home, a new wave of workers from the same countries would replace them ... Workers who have accumulated know-how, skills, networks, and savings in rich countries could be true agents of change for their societies upon returning. (Emphasis in original)[29]

We know one thing for certain: we cannot do nothing and allow business-as-usual to continue to exacerbate inter- and intra-generational inequalities. Capital is too mobile in part because it is too cheap. Sooner or later we will need to return to a more labor-intensive economy. Let's make that change now, before it is too late.

9 Implement a maximum wage

There is a lot of talk these days about minimal wages, especially in the United States. And for good reason: the current rate of US$7.25 doesn't buy you much. It is certainly a far cry from the US$10.56 rate, in *today's* dollars, in place back in 1968.[30] Let me put that US$7.25 into some global perspective. The world's highest minimum wage is in Australia, where workers are paid at least 15.96 Australian dollars, or US$16.91, an hour. In France, the minimum wage is €9.43, or US$12.68, an hour. In the UK, you can't work less than for £6.11, or about US$9.50, an hour. And while Canada does not have a national minimum wage the lowest provincial minimum wage is in Alberta, where workers receive at least 9.75 Canadian dollars, or US$9.73, an hour.[31]

Yet while US politicians are quibbling over a dollar or so (President Obama's "bold" vision is to increase the national minimal wage to US$9.00 an hour) the CEOs of companies profiting wildly from these low wages are making in excess of a *thousand times* more an hour. These pay inequalities were tackled in Chapter 9, where they are shown to make no sense, as they, in the end, make everyone worse off. Focusing exclusively on minimum wage is a bit like using a five-gallon bucket to bail out the *Titanic*. In either case, you are going to sink; a fact that would go unchanged by the captain handing you a one-gallon "raise" by offering you a larger six-gallon pail.

Take the world's highest paid CEO in 2011, John H. Hammergren. Hammergren, CEO of McKesson (a pharmaceutical firm), made US$131.19

million in that year.³² Let's put those "earnings" – using the term loosely – into some perspective. A person working full-time (40 hours per week for 52 weeks) at US$7.25 per hour earns US$15,080 annually. Hammergren would have to work 14.5 *minutes* to make that same amount. Conversely, it would take a minimum wage earner 8,699 years and seven months to make what Hammergren made in 2011. Assuming an average life expectancy of 65 years, since minimum wage workers can't get the same nutrition and healthcare as everyone else, that's 134 *entire lifetimes* of nonstop minimum wage work, from infancy to death, just to make what Mr. Hammergren made in 2011.

Before writing off the prospects of a maximum wage as unrealistic and untested let's not forget those instances where it is already in place.

- The National Football League (NFL). The NFL salary cap keeps the sport exciting and entertaining. It assures that the John H. Hammergrens of the world can't just buy Super Bowl ring after Super Bowl ring, while also allowing little ol' Green Bay, Wisconsin, home of the Green Bay Packers, and roughly 100,000 people, to continue to have a professional sports team in their town. Salaries are still outrageous, especially when looked at relative to the minimum wage. The top five paid NFL athletes each make over US$17 million a year.³³ And don't tell me, for example, that hotel housekeepers or janitors, working 12 months out of the year for a lifetime, experience less wear and tear on their body (NFL salaries are often justified by the physical stress placed on these athletes). But still, salaries for each franchise are capped and the sky isn't falling down.
- The clergy. All Methodist bishops in the United States, for instance, receive the same salary. The salary for US bishops for 2012 was $135,880, plus each is provided an episcopal residence.³⁴ Or take US Catholic priests. While it can vary by length of service and size of congregation, salaries do not exceed the mid-US$30,000s.³⁵
- The military and government. Salaries around the world for government officials, civil servants, and the military follow a pay scale, dictating clear minimums and maximums. While some like to talk about "government waste" the salaries earned by government officials belie this argument. For example, the highest paid person in the US government, the president, makes a relatively modest US$400,000 a year. Or take the UK: the prime minister's salary is £142,500 – that's less than US$250,000. I'd say they earn every penny.

10 More accurate pricing while recognizing this practice's limits

It is laughable to hear arguments about how the market, if left to its own accord, would solve the world's ills. That's not how markets work. Only people are paid for their work. Therefore, any work the environment does, and it's a heck of a lot – for instance, 12 atmospheric services vital to human well-being and all life on earth were valued at between 100 and 1,000 times the gross world product (or US$6,850 trillion and US$68,500 trillion annually) – doesn't so much as get a "thank you" from the market.[36] The contribution of the real wealth of the oceans, forests, fertile soils, insects, the atmosphere, and aesthetic nature is abundant, while their (market) prices are *low*. Market values of environmental services are inverse to real the wealth contributions that go toward making life worth living.[37]

As explained by Brian Czech, founding President of the Center for the Advancement of the Steady State Economy, there is a colossal "mismatch between trophic levels (with profound value at the bottom) and GDP figures (with big money spent at the top)."[38] The reference to trophic levels refers to the *law* – the second law of thermodynamics – that no trophic level may consist of more biomass than its underlying level. (A trophic level refers to a group of organisms that occupy the same position in a food chain.) A general rule of thumb among ecologists is that each trophic level consists of roughly ten percent of the biomass of the next-lower level.[39] To give a simplified example involving three species and three trophic levels, it is possible to have 10,000 tons of grass (first trophic level), 1,000 tons of deer (second trophic level), and 100 tons of mountain lions (third trophic level). In ecology, value *diminishes* the further up the levels one goes. We have the second law of thermodynamics to thank for this, which explains that energy is *always* dissipated when something (e.g., grass) is transformed into something else (e.g., deer meat). According to current measures of economic growth, conversely, greatest value lies at the top. *That's* the unsustainable mismatch. The mulch the grounds crew is now scattering around my building's flower beds cost the university a lot more than the tree whence it came. In fact, the tree was probably "free" thanks to a recent storm knocking many down. And there's the problem. The market currently only values those services generated by human hands and ignores the rest, even though "the rest" contribute most to our lives and the overall functioning of the planet.

There are different ways we can work to right this wrong. The American ecologist Howard Odum, for example, provocatively suggested the "emdollar." The emdollar is a hypothetical form of currency centered on the amount of solar energy embodied in a good or service.[40] Fortunately, I think similar ends can be achieved without having to adopt an entirely new form of money. One such option, which is advocated for in earlier chapters, would involve higher ecological taxes. While proponents of cheaponomics will undoubtedly express abhorrence to such a proposal it is based on a relatively uncontroversial (at least as far as the general public is concerned) economic principle: namely, that it is better to tax bad things than things that generate societal value. As stated repeatedly, a key ingredient to making things affordable and society affording is labor-intensity, and then, just as importantly, spreading all that labor out over the world's population so that the entire working aged population works roughly 20 hours per week. We are not going to get there as long as energy – and capital intensity – remains grossly underpriced.

The thing about cheaponomics is that the facts are not on its side.[41] Indeed, as I've already explained, it flies in the face of certain physical laws of the universe. But I am hopeful we can change, that is, before it is too late (for eventually we'll *have* to change or …). This sincere hope is rooted in the soil of not only what might be but of what already is. The path toward affordability is not paved with things we have never done – or it doesn't have to be at least. Consuming collaboratively; working less; taxing bads/rewarding goods; democracy; creating walkable communities; making repairable goods; enforcing antitrust laws; a maximum wage (and on and on): these are all things we as a society have, to various degrees, experimented with. And we've experimented with them because they work, which is to say they have the ability to make us, the planet, and future generations better off. These experiential realities ought to trump opinions and half-baked cheaponomic theories.

So: what are *you* going to do and with *whom*? And how soon can you start?

Notes

1 Copper, Richard (1997) "The general theory of employment, money, and interest," *Foreign Affairs*, September/October, www.foreignaffairs.com/articles/53257/richard-n-cooper/the-general-theory-of-employment-money-and-interest, last accessed July 13, 2013.
2 Keynes, J.M. (2006 [1936]) *The General Theory of Employment, Interest, and Money* (New Delhi: Atlantic), p. vii.
3 To paraphrase Sen, Amartya (1999) *Development as Freedom* (New York: Alfred A. Knopf), p. 6.
4 See, for example, Carolan, Michael (2011) *Embodied Food Politics* (Burlington, VT: Ashgate).
5 See, for example, Carolan, Michael (2013) *Society and the Environment: Pragmatic Solutions to Ecological Issues* (Boulder, CO: Westview Press).
6 Bartels, Larry (2008) *Unequal Democracy: The Political Economy of the New Gilded Age* (New York: Princeton University Press), p. 20.
7 *The Economist* (2006) "The rich, the poor and the growing gap between them," *The Economist* June 15, www.economist.com/node/7055911, last accessed November 11, 2013.
8 Ibid., p. 20.
9 Papadopoulos, Anestis S. (2010) *The International Dimension of EU Competition Law and Policy* (New York: Cambridge University Press), pp. 9–10.
10 Stiglitz, J. (2012) *The Price of Inequality* (New York: W.W. Norton), p. 271.
11 Boyle, David and Andrew Simms (2009) *The New Economics: A Bigger Picture* (London: Earthscan), p. 147.
12 The World Bank (2012) "Global development finance: External debt of developing countries," World Bank, Washington, DC, p. 1, http://data.worldbank.org/sites/default/files/gdf_2012.pdf, last accessed July 17, 2013.
13 See Stiglitz (2012), p. 274.
14 Buffett, Warren (2011) "Stop coddling the super-rich," *New York Times*, August 14, www.nytimes.com/2011/08/15/opinion/stop-coddling-the-super-rich.html?_r=0, last accessed July 17, 2013.

15 Warren, Elizabeth and Amelia Warren Tyagi (2004) *The Two-Income Trap: Why Middle Class Parents are Going Broke* (New York: Perseus Books).
16 Watson, Bruce (2013) "The higher cost of higher education is explained in one simple graph," *DailyFinance.com*, March 16, www.dailyfinance.com/on/college-costs-tuition-rising-student-debt-infographic/, last accessed July 17, 2013.
17 Kim, Richard (2013) "What's the matter with Graham Hill's 'Living with Less'," *The Nation*, March 13, www.thenation.com/blog/173328/whats-matter-graham-hills-living-less#axzz2ZKtaBrMf, last accessed July 17, 2013.
18 Handley, Meg (2010) "Europe's education crisis: College costs soar," *Time*, April 4, www.time.com/time/world/article/0,8599,1976724,00.html, last accessed July 17, 2013.
19 Fox, Maggie (2013) "Americans live a little longer, still lag other rich countries," *NBCnews.com*, July 10, www.nbcnews.com/health/americans-live-little-longer-still-lag-other-rich-countries-6C10588107, last accessed July 17, 2013.
20 Mahon, Mary (2012) "US spends far more for health care than 12 industrialized nations, but quality varies," *The Commonwealth Fund*, May 3, www.commonwealthfund.org/News/News-Releases/2012/May/US-Spends-Far-More-for-Health-Care-Than-12-Industrialized-Nations-but-Quality-Varies.aspx, last accessed July 17, 2013.
21 Adapted from Coote, Anna, Jane Franklin, and Andrew Simms (2010) "21 hours: Why a shorter working week can help us all to flourish in the 21st century," New Economics Foundation, London, pp. 2–3, http://dnwssx4l7gl7s.cloudfront.net/nefoundation/default/page/-/files/21_Hours.pdf, last accessed July 18, 2013.
22 See, for example, Frohwein T. and B. Hansjürgens (2005) "Chemicals regulation and the Porter hypothesis: A critical review of the new European chemicals regulation," *Journal of Business Chemistry*, 2(1), pp. 19–36.
23 Carolan (2013), p. 224.
24 Raffensperger, C. and J. Tickner (eds) (1999) *Protecting Public Health and the Environment: Implementing the Precautionary Principle* (Washington, DC: Island Press), p. 8
25 Wynne, B. (2002) "Risk and environment as legitimatory discourses of technology: Reflectivity inside and out?" *Current Sociology*, 50, pp. 459–77.
26 Stiglitz (2012), p. 61.
27 Ibid., pp. 61–2.
28 Rodrik, Dani (2011) *The Globalization Paradox: Democracy and the Future of the World Economy* (New York: W.W. Norton), p. 268.
29 Ibid., pp. 268–9.
30 Kurtz, Annalyn (2013) "A history of the minimum wage since 1938," *CNN Money*, http://economy.money.cnn.com/2013/02/14/minimum-wage-history/, last accessed July 18, 2013.
31 Isidore, Chris (2013) "On minimum wage, U.S. lags many rivals," *CNN Money*, February 13, http://money.cnn.com/2013/02/13/news/economy/minimum-wage-countries/index.html, last accessed July 18, 2013.
32 *Forbes* (2012) "CEO compensation," *Forbes.com*, www.forbes.com/lists/2012/12/ceo-compensation-12_John-H-Hammergren_ESV7.html, last accessed July 18, 2013.
33 Rosenthal, Gregg (2013) "Top 10 NFL salary-cap numbers: Quarterbacks on top," *NFL.com*, July 15, www.nfl.com/news/story/0ap1000000217898/article/top-10-nfl-salarycap-numbers, last accessed July 18, 2013.
34 United Methodist Church (n.d.) "Frequently asked questions about the Council of Bishops," *United Methodist Church*, www.umc.org/site/c.lwL4KnN1LtH/b.4572065/#Compensation, last accessed July 18, 2013.
35 Byron, William (2007) "How much money does a parish priest make?" *Catholic Digest*, October 1, www.catholicdigest.com/articles/faith/knowledge/2007/10-01/how-much-money-does-a-parish-priest-make, last accessed July 18, 2013.

36 Thornes, J., W. Bloss, S. Bouzarovski, X. Cai, L. Chapman, J. Clark, S. Dessai, S. Du, D. van der Horst, M. Kendall, C. Kidda, and S. Randalls (2010) "Communicating the value of atmospheric services," *Meteorological Applications*, 17, pp. 243–50.
37 Odum, Howard (2003) "Emergy accounting," in *Unveiling Wealth*, edited by Peter Bartelmus (Dordrecht: Springer), pp. 135–46.
38 Czech, Brian (2012) *Supply Shock: Economic Growth at the Crossroads and the Steady State Solution* (Gabriola Island: New Society Publishers), p. 183.
39 Ibid., p. 181.
40 Odum (2003).
41 See Kubiszewski, Ida, Robert Costanza, Carol Franco, Philip Lawn, John Talberth, Tim Jackson, and Camille Aylmer (2013) "Beyond GDP: Measuring and achieving global genuine progress," *Ecological Economics*, 93, pp. 57–68.

Index

access, freedom of 15, 23, 35, 37–38, 60, 106, 136–38, 140, 155, 157, 161, 181, 183, 197, 200; *see also* ownership, weight of
advertising: as something that ought to be tax 187; as a taxable business expense 69; and children 69, 189; food consumption 69; hyper-consumption 133, 188; values 188
air travel 11: pollution from 30, 97
antitrust laws 198–99, 208
apolitical ecology 74
apparel 147, 148; *see also* fashion, fast
Apple 27–29, 30, 32
Argentina: nutrition transition 72
Australia: automobility 94; bees 82; coltan 24; minimum wage 205; obesity 73; waste 154
automobile: and accidents 9–10, 51, 95–97, 104, 105; air pollution 10; climate change 10, costs of 9–10, 91–107; congestion 10, 95, 104, 105, 106; effective speed of 93–95; fuel economy 150; free parking 98–100; obesity 74; insurance 10, 92, 94, 155; planned obsolescence 36, 47; traffic 9, 93–95, 97, 102; transitioning away from 156–57; *see also* peek car
Ayres, Robert 131, 168

bankruptcy law: domestic 199–200; international 200
banks: local 115–16; too big to fail 173; *see also* credit
Becker, Gary 139
bees, honey 81–82
Benjamin, Walter 32–33

bike: effective speed of 93–94; increasing use of 156; links to well-being 107, 120, 141
biodiversity: plastic bags 43; agricultural subsidies 70; conventional agriculture 81
Botsman, Rachel 155
Botswana: car fatalities 96
Buffet, Warren 200
Bulgaria: car ownership rates 106; fracking ban 58
buycott 161–62; *see also* carrotmob

cadmium exposure/poisoning 8, 34
Canada: car accident rates 96; minimum wage 205; obesity 72
carbon intensity 151–52: *see also* energy intensity
car sharing 155–56, 161
carrotmob 161–62; *see also* buycott
celluloid 49–50
China 1, 111, 175; and air pollution 97–98; antitrust law 199; automobile sales 105–6; carbon dioxide emissions 153; coal 2, 57, 98; emissions standards 106; e-waste 8, 31, 33–34, 37; food waste 82; inequality 176; labor abuses 27–29; mobility 106; obesity 73; road fatalities 96
Citizens United 197
clean rooms, and semiconductor chips 25–27
climate change 2, 10, 12, 13, 202; and the automobile 10, 98; agriculture 77, 82; costs 31, 173; discounting 53; food security 74–75; livestock 77; obesity 74–75
CO_2 emissions: agriculture 82; automobile 10, 98, 100; food waste 82; global

212 Index

emissions 153; livestock 76; cloud computing 21, 23, 24, 30–31; fracking 59–60; China, economy of 152; India, economy of 152; Japan, economy of 152; Russia, economy of 152; United Kingdom, economy of 151; United States, economy of 135, 151, 152, 155

coal: China 2, 57, 98; in electricity production 1–2, 8, 21, 23, 29–32 151; in plastic production 57; production efficiency 148–49

Coca Cola 69, 72; see also soda

collaborative consumption 12, 16, 38, 138, 142, 155–57, 159, 161

coltan 24–25

comatose server 30

Common Agricultural Policy, EU 65, 68, 70

common property regime/ resources 157, 159

compact fluorescents (CFLs) 149–51

comparative advantage 4

compositional effect 135–36; see also scale effect

concentration: market 120–24; media 199

conflict 2, 126; and electronic industry 24–25

Congo: coltan 24–25

cost-benefit analysis 8, 50–53, 203

credit: access to 200; agriculture 124, 200; "cheap" 131, 200; and collaborative lending 161; score 160; see also banks

Czech, Brian 207

Daly, Herman 178

decoupling 152–53: absolute 152; relative 152

debt: and credit card 200; ecological 3; national 3, 200

debt service 200

Delucchi, Mark 104–5

demand-side prosperity 4; see also supply-side economics; supply-side prosperity

democratic leisure 140, 141; see also leisure

democracy 10, 13, 91, 164, 187, 197–98, 199, 208: consumption as type of 101, 164, 190; see also governance

disaster capitalism 14

discounting, the economic practice of 52–53, 203

disposability 8, 46–47

Dow Jones Industrial Average 14, 168–69, 174

down-cycling 56, 197; see also recycling

economies of scale 22, 78,111

effective speed 93–95

efficiency 16, 30, 36, 70, 79, 148–53, 162, 170,

electricity 12, 24, 100, 187: and cloud computing 29–32; coal 1–2, 8, 21, 23, 29–32 151; lighting 149–51

emdollar 207

energy intensity 151; see also carbon intensity

Enron 172

environmental racism 52

e-waste 8, 37: and planned obsolescence 35–38; costs of 32–35; recycling of 8, 34,

externalization, cost 4, 7–8, 23, 29, 47, 50, 186, 187

Facebook 29, 30, 31, 138, 156, 160, 187

Farm Bill, US 65

farms, agriculture 68, 70, 79, 81, 122–24

farms, server/data 21, 30–32, 131, 187

fashion, fast 147–48, 150

food: deserts 9; security 3, 12, 25, 71–72, 178; waste 78, 82–83

fracking 57–60; see also natural gas

France: car use 106; fracking ban 58; obesity 73; minimum wage 205; price of food 65

Frederick, Christine 46

Friedman, Milton 14, 164, 177, 180

fundamental law of road congestion 95

Galbraith, John Kenneth 133

general theory of second best 180–81

Germany: obesity 73; Walmart 122; workweek 134

Goetz, Stephan 114–15

golden parachutes 178

Google 21, 23, 29–30, 32, 160, 187

governance 38, 60, 181, 184–85; and corporate 198; see also democracy

Great Depression 132, 134, 175

Great Pacific Garbage Patch 44–45, 48; see also North Pacific Gyre

Great Recession 14, 168

Green Revolution 12, 65

Index 213

happiness: and commuting time 102; growth 13, 126, 141, 170–72, 177, 188
Happy Planet Index 107, 173
Hardin, Garret 158–59, 190
Hayek, Friedrich 180
healthcare 9, 31, 105, 131: and foodborne disease 77; obesity 72–74; Medicare 4, 112–13; rising costs of 9, 134, 201
heat island effect 100
high fructose corn syrup 68–70; *see also* sugar
Hirschman, Albert 185
hunger 2, 9; and access 72

idling capacity 154; of space 155
ignorance 5: social construction of 6–7
Illich, Ivan 94
India: automobile emissions 106; CO_2 emissions 152; e-waste 8; mobile phone use 31; population 175
inequality: costs of 174–80; rising levels of 3, 15, 16, 74, 83, 106, 126, 134, 174–80, 181, 183, 202;
International Monetary Fund 198, 200

Jackson, Tim 151
Jacobs, Jane 101
Japan: automobile fuel standards 106; CO_2 emissions 152; food waste 82; healthcare 201; transportation 106; work week 134
Jevons paradox 12, 149; *see also* rebound effect
Jevons, William Stanley 149
Jordan: car ownership rates 106

Kenya: transportation 94, 96
Keynes, John Maynard 5, 11, 133, 195–96
Korea, South: food waste 82; happiness 173; semiconductor manufacturing 27
Kurzweil, Raymond 36

labor: and electronics industry 27–29; e-waste industry 37; food system 71, 79–81; -intensity 15, 71, 139, 187, 202, 204–5, 207; links with leisure 129; mobility 140–41, 204–5; productivity 131, 133, 140; substitute capital for 131–32, 187; taxing of 186–87; the reduced work week 132–34; unpaid 28, 139; Walmart 112
landfill: e-waste 33, 35, 37; food waste 78; plastics 48, 54, 56–57; plastic bags 43

leisure 5: and community involvement 129–30, 140, 141; creating more time for 5, 11, 129–30, 135, 138–40, 141; resource-intensive 130, 138, 139: *see also* democratic leisure; manufacturing leisure
Leonard, Annie 33
Litman, Todd 105
livestock, agriculture: animal transportation 77–78; animal welfare 78; climate change 77, 70; food waste 78; impacts on community, large-scale 80–81; overgrazing 158–59; risks to public health 77–78; risks to worker health 79; subsidies 70; water footprint 76, 78
London, Bernard 46

macroeconomics 111, 195: broken links to prosperity 117–20
malnutrition 9, 180
manufacturing leisure 141; *see also* leisure
market failure 16, 91, 92, 180, 198
maximum wage 178, 205–6, 208; *see also* minimum wage
McDonald's 65, 76, 118, 120
mercury exposure/poisoning 8, 31, 34
mesh-based economy 157; *see also* sharing economy
methane emissions: and food system 81, 82; fracking 58
Mexico: automobile 101; nutrition transition 72; obesity 72
Middle East 1
Midway Atoll 45
Miguel, Edward 140
Mill, John Stuart 45
minimum wage 134, 178; and Australia 205; Canada 205; France 205; United Kingdom 205; United States 4, 205, 206; *see also* maximum wage
Mishan, Ezra 133
Molotch, Harvey 37
monocultures 71
monopoly: 120–22; *see also* monopsony
monopsony 120, 122; *see also* monopoly
Moore's law 36

nutrition transition 72
natural gas 57–60; *see also* fracking
Netherlands, the 47, 107, 68
network enabled sharing 157

214   Index

New Zealand: car ownership rates 106; food system concentration 122–23; healthcare 201
nitrous oxide emissions: agriculture 81, 82
noise pollution 10, 97
North Pacific Gyre 44; see also Great Pacific Garbage Patch
Norway: advertising in 189; economy of 111; healthcare 201
nuclear power 30,

Obama, Barack 24, 205
obesity: and automobile 97; climate change 74–75; costs of 71–75, 172
Odum, Howard 207
oikonomia 119, 184
open access regime/resources 159
opportunity costs 100; see also social opportunity costs
Ostrom, Elinor 157, 160, 190
ownership, weight of 15, 23, 35, 37–38, 60, 106, 136–38, 140, 155, 157, 161, 181, 183, 197, 200; see also access, freedom of

parking, free: cost of 98–100
participatory budgeting 184–85
Patel, Raj 76, 181
peek car 105–7; see also automobile
peer-to-peer lending 161
peer-to-peer renting 138, 155, 161, 202
petroleum 1; and firms 111
Pigou, Arthur Cecil 186
piranha baths 22, 26
planned obsolescence 8, 35–38, 46, 60, 130, 133; history of 46–48
plastics 1, 7, 8, 33, 53; and bags 43–45; biodegradable 57; fracking 57–60; Great Pacific Garbage Patch 44–45; origins 49–50; pre-molded 36; recycling 53–57
Poland: car ownership rates 106
polybrominated diphenyl ethers (PBDEs) 34–35
Porter Hypothesis 202–3
positional good 50
Posner Richard 139–40
precautionary principle 203
Prisoner's Dilemma 159, 190
productivism, ideology of 12, 142
Putman, Robert 101

Rawls, John 182–83
Reagan, Ronald 4; see also Reaganomics; Reaganism
Reaganomics 4; see also Regan, Ronald; Reaganism
Reaganism 50; see also Regan, Ronald; Reaganomics
rebound effect 12, 148–50, 153; see also Jevons paradox
recycling: e-waste 33–35, 37; design 37, 197; global rates 33; links to increased consumption 53–57; plastic bags 44; see also down-cycling
Rees, William 104
regulation 12, 37, 44, 53, 70, 134, 169, 187, 189, 202–3
renewable, resources/energy 12, 30, 31
resin codes 54–56
responsibilities, individual 13, 181–84; see also rights, individual
rights: individual 13, 181–84; negative 183; positive 183; see also responsibilities, individual
Rodrik, Dani 186, 204
Ryan, Paul 174

sacrifice, discourse of 169
Samuelson, Paul 159
Sandel, Michael 181
scale effect 135; see also compositional effect
Schor, Juliet 134, 136, 140
Schwartz, Barry 163
semiconductor, manufacturing of 25, 34
Sen, Amartya 178, 181–83
sharing economy 155, 157–58, 159–62, 181, 189, 200; see also mesh-based economy
Simon, Julian 177
Sloan, Alfred 36
smoking 51, 95: automobile comparable to as health risk 97
social capital: amateur economy 139, 202; automobile 130; economic growth 115, 139–41; governance 157–59; Walmart 119–20
social opportunity costs 105; see also opportunity costs
soda: consumption 66–67, 72; manfacturers 69; see also Coca Cola
solar power 29, 30, 100, 162, 207
South Africa: bee populations 81; inequality 175–76

Spain: air pollution 97
Speth, James 174
sprawl 12, 97, 101, 103–5
Stevens, Brooks 48
Stiglitz, Joseph 204
storage space: rental 137, 154; in the home 153–54
subsidies, agricultural 67–71, 200
subsidies, corporate 30, 32, 67–71, 104, 106, 111–15
sugar 65–67, 69–70, 72, 75, 163; *see also* high fructose corn syrup
Summers, Lawrence 52
supply-side economics 4; *see also* supply-side prosperity; demand-side prosperity
supply-side prosperity 4; *see also* supply-side economics; demand-side prosperity
Sustainable Apparel Coalition 147–48
Switzerland: obesity 73; healthcare 201; inequality 178
Syria: car ownership rates 106

taxes 2, 3, 12, 15, 99, 176: and gas 106; on advertising 189; on capital 204; on labor 186, 204; on plastic bags 45; Pigovian 186; pollution 186–87; property 32; reform 200–201; Walmart 113;
Thatcherism 50
Thompson, E.P. 183–84
Toffler, Alvin 21, 189
Tragedy of the Commons 158–59
Tranter, Paul 93
TrustCloud 160

Twain, Mark 50, 92–93
tyranny of small decisions 164

uneconomic growth 126
United States: and breast cancer rates 27; car ownership 9–10; e-waste 35, 37; food prices 4; fracking 57–60; frontier designation 47; plastic bags 43; plastics industry 53, 56, 57–60; recycling rates 54; retail in 8, 10; welfare 10

vacation 11, 129–30, 138, 150
Victor, Peter 180
Vietnam: road accidents 96

wages: and low 2, 10, 28, 125, 130–33, 187, 204; equity 178–80, 205–6; food system 79–80; middle class 106; Walmart 114–16, 118
Walmart 1, 2, 10; and community well-being 117–20; market concentration 111, 120–24; poverty 114–16; prosperity 124–26; welfare 4, 112–14
Warren, Elizabeth 201
welfare economics 52
willingness to pay: to save marine animals 43
wind power 30
work day, reduce length of 132, 202
work and spend cycle 136
World Bank 52, 98, 198, 200
World Health Organization 66, 69, 95
World War II 4, 14, 132, 138, 168, 175

Zipcar 155–57; *see also* car sharing
zoning 99–100